BOOK 1

A Moment in Time

in Time

Words of Encouragement
for Parents

BOOK 1

A Moment in Time

Words of Encouragement for Parents

FAMILY

 Carl Willis

AMG
PUBLISHERS

A Moment in Time:
Words of Encouragement for Parents (Book 1)

Copyright © 2019 by Carl Willis
Published by AMG Publishers, Inc.
6815 Shallowford Rd.
Chattanooga, Tennessee 37421

ISBN 13: 978-1-61715-537-6

First Printing—September 2019

Scripture quotations taken from the New American Standard Bible® (NASB), Copyright © 1960, 1962, 1963, 1968, 1971, 1972, 1973, 1975, 1977, 1995 by The Lockman Foundation. Used by permission. www.Lockman.org

Cover designed by Daryle Beam, Bright Boy Design, Chattanooga, TN.

Editing, interior design, and typesetting by Rick Steele Editorial Services (https://steeleeditorialservices.myportfolio.com).

Printed in the United States of America

To Christine,

my "gap-filler" since 1985 and truly my best friend.

ACKNOWLEDGMENTS

There are far too many people who deserve to be acknowledged for inspiring me to begin writing these devotional thoughts back in 2016. But first and foremost is my precious bride of over three decades, Christine.

Secondly, I want to thank all my *Every Man A Warrior* (EMAW) colleagues (again, too many to name) for being there for me as I began and continued this journey. EMAW gave me the passion to start writing, which has not diminished. And these men were my literal sounding board as I shared many of these thoughts with them.

And finally, I want to thank all my family, who are the subject of many of these devotions. You are my delight and true loves. Thank You, Jesus, for blessing me with such awesome people in my life.

INTRODUCTION

This is the first book (Year One) of a three-part series of *A Moment in Time* daily devotions. What started out as simply my efforts to be obedient to the Lord has resulted in the pagination of my thoughts and prayers throughout the Word.

Back in 2015, I began journaling my quiet times as part of a men's small group that was using the *Every Many A Warrior* study. This study gave me a renewed passion to study and memorize God's Word. In January 2016, at the urging of the Holy Spirit, I began the journey to write a short devotional blog for moms and dads in which I would cover every chapter of the Bible, all 1,189 of them! In total, these blog posts produced three years worth of daily devotionals.

Through a series of events, I was led to AMG Publishers, who has walked me in this process of publishing (something I never dreamed of) these blogs for families.

It is my prayer that you will read these as intended—to inspire you to see God working in each and every word of the Bible. We can't pick and choose which verses we want to live by. They all have purpose and application in our lives. Read, be encouraged and live it out!

BE THE LAST ONE

Matthew 20

BEST VERSES: 16, 26–28

16: So the last shall be first, and the first last.

26–28: It is not this way among you, but whoever wishes to become great among you shall be your servant, and whoever wishes to be first among you shall be your slave; just as the Son of Man did not come to be served, but to serve, and to give His life a ransom for many.

What a lesson to teach our children! And probably one of the most difficult. Twice in this twentieth chapter of Matthew, Jesus mentions the last being first and the first being last. However, we know that little Elrod and Gertrude ALWAYS want to be first. When they surprise us and allow someone else (yes even their sibling) to go first we almost pass out!

TEACHING MOMENT

Humility! It's all about humility. Did you know you can't teach humility, but it can be learned? You are probably thinking, "Huh? What do you mean?" Humility is a characteristic that is caught, not taught. And guess who models that behavior. That's right—YOU! Mom and Dad!

So, let me ask you a question. Are you being humble? Are you letting others go before you? Do you give up that parking space in the mall parking lot when someone else wants it? Do you let the person in line at the grocery go before you?

Your kids are watching. They are learning from your actions, not your words. Be last! For Jesus!

Father, I know these words are true, but it's hard to not go first. Give me the desire to go last. Give me the desire to put others in front of me.

THE HANDS OF A WOMAN

Judges 4

BEST VERSE: 9

She said, "I will surely go with you; nevertheless, the honor shall not be yours on the journey that you are about to take, for the LORD will sell Sisera into the hands of a woman." Then Deborah arose and went with Barak to Kedesh.

I can't help but wonder what would have happened if Barak hadn't asked Deborah to go with him to fight against Sisera. I bet he thought she was referring to herself, and he was pretty sure he could outfight her. Nope, Deborah was referring to another woman, Jael.

You really need to read the rest of the chapter. Jael tricks Sisera, who had fled from the battle, and then killed him with a hammer and tent peg while he slept. Pretty gruesome. Jael must have been some woman!

TEACHING MOMENT

You may be thinking, Come on, Carl, how in the world do I apply this verse to my kids? Well, think about it. Do you think for a second that Sisera ever considered Jael a threat to his safety? God can use anyone He desires to accomplish His will. He chose to use Jael to be the one to kill Israel's chief enemy at the time. Your sons and daughters might just be the one to accomplish His will in some way no one expects.

What are your desires and wishes for your children? I am sure you have them. Ask the Lord to expand those. Ask the Lord to use them to accomplish incredible feats of faith to lead thousands to Christ. Wouldn't that be the best answered prayer ever? Teach your children to submit and trust.

What does the Lord want to use you for? Are you willing to pick up the hammer and tent peg to defeat His enemies? Are you willing to lay down your life for your God? He will lead you if you trust Him.

O God, I know you can use anyone if we will allow You to do so. Help me to yield. Help me to teach others to trust Your leading.

YOUR CALLING

Exodus 35

BEST VERSES: 30–33

Then Moses said to the sons of Israel, "See, the LORD has called by name Bezalel the son of Uri, the son of Hur, of the tribe of Judah. And He has filled him with the Spirit of God, in wisdom, in understanding and in knowledge and in all craftsmanship; to make designs for working in gold and in silver and in bronze, and in the cutting of stones for settings and in the carving of wood, so as to perform in every inventive work."

Most people think that when someone is "called" by God that means they are going into the ministry. God only calls people to be preachers or missionaries, right? Wrong! Look at today's passage. Bezalel was called to be the artist for the tabernacle. God gave him specific gifts and abilities to be used for His glory. He even said, "He has filled him with the Spirit of God." Wow! A Spirit-filled artist. That's just cool.

Can you imagine how Bezalel felt when he heard Moses saying God had called him to serve Him in this way. He was probably thinking, How can I be used of God in the desert? There's not much need for an artist in the wilderness.

TEACHING MOMENT

Your children will be given gifts by God through the Holy Spirit at salvation. I truly believe that. I am not talking about talents or abilities. I am talking about spiritual gifts that can be manifested through talents and abilities. As parents, it is our job to nurture those gifts and give them opportunities to develop them.

I bet Bezalel's parents encouraged his artistic talents as a child, not knowing that God would one day take those and through His Spirit use them to help build the tabernacle. Only God knows how He will use your child to honor Him.

I pray you are using your gifts to honor your Father in heaven. It is sad to see someone neglect the gifts God has given them. And I know it saddens the heart of God for Him to see His children not use what He has given them to further His kingdom. Be obedient with your gifts.

Father, thank You for the gifts You have given me. My heart longs to use them for Your glory!

READ IT FOR YOURSELF

Luke 16

BEST VERSE: 31
But he [Abraham] said to him, "If they do not listen to Moses and the Prophets, they will not be persuaded even if someone rises from the dead."

Do your children want you to do everything for them? Do they wait for you to help them do their homework when you know they are capable of doing it themselves? Do they complain they don't know how to do that chore you have shown them fifteen times? Now there is nothing wrong with helping your child, but they must learn to do these things on their own at some point.

The rich man in this story begs God to make special efforts to show his brothers, who were still alive, how to get to heaven. He doesn't believe his brothers will recognize the need for salvation on their own. God essentially says through Abraham, "They have all the instructions they need. They just need to listen to My Word." Wow! That's kind of harsh, isn't it?

Not really. God is a just and fair God. He loves each of us the same and shows each of us how to surrender to His Will. He knows that many will reject Him but will, at the last minute, want to negotiate a deal. Oops! Too late!

TEACHING MOMENT
Our children have to learn from us that there are some things in life that are nonnegotiable. Salvation is one of those. There is only one way to the Father. That is through Jesus Christ His Son. No matter what the world does to try make it fit the culture of today, there is only one path to God.

Teaching our children to rely on God for everything is the key. They will all reach a point when they will not need us anymore, but they will always need their heavenly Father. They will always need His Word. They will always need the Holy Spirit's guidance. But we must let them come to

Him on their own. By that I mean we can't force-feed salvation. We must pray for God to draw them to Himself. And then we leave the rest up to Him. Remember, it is God's will that all should come to repentance (see 2 Pet. 3:9). That includes your child.

God, Redeemer of all mankind, I know salvation is Your work. But Lord, use me as your instrument to draw others to Your grace and mercy. I want to be used by You.

JANUARY 5

LEAKY ROOF

Mark 2

BEST VERSE: 4
Being unable to get to Him because of the crowd, they removed the roof above Him; and when they had dug an opening, they let down the pallet on which the paralytic was lying.

This is one of those Bible stories that has been taught over and over. Almost anyone who has been to Sunday School or Church has heard the story of the friends who dug a hole through the roof to get their friend healed. But have you ever thought about those men?

The focus seems to always rest on Jesus (as it should), the paralyzed man or the ones who questioned Jesus. But these men had the faith to believe that Jesus could heal their friend. They hastily made a hole in the roof for him. I bet they even believed that Jesus could fix the roof. Maybe He did. We don't know. But these friends went to extreme measures to get their friend in front of Jesus.

TEACHING MOMENT
To what extreme are you willing to go to get your children in front of Jesus? "Well Carl, I would do anything." Really? How about getting rid of your television so you and your children can spend more time with Jesus? How about giving up weekend soccer so you can make sure your children are in church on Sunday?

Ouch, did that hurt your toes? You see, we are willing to do anything—unless it inconveniences us. We say we want them to walk with Jesus and live holy lives, but only if it doesn't hamper our lifestyles.

What do you need to give up today in your family to make sure your children (and you) spend more time with the Lord? I guarantee there is something. We ALL have something. Don't compromise your walk with Christ to make sure your children have all the opportunities to be a success at soccer or tennis or piano or . . . you name it.

Ask yourself what is more important, that activity or their eternity. I don't think there is any question which is the most important. Now, are you willing to dig that hole through the roof?

O Father, give me the courage to get rid of the things in my family's life that hamper us from fully seeing you. Give me the boldness to dig a hole through my neighbor's roof to get my family in front of Jesus.

JANUARY 6

FIG SEASON

Luke 21

BEST VERSES: 29–30
Then He told them a parable: "Behold the fig tree and all the trees; as soon as they put forth leaves, you see it and know for yourselves that summer is now near."

When I was growing up in South Georgia, I used to love to go visit my Grandma Carter's house in the country. She lived on this farm where we could run around and explore. There was a chicken coop, a couple of barns, and cows. But there was also this awesome fig tree.

This fig tree had those large brown figs. I couldn't wait until it was fig season. I would go to that tree which was right beside the well house and eat those figs right off the tree. I would find the biggest one, split it open, and eat the insides first. Fig season was indeed sweet!

However, in this parable Jesus refers to the fig tree and other trees as a way we know the seasons. He is telling them that just like that, when we see the events He talked about concerning the Last Days, we will know the "season" has come.

TEACHING MOMENT

Have you listened to the news lately? We need to be preparing our children for these last days. All around us the events are lining up for His return. But oh, moms and dads, these are not times to be feared. Just like I eagerly anticipated fig season, we too should be eagerly anticipating His return.

So, may I ask you a question? Are you ready? Have you asked the Lord Jesus to be your personal Lord and Savior? Have you prayed for your children to do the same? Have they? Don't delay. It's almost fig season!

I am looking forward to that day, Jesus, when I see You face to face. It may be here, or it may be there. But I can't wait to spend eternity with You.

JANUARY 7

BONE KILLING

Judges 15

BEST VERSE: 15
He found a fresh jawbone of a donkey, so he reached out and took it and killed a thousand men with it.

Samson was definitely a controversial judge. Some of his antics will cause you to raise an eyebrow. But judge he did, for twenty years. This story is one of those eyebrow-raising stories. The Philistines came to kill him for burning their fields with three hundred foxes tied together with torches (another interesting tale, no pun intended). He agreed to be turned over to them, tied with two ropes, which he quickly broke.

The only problem was Samson didn't have a sword, shield, bow, or arrows. How would he fight them? He used what he had around him. He saw a bone on the ground, picked it up and slaughtered a thousand Philistines.

Pretty gruesome, I know, but warfare is gruesome. God used Samson in His own way to defeat Israel's enemy.

TEACHING MOMENT

"Okay, Carl, show me how to teach this to my little Susie." Glad you asked. God puts things in our life to use to serve Him. For Samson, it was a donkey's jawbone. For your little Susie, it could be her musical talent. It could be her oratory skills. It could be her gift of service. God equips us all in different ways. But He will use us all, if we surrender.

What skills and talents do you see in your children? Help guide them in honing those for use to God. Now, He may choose to develop a whole new gift in them. That's okay. But prepare them for God's service. They should feel natural in their service to Him, not awkward or nervous.

What has God put in your hands to serve Him? Are you using it? Pick up that jawbone. Serve Him with vigor and energy. Don't say, "I can't do that." You don't have to. God will through you. Let Him.

Father, You are the gift giver. You are the One who equips us for service. Show me how to use what You have placed around me.

JANUARY 8

PROUD OR HUMBLE?

Luke 14

BEST VERSE: 11

For everyone who exalts himself will be humbled, and he who humbles himself will be exalted.

How many times have you seen little children push and shove to be first in line? That is especially true if they are waiting in line for a snack or to go out for recess. They just have to be first in line. Somehow, they think if they are first, they get something special.

The people in the room with Jesus were jockeying for position at the table. They were trying to be in that special position near Jesus. They wanted to be seen as being close to Him. But Jesus puts them in their place with these words we just read. Do you think they heard Him?

O Jesus, I can't wait to hear the rest of Your story. I can only imagine all the other things You did. But I am thankful most of all for the ONE thing You did that changed my life—You died for me.

WAITING ON THE GREEN LIGHT

Judges 8

BEST VERSE: 27
Gideon made it into an ephod, and placed it in his city, Ophrah, and all Israel played the harlot with it there, so that it became a snare to Gideon and his household.

After successfully defeating the Midianites and leading the nation, Gideon made a terrible mistake. He forgot the Second Commandment. You know that one, don't you? Don't make any graven images. Now, I don't know Gideon's motive behind making the ephod, but I really don't think he meant it to be worshiped. Perhaps he just wanted a reminder of the great victory over the Midianites. Perhaps he just wanted the people to see it and remember the mighty act of God in that battle.

Whatever his motive, it backfired. The people began to worship it. The passage says it "became a snare to Gideon and his household." So somewhere between defeating the Midianites and death, Gideon messed up.

TEACHING MOMENT
Your children may do something with good intentions that is NOT what the Lord intended. Pursuing a career that provides well may seem harmless unless it is not what the Lord would have them do. We, as Mom and Dad, are the ones to direct them in their early years toward seeking the Lord's will in everything. Sometimes that means waiting and waiting and waiting.

I don't know about you, but I hate to wait. I hate waiting at red lights, restaurants or . . . on God. But I have to wait. I have no choice. Our children have to learn to wait. After all, life is a lot of red lights with very few blinking green lights. God will tell us to go when we He is ready. Don't let your kids jump the red lights in life. That can lead to disaster.

The next time you are with your kids at a red light, instead of getting anxious about the wait, how about asking your child to pray? Pray for the person in the car next to you or the business or house you just passed. You never know what may happen.

O God, I know better than to pray for patience. That is built through trials, and I sure don't want more of them. But I want to be more patient as I wait on You.

THERE YOU WILL SEE HIM

Matthew 28

BEST VERSE: 16
But the eleven disciples proceeded to Galilee, to the mountain which Jesus had designated.

This passage continues with the much-quoted verse where Jesus tells His disciples to go make disciples in all nations. We quote that verse a lot, but verse 16 caught my attention.

Jesus did not appear to them and tell them to go to Galilee. He appeared to some women (Mary Magdalene and the other Mary) and told them to tell the disciples. When the disciples heard Jesus' command they obeyed. They just went where He said He would meet them, and then they received this "Great Commission." This was perhaps one of the greatest things He said to them in all the time He was with them.

TEACHING MOMENT
Parents, your children need to learn to obey you even when you are NOT around. They need to know that the directions you are giving them are for their good. They don't need to know the "why" every time. The disciples didn't know why they were going to Galilee. They just know He said, "Go!"

Don't get me wrong. We need to talk to our kids and explain things to them, but I have seen too many parents who are too "wordy" when it comes explain our actions. The trouble is, there is no excuse for disobeying God's instructions.

TEACHING MOMENT

Your children will do the same thing. But don't let them get by with this. Sometimes they can make up some pretty funny excuses like "I accidentally ate the cookie" or "My hand just slipped and punched my brother." They can really crack you up with their imagination.

But remember, there are no excuses. Sin has consequences. Mercy can be shown, but recognition of sin is so important. God could have killed Aaron for leading Israel into idol worship, but He showed mercy instead. Moses begged God to forgive the people and not wipe them out. And God listened to him. Grace was given.

What sin are you justifying right now? How good are you at rationalizing your disobedience? We get good at it, don't we? Stop! Confess! Rid yourself of the lies and seek to follow Him.

Grace Giver, thank You for forgiving me of those times when I have lied about my sin. Thank You for convicting me of my disobedience. Help me point others to You.

JANUARY 28

A PARENT'S LOVE

2 Samuel 18

BEST VERSE: 33

The king was deeply moved and went up to the chamber over the gate and wept. And thus he said as he walked, "O my son Absalom, my son, my son Absalom! Would I had died instead of you, O Absalom, my son, my son!"

Even after Absalom's attempted coup of David's reign, David still loved him. He was grieved over his death. If you are a parent, you understand this. No matter what our children do, they are still our children. We will love them regardless.

The Lord is that way with us also. He loves us unconditionally. He loves us with an everlasting love. But He won't force us to love Him back. He won't force us to obey. David could have forced Absalom back into exile or could have imprisoned him, but that certainly would not have led Absalom to love his father any more.

TEACHING MOMENT

We teach our children this kind of love by telling them we love them over and over and over. We teach them this by hugging and kissing them. Parents, heed my words: you can't love your kids too much. Now, I didn't say to spoil them. I said to love them.

Kids need love. Believe me. I'm in my fourth decade of working with kids and families. You can't tell people too much that you love them. They need to know when they see you that you are going to tell them that. They need to know that if they need a hug they can come to you.

Are you in need of a hug today? How about a holy kiss? Here it comes—muah! Don't you feel better. And just think. God is always ready to hand those out. Just ask.

O Lord of love, thank You for unconditional love. Thank You that I know You are always ready to hand out hugs and kisses to me through Your Spirit.

JANUARY 29

WELL, HOW ABOUT THAT?

Genesis 29

BEST VERSE: 9
While he was still speaking with them, Rachel came with her father's sheep, for she was a shepherdess.

Many times, we run right past these verses. We read it and think "oh that's sweet, he met Rachel." No! Look at the importance of this verse.

Jacob had traveled to a foreign land to find a wife from the family of his mother's brother, Laban. He comes to a well that "just happens" to be the well which Rachel used to water her flocks. Just a coincidence, right?

I don't believe in coincidences. I hope you don't. The sovereignty of God determines the events of our life. He has a plan which He wants to unfold before our eyes if we will just get out of the way. Jacob went as he was directed, and God presented his wife to him by a well.

TEACHING MOMENT

What do you think God has in store for your children today? Are you willing to let them go wherever or to whomever to receive His blessing? Are you praying for their future spouse? They probably won't have to go to a well to find their husband or wife, but they may be led away from you. They may find them at college or on the mission field. God may direct them to a place that we, as parents, would never choose. Our job is to teach them to follow God. The rest is up to Him.

Let God direct your steps today. Let Him be in complete charge for once. What happens might just surprise you.

Thank You, Lord, for directing me to my bride. Thank You for allowing our paths to cross over thirty years ago. You have blessed me beyond what I deserve.

JANUARY 30

JUST DO WHATEVER

Judges 10

BEST VERSE: 15
The sons of Israel said to the Lord, "We have sinned, do to us whatever seems good to You; only please deliver us this day."

When someone says, "I don't care, just do whatever," that usually implies they really just don't care, or they are just tired of arguing about the issue. Right? Well, this is NOT the case here. In the pattern in which the Israelites had fallen, they had once again begun worshiping pagan gods, had been given into the hands of an enemy for judgment, and now were crying out to God for deliverance.

But look at their words. "Do *whatever* seems good to You." Those are dangerous words. I have prayed those words before. Desiring brokenness and humility, I have prayed, "Lord, do whatever You need to do to bring me where You want me." I am not sure I understood what exactly those words implied when I said them. I am sure I meant them, but did I fully understand them?

TEACHING MOMENT

Your child may throw similar words at you, but with more of a flippant attitude. Like the Israelites, they have done something wrong, and you have to discipline them. They get mad, rather than sorrowful, and say, "I don't care. Just do whatever." That is the perfect time to pull out this verse. Show them what those words could mean. Asking someone to "do whatever" can be a good thing, or it can be a bad thing. But when they ask God to do "whatever," especially with a sincere attitude, He can literally turn their world upside down. Is that what they want?

When we discipline our children, it is not to break them. But it should lead to brokenness and confession. We should see repentance and a desire for deliverance. As bad as we want it, however, we can't force this on anyone. That has to be desired and asked for by the person. We just set the table.

I don't know about you, but I truly desire having a contrite heart. I want to be vulnerable enough to be used by God and not be seen in the process. I want others to just see Jesus.

O Lord my God, as dangerous as it sounds, break me. Make me into Your perfect image. Let others ONLY see You in me.

THE ROCK

Mark 12

BEST VERSES: 10–11
Have you not even read this Scripture: "The stone which the builders rejected, this became the chief corner *stone*; this came about from the Lord, and it is marvelous in our eyes"?

I just love the fact that here in this passage Jesus basically calls Himself a rock. What do you think about when you hear the word "rock"? I have

PROTECTION THROUGH OBEDIENCE
Joshua 20

BEST VERSE: 6

He shall dwell in that city until he stands before the congregation for judgment, until the death of the one who is high priest in those days. Then the manslayer shall return to his own city and to his own house, to the city from which he fled.

The cities of refuge idea in Old Testament Israel is pretty cool when you think about it. Here's why. Back then, if someone killed someone, the victim's family was normally pretty quick to seek revenge. It didn't matter if it was an accident or not. The accused would be hunted down and murdered for killing their family member.

Cities of refuge provided safe places for the accused to state his innocence. The elders of a refuge city would not allow him to be killed. But . . . there was one stipulation. The accused had to stay in the city until the death of the current high priest. That might be years! But the umbrella of protection was only good if they abided by the rules.

TEACHING MOMENT

Children need to understand that the protection you provide them is only as good as their willingness to obey. If they refuse to listen to your guidance, they place themselves in harm's way. You can only protect those who want to be protected.

I have seen far too many parents enable their rebellious children simply by continuing to bail them out of trouble. The problem with this is the trouble gets deeper and deeper. Teach your children the rewards of obedience and the consequences of disobedience. That's biblical!

Are you suffering the pain of disobedience in your life right now? Turn back to the One who can provide you protection. He wants to defend you. He wants to give you refuge, but you must follow His commands. He cannot protect those who refuse to follow.

O God, I know far too well the pain of not following You. I am grateful for Your arms of protection over me when I submit to Your leadership and direction. Help me show others the benefits of being under Your protection.

THE GRASS ISN'T ALWAYS GREENER

Genesis 13

BEST VERSE: 10

Lot lifted up his eyes and saw all the valley of the Jordan, that it was well watered everywhere—*this was* before the LORD destroyed Sodom and Gomorrah—like the garden of the LORD, like the land of Egypt as you go to Zoar.

Didn't you just love it when someone gave you first pick? Like when your mom or dad let you pick first because it was your birthday. Of course, you picked the best piece of chicken or the biggest piece of pie. Lot thought, "Oh boy, Abram has given me first pick. I can't believe this."

If he had only known what was coming as a result of his pick. Had he known that ahead, do you think he would have chosen to remain with Abram while ordering his servants to stop quarreling with Abram's? I bet he would have. But obviously, he did not have that kind of foresight, and his life became a mess. His home and city ransacked, wife turned to salt, everything consumed by fire and brimstone! Wow! The grass definitely isn't always greener.

TEACHING MOMENT

What a perfect lesson for your kids when they want to pick first. Take a moment and tell them this story—the whole story. Not just the part of Lot getting what he wanted. They need to hear the rest also.

It is always better to go second or third. Put others before yourself. Your children need to learn that kindness and compassion will go a long way in life. Don't you agree?

Are you always pushing for first? Are you so busy climbing up that you ignore those below you? Jesus was God, but He put Himself in a lowly place so He could serve others. Be like Him.

Lord, teach me to put others before me. Let me see them as You do, and I know I will put them first. And let my children and others around me see it too.

ASK THE LORD

2 Samuel 2

BEST VERSE: 1

Then it came about afterwards that David inquired of the Lord, saying, "Shall I go up to one of the cities of Judah?" And the Lord said to him, "Go up." So David said, "Where shall I go up?" And He said, "To Hebron."

I just love the fact that one of the very first things David did after Saul died and he became king was to ask the Lord for direction. He asked Him where he should live. Come on, now! He's king. He could live anywhere. But David wanted to know what the Lord thought. So, he asked the Lord, and the Lord told him exactly where to go.

I read a quote the other day by A.W. Tozer that says, "Most people don't hear God's voice because we have already decided we aren't going to do what He says." Not David! He wanted to hear God's voice and do what He said. Hmmm, we could learn something here, couldn't we?

TEACHING MOMENT

Teaching our children to listen to us is important. But even more important is to teach them to do what we say, especially when it comes to following the Lord. Have you ever grabbed your little one's face and held it in your hands so she would look at you and listen? That's exactly the kind of attention we should give the Lord. We should have our eyes on Him, just waiting for His direction.

The next time your child nonchalantly asks you a question, without really listening for the answer, give them an off-the-wall answer, just to see if they are listening. "Mom, what's for dinner?" "Oh, I thought I would fix snails and toads." Sometimes, we ask God for direction and then totally ignore His answer. Later, we complain that He hasn't heard our prayer. In reality, He heard, and may have already answered. We just weren't paying attention.

What have you been asking the Lord lately? Have you been listening for His answer? Are you willing to hear His answer? Will you do what He says?

David did. He could have lived anywhere, but he went to Hebron because God said so.

Oh Lord, show me how to listen better. Open my ears and my heart to hear Your voice. And give me an obedient heart to follow wherever You lead.

FEBRUARY 6

FORGIVENESS

Luke 22

BEST VERSES: 31–32
Simon, Simon, behold, Satan has demanded permission to sift you like wheat; but I have prayed for you, that your faith may not fail; and you, when once you have turned again, strengthen your brothers.

This is one of the most precious things the Lord said to any of His disciples. He knew Satan wanted to bring down, not only Him, but also Peter and His other disciples. You see, Satan knew that those followers of the Son of God might just continue to tell the story after Jesus died. He wanted to "sift" them like wheat. In other words, Satan wanted to tear them apart.

But of all things, Jesus tells Peter that He has prayed for him. Jesus prayed specifically that once he had denied Him (Luke 22:47–53), he would return and be used to strengthen the other disciples. How would you have felt if Jesus had told you He had prayed for you?

TEACHING MOMENT
Our children are going to disappoint us. They are going to make mistakes. However, they need to know, just like Peter, that we will forgive them, and that God has great plans for them. Don't you think Peter remembered these words of Jesus after he denied him, and that rooster crowed?

How can you show your children to trust the Lord, even when they have "denied" Him? When they make those foolish decisions to go against God's will and your desires for them, they still need to be loved and prayed for. That does not mean that we condone their behaviors that are contrary to God's Word. But it does mean that, just like Peter, they can still be used to "strengthen" their brothers.

Forgiveness is a hard thing. Our flesh wants to seek revenge, not forgive someone. But we must follow the Lord's example. In the hour of His greatest need, Peter abandoned Him. But Jesus loved him anyway and prayed for him. Will you pray for your children, knowing that they will disobey and disappoint? Jesus does, for them and for you.

Protect my children today, O Lord. Cause them to walk with You on the straight and narrow road. And when they stray, bring them back to You quickly.

FEBRUARY 7

WHATEVER HAPPENS
Daniel 3

BEST VERSES: 16–18
Shadrach, Meshach and Abed-nego replied to the king, "O Nebuchadnezzar, we do not need to give you an answer concerning this matter. If it be so, our God whom we serve is able to deliver us from the furnace of blazing fire; and He will deliver us out of your hand, O king. But even if He does not, let it be known to you, O king, that we are not going to serve your gods or worship the golden image that you have set up."

Have you ever been faced with an impossible decision? It seemed no matter which answer you decided on was going to end wrong. Well, that's exactly the story today. If Shadrach, Meshach, and Abed-nego bowed to the statue, they were disobeying God. If they didn't bow, they were disobeying the king.

There may come a time in your life when you are faced with such a dilemma. Then what? What will you choose? Will you obey God or man? Will you choose to live or possibly die? All around the world right now, brothers and sisters in Christ are faced with that decision because of persecution in their countries. Many choose to compromise and live. Others choose to obey their Lord and are beaten or even killed.

TEACHING MOMENT
I pray this is a choice our children never have to make. Children should not have to worry about life and death decisions. But the way the world is

going, they very well could face a decision like this. So, how do you talk to your kids about this subject. Just use the Word. Read them this story and ask them what they would do. Ask them if they thought Shadrach, Meshach, and Abed-nego were scared when they approached that furnace.

It's okay to be scared in the face of danger. But it is also a time to trust the God who grants us salvation. Let them see your courage when you face uncertain times. Let them know you are trusting in God who has promised us peace through His Son.

Are you struggling today at trusting Him? Are you facing some hard times right now and feel He is nowhere near you? Stop and listen. He may just be calling your name right now.

I trust You, Lord, even in the darkest hours. I trust You to bring me through, one way or the other. I know I can depend on You.

FEBRUARY 8

NOT FINISHED

Joshua 18

BEST VERSES: 1–2
Then the whole congregation of the sons of Israel assembled themselves at Shiloh, and set up the tent of meeting there; and the land was subdued before them. There remained among the sons of Israel seven tribes who had not divided their inheritance.

It's hard to understand why the sons of Israel hesitated in taking the land that had been given to them. God had done so many miracles in their midst, and yet, they were still slow about claiming what was theirs. Only the descendants of Judah and Joseph had claimed their land in the Promised Land. The rest of the people were just hanging out, I guess. They had not completed their tasks.

I will never forget a dear friend of mine who passed away in his eighties. He was in church the night he died. It was a Wednesday night, and the congregation was sharing testimonies. He had stood up to give his when he collapsed. When the person next to him knelt down to him he heard him say these last words, "But I'm not done yet!" I have thought of that often. This friend of mine had much more living to do for Jesus, he thought, but the Lord called him home.

TEACHING MOMENT

Children have to be taught how to complete chores, don't they? You can't just tell them to do something and expect it to get done. You take the time to show them how to do it and how it should look when they are finished. A half-mowed lawn does not look good. A half-loaded dishwasher won't get the dishes clean. They must learn to follow through to the end. Complete the task. Finish the job.

We are preparing them for their future. This applies not only to their jobs, school work or hobbies, but it also applies to the task they will receive from the Lord. Finishing well pleases Him. Notice I didn't say it has to be perfect. Only God is perfect. But He does want us to do our very best and complete the tasks He gives us.

Are you putting off something the Lord has asked you to do? What have you started and not finished? Commit today to finish that task. Let the Lord show you exactly how and what He wants you to do for Him. He is a great teacher.

Finish the job! Complete the work! Then rest in knowing you have pleased the Master.

I want to finish well. I desire to serve You to my fullest and hear those words from You when I see You in heaven, "Well done, good and faithful servant."

FEBRUARY 9

JUST A TOUCH

Matthew 14

BEST VERSES: 35-36

And when the men of that place recognized Him, they sent word into all that surrounding district and brought to Him all who were sick; and they implored Him that they might just touch the fringe of His cloak; and as many as touched it were cured.

It never ceases to amaze me how I find "brand new" verses in the Bible every year. But it has happened again. I don't recall reading this passage before, even though I know I have. We all remember the woman who had the issue of blood sneaking up behind Jesus and touching His robe and receiving healing. But look at this passage. It says, "as many as touched *it* were cured."

How many touched it? Who were they? What ailments or diseases did they have? It doesn't mention that Jesus asked who they were. It just says when the people knew He had come, they sent word and brought all the sick to be healed. All they needed was just a touch of His robe. Now that is power.

TEACHING MOMENT

What's the point for us? How do we teach our children this truth? Our children need to know that Jesus is there and that He is perfectly fine with them touching Him. I don't mean He is physically present, of course, for them to touch. But He is always available for us to reach out and touch through prayer. He invites us to touch Him.

One of the best truths we can teach our children is the reliability of the healing power of Jesus. Now, don't get me wrong. I am not saying you should emphasize that Jesus is going to heal every boo-boo or scrape they have, as His healing goes much deeper than that. His healing can remove the grief and pain of heartache. His healing can take away the hurt and anger we have towards someone who has hurt us. His healing can. . . .

Mom and Dad, do you need to reach out today and touch the fringe of the garment? Do you need a fresh touch of Jesus? Won't you allow Him to send His healing power surging through you today? He wants to. He, in fact, is inviting you to do just that. Touch Him today!

O Lord God, touch me today. I need Your touch. I want to touch You. Send Your healing power surging through me!

FATHERLY ADVICE

Exodus 18

BEST VERSES: 17-18

Moses' father-in-law said to him, "The thing that you are doing is not good. You will surely wear out, both yourself and these people who are with you, for the task is too heavy for you; you cannot do it alone."

I never had the chance to get a lot of advice from my father-in-law. Pop died a few years after my wife and I were married. I regret that. But my dad lived until he was 84 and was always there to give me advice when I needed it. Having a father figure in your life with whom you can talk is priceless.

Moses was thrilled to see Jethro when he brought his wife and sons to him. Obviously, Jethro thought highly of Moses and was proud of him. So, when he observed Moses spending the whole day hearing complaints, he gave him some fatherly advice—you can't do this alone. That's good advice.

TEACHING MOMENT

I want to encourage you to tell your children the same thing. They can't do life alone. They may say when they are young that they don't need any help. I bet your two-year-old said that at least once. Am I right? And we know that teenagers don't usually want the help of mom or dad. Independence begins with interdependence. We need each other.

Dads, make sure your son understands that. Girls naturally have girlfriends to talk to. Guys, on the other hand, keep their emotions and thoughts close to the vest. We need to develop friendships with other guys that will allow us to turn to them when we need advice. Your son won't always have you around.

I miss my dad's advice. When he got older, I would call to ask his advice on something just so he would know I still needed him. In his last few years I had the privilege to give him spiritual advice. What a joy! Who will you turn to when you need a listening ear? If you can't name someone, find someone today.

O God, I am so grateful that You are always there to hear my pleas for help. I thank You also for those You have put in my life to influence me. I praise You for their godly advice.

HIDING FROM GOD

1 Samuel 10

BEST VERSE: 22B
So the LORD said, "Behold, he is hiding himself by the baggage."

Some people will go to great lengths to hide from God. They know God is talking to them. They know He is seeking them, but they just hide. Or at least they attempt to. I love this part of the story of the calling of Saul as the first king. There had never been a king of Israel. Saul wasn't sure about this whole king thing, so he hid in the baggage.

But who found him? God. God said, "He's hiding in the Samsonite." Not really! But Saul, this tall, good looking, young man, whom Samuel had anointed as king, was hiding from God. He was afraid of what was asked of him.

TEACHING MOMENT
This is a great lesson for kids. Read them the whole chapter and talk about what they might have done if it were them in this situation. How would they have reacted when all the things came true that Samuel told Saul would happen on the way home? Ask them if they have ever hidden from someone?

Explain to them how important it is to obey God. When He calls them to do something, it is best to yield to Him and just do it. God wants obedient children (just like you do), but He won't force obedience. Also explain that through obedience comes blessings. All kids want blessings.

Which baggage pile are you hiding in? Has the Lord called you to do something? Are you putting it off or ignoring it? Stop hiding. Do exactly what He asks of you. I promise you won't be disappointed at the outcome. Trust Him to see you through.

I am not worthy to be used by You, Lord. I thank You that You see me as worthy. Help me to respond quickly and obediently each time You call.

BE STRONG

Daniel 11

BEST VERSE: 32B

But the people who know their God will display strength and take action.

Daniel 11 is all prophecy. The man who appeared to Daniel (whom I believe is Jesus, but that's a another study in itself) is telling Daniel what is going to happen in the future. But the last half of verse 32 caught my eye. Even in the midst of all the trouble God's people will face, it says, "but the people who know their God will display strength and take action."

Now what does that mean? God wants us to be strong and do what He says. There will come times in our lives when we are facing unimaginable obstacles and foes. Regardless, God tells us to trust Him. Be strong! Do what He says! No matter what! When He says move, move. When He says speak, speak. When He says—well, you get the picture.

TEACHING MOMENT

And this is something our children need to be taught at an early age. When God speaks to them, and He will, they need to do what He says—period. How do they learn to do that? By obeying us. That is preparation for obedience to God. As a parent we are to teach our children to obey those whom God has placed over them. Submission to authority is a critical skill in maturity.

No one likes to obey, right? We all want to do it our own way when we want to do it. We often think our bosses or superiors are just plain stupid and don't know what they are doing. We KNOW we could do it better. But wait! God wants us to learn to obey from these people. So, teach your children now to obey.

I bet you are complaining right now about someone. Am I right? I have learned to submit to authority because when I don't, God just lets me keep repeating that learning experience. I don't always do it, though. I am stubborn and opinionated. Yep, me! I want to encourage you today to be strong and take action. But only take the action God instructs you to take. That may involve simply submitting.

Lord, You know my stubborn streak. You know I prefer to do it my way. Teach me today to submit to those whom You have placed in my life to direct me. Help me trust You in the process.

IGBOK

Haggai 1–2

BEST VERSE: 2:9
"The latter glory of this house will be greater than the former," says the LORD of hosts, "and in this place I will give peace," declares the Lord of hosts."

In the days of Haggai, he was prophesying about the temple. The people had neglected the House of God, so the Lord sent Haggai to remind them of a few things. Their suffering and hard times came because they had failed to follow Him and worship Him. Haggai brought this message to the people and said, "Rebuild."

However, many of them saw the rebuilt temple as inferior to the original. This verse today may have been heard and interpreted as referring to the physical temple, but it meant so much more. Jesus would come, the very Son of God, and fulfill this prophecy. He, indeed, was far more glorious than the temple. He was and is the very essence of God. He was the walking temple of God.

TEACHING MOMENT
When your little one is having a bad day, you may say, "It's gonna be okay." That's the meaning of the title of this devotional (IGBOK). You may have seen those bumper stickers around. Let me just say, however, that the acronym is not true. Unless . . . you know Jesus. Just as Jesus's presence on earth brought salvation to mankind and "made things better," when we know Him as our personal Lord and Savior, we have the hope of eternity.

Teaching our children real hope is so important. I am not talking about hoping for something tangible. I am talking about hope in Christ, hope in eternity, hope in a life filled with the joy of Christ. When those things are present through Christ, IGBOK!

When you see one of those stickers, pray for that person who is driving that car that they truly know how to be okay. Pray that they will come to Christ. Pray they will not let the circumstances of this world dictate their joy. It never will produce that.

Thank You, Lord, that it is going to be okay. Thank You for reassuring me through Jesus. Thank You for the promises in Your Word.

LOST OR NOT

Luke 2

BEST VERSE: 49
And He said to them, "Why is it that you were looking for Me? Did you not know that I had to be in My Father's *house?*"

Have your kids ever disappeared from your sight? I will never forget the time when our daughter, who was probably 2 or 3 at the time, vanished inside our home. We couldn't find her anywhere. I was frantically calling her name and looking in every nook and cranny in our house. I knew she couldn't have gotten out the door, but she was nowhere to be found. Finally, we heard her. She was hiding inside the fold of our bi-fold closet doors. She had become so frightened when she heard me hollering and getting more excited that she was afraid to come out.

My first thoughts as I read this familiar passage is how my parents would have responded. Man, I would have been in so much trouble. My bottom would have been warm for a week. But of course, I also wasn't the Messiah. I would have disappeared out of disobedience, not obedience.

Jesus wasn't lost. He was exactly where He should have been. He was far more at home in the temple than He was with His earthly parents. We can only speculate on what kind of child He was. Scripture is noticeably silent on His childhood years. But it is apparent from this passage that He was familiar with the surroundings in which they found Him after their three-day search.

Are your children at home in God's house? Are they familiar with the surroundings? Do they know their pastor(s)? Are they so comfortable at church that they had rather be there than anywhere? Jesus felt at peace in the temple because of His relationship with His Father. How about your kids? Are they at peace with their heavenly Father? If not, maybe it's time you introduce them.

In Your house, Lord, is where I belong. I am "at home" there, but I can't stay there. Give me the burden to invite others to come home with me and meet my Father.

FEBRUARY 15

IGNORANCE IS NO EXCUSE

Exodus 5

BEST VERSE: 2
But Pharaoh said, "Who is the LORD that I should obey His voice to let Israel go? I do not know the LORD, and besides, I will not let Israel go."

Have you run into people with this same attitude? "I don't believe in God, so I don't have to abide by His laws." Unbelief does not negate His existence. Nor does it do away with the need to obey His commands. Pharaoh found that out the hard way, remember? Ten plagues ending with the death of all first born! Pretty tough way to learn, huh?

Even after going through all that, Pharaoh still hardened his heart and came after the people Moses was leading out of Egypt. Some people just don't learn. But before you are so quick to judge, think about how hardheaded you are sometimes.

TEACHING MOMENT

Children can be hardheaded, too. Guess whom they learn that from? Yep, you! We model bad behavior so often that we don't even recognize it. The next time your son or daughter bows up at you, stop and think, "Did I give them this example?" You may be surprised at what you discover.

Teaching our children to abide by the Lord's commands shouldn't be all that difficult if we are living by them ourselves. As we model obedience, they will learn to obey. As we bow to His direction, they will learn to follow Him in their choices. Teach them by leading them, not preaching to them.

Are you obeying today? Are you abiding in Him? Don't be a Pharaoh with the hard heart who thinks he knows best. Be the one who obeys without questioning because you know if the Lord gives you a command, it is always for your good.

O Lord, show me the ways I am not obedient to you. Show me the right way to live. Show me the truths to teach my children and others.

FEBRUARY 16

SHOULDA, COULDA, WOULDA

Judges 1

BEST VERSE: 19

Now the LORD was with Judah, and they took possession of the hill country; but they could not drive out the inhabitants of the valley because they had iron chariots.

I want to you to take a look at this verse today and then also look at the following verses: 21, 27, 29, 30, 31, 33, 35. What do they have in common? The sons of Israel failed to drive out the inhabitants of Canaan and disobeyed what the Lord told them to do. The task got a little hard, and they quit.

God had clearly told them to clear the land of the current inhabitants. He knew what would happen if they didn't. As you read Judges, you see how they were influenced by these pagans to compromise and incorporate their gods into their lives. Hmmm, sounds familiar.

TEACHING MOMENT

If there is one warning we need to give our children, it is this—DON'T COMPROMISE YOUR FAITH. The church has been doing that too long. Our children are pressured to accept all kinds of "faith" as valid that are clearly not. Only Jesus can save. Only Jesus can give life. Only Jesus can lead people to the Father.

When your little one comes home from school stating how they learned that all religions are equal, correct that quickly. When they tell you that their teacher or friend says there is more than just one way to heaven, correct that on the spot. Don't let these "false teachings" gain a foothold in your child's life.

What have you allowed to water down your faith? What have you compromised on in your spiritual walk with Christ? "Well Carl, it's just too hard to be so dogmatic." Well yes! Of course, it is! What did you expect when you surrendered to Him? He demands obedience. He expects us to follow ONLY Him.

I want to challenge you today to take a look at what you believe and why. Do all your beliefs and convictions hold up to Scripture? There is only one absolute truth—His Word!

FEBRUARY 17

DO I HAVE TO SIT BY HIM?

Mark 14

BEST VERSE: 3

While He was in Bethany at the home of Simon the leper, and reclining at the table, there came a woman with an alabaster vial of very costly perfume of pure nard; and she broke the vial and poured it over His head.

When you read this story in Matthew and Mark what do you focus on? I don't know about you, but most everyone zeroes in right away on the alabaster vial. There have been songs written about it. Babbie Mason even entitled a Christian album by that name.

But did you notice the first phrase, "While He was in Bethany at the home of Simon THE LEPER"? Jesus was reclining at the table with a leper? Really? Most scholars agree that Simon was probably a former leper who was still known as Simon the Leper. And since Jesus was the guest of honor, He was probably reclining right next to Simon. Perhaps Jesus had healed Simon, and thus the reason He was at his home. We don't know for sure, but the fact remains, Simon was known as "Simon the Leper." What a nickname!

So, what's the lesson we can teach our kids from this passage? Nicknames stick? Be careful whom you eat with? No! The lesson is that Jesus loved Simon, no matter what people called him. People probably shunned him. People probably avoided shaking Simon's hand. Not Jesus. He reclined right next to him and ate with him. And we can assume Simon loved Jesus.

We need to teach our kids to accept others who may be different than us. We need to love on the unlovable. We need to accept those who the world may shun. Why? Because Jesus did! And He asks us to do the same. Why don't you reach out this week to someone you normally wouldn't? Show your kids that you too can love a "Simon."

Lord, I know You love the unlovable. Give me that same kind of love. I want to love others to Christ and I can through You.

FEBRUARY 18

PROMISES, PROMISES

Genesis 21

BEST VERSE: 1
Then the Lord took note of Sarah as He had said, and the Lord did for Sarah as He had promised.

Back in Genesis 17 God had told Abraham that Sarah and he would conceive and have a son. Unlike us, God does not forget His promises. God is faithful and will ALWAYS keep His word. Sarah became pregnant and had a child when she was in her 90's. Hey moms, how would you like that?

Sarah was excited. She even remarked later how God had made them laugh. In fact, Isaac means "He laughs." Even though Abraham and Sarah had both laughed at the idea of God giving them a child in their old age, God had given them laughter of joy through the birth of a son.

TEACHING MOMENT
But this devotional isn't about laughter. It is about keeping your word. Our children need to know our word is our bond. They need to know if we promise something that we will follow through. Why? Because if we don't, they

can't trust us. They can't trust what we say. They can't trust us when we tell them God promises us eternal life. They won't believe anyone's promises.

You see, we are responsible for building their trust in people when they are small. When they are older, they will learn to keep their word. Promises spoken should be promises kept. What have you promised your child this week? Did you have any intention of keeping that promise? If not, shame on you! Yep, I said that. Sorry! If you have broken a promise to your child, even a small one, make it right.

The other day, I found out a child at church was mad at me for something I said. I had told all the kids we were going to have cookies after a Christmas church service. Well the service was postponed due to weather, and all the homemade cookies had been dispersed to a downtown mission effort our church does weekly. So, when we rescheduled the church service the cookies were gone. But this little boy had not forgotten those cookies. I need to make that right, even though it was out of my control. He heard me promise something, so I needed to make good on that promise.

DON'T BREAK IT, KEEP IT!

Lord, may I exhibit Your character through my words, promises and deeds. I am thankful You always keep Your promises.

FEBRUARY 19

DIDN'T YOUR MOM ALWAYS KNOW?

Joshua 7

BEST VERSES: 16-18

So Joshua arose early in the morning and brought Israel nearby tribes, and the tribe of Judah was taken. He brought the family of Judah near, and he took the family of the Zerahites; and he brought the family of the Zerahites near man by man, and Zabdi was taken. He brought his household near man by man; and Achan, son of Carmi, son of Zabdi, son of Zerah, from the tribe of Judah, was taken.

I truly believe God gives moms a sixth sense about some things. My mom always seemed to know when I was lying when I was a little boy. She could spot a lie from a mile away. As I got older, I learned how to lie better, but I believe she always knew when I was doing wrong. I think she was the first one to say, "Be sure your sins will find you out."

Seriously though, that saying is very true. Just look at the passage for today. Achan knew the rule. Don't take any spoils from Jericho! But he just couldn't help himself. He saw something he wanted and took it. That foolish choice cost him and his entire family their lives. Consequences!

But the point I wanted to make about this passage is how Joshua found out who was the guilty party. As the tribes, families and men came forth, God revealed to him who it was. Verse 14 tells us that they "threw lots" to find out. God told them to do that, so He was the one directing the choice. First the tribe of Judah, then the family of Zerah, and then Achan. Don't you know Achan was sweating, as the choices narrowed?

TEACHING MOMENT

Our children need to learn early that even if they do manage to fool us, no one can fool God. He knows the choice they are going to make before they make it. He knows we are going to make poor choices sometimes. All He wants is for us to come to Him in repentance and ask for forgiveness. There may be consequences for our sin, but even in that there is His mercy. Rest little children knowing God loves you and has set up guidelines to protect you.

Father, I want to come clean of all my sins. Forgive me in all the way I have failed You. Forgive me of being critical and rebellious towards others.

CLAP AND SHOUT

Psalms 47–48

BEST VERSE: 47:1
O clap your hands, all peoples; shout to God with the voice of joy.

I have the privilege to travel to Uganda and Kenya each year to teach at a pastors' conference. Oh, the joy! Worship with my Ugandan and Kenyan brothers and sisters is filled with clapping and "shouting" for joy. Needless to say, their worship is lively and invigorating.

Then I come home (insert sad face here). Our worship isn't nearly as exciting. Let me explain quickly. I don't mean you have to clap and shout to have worship. Please hear me. But the Spirit in which my African brothers and sisters worship is in freedom. Their culture does not look at someone strange if they sway, jump, or dance to the songs. It's not about what they do in worship. It's about the Spirit in which they do it.

TEACHING MOMENT

Children don't have to be encouraged to move to the music. Sometimes they just have to move. I believe, as long as they are not distracting others, we should allow our children to worship as the Spirit leads them. You have to teach them what is appropriate for the setting. But give them some freedom.

Why not have a worship time at home and tell them that while singing songs they are free to respond to the music however they want? After you do that, ask them why they responded the way they did. What a great teaching moment for them! Individual worship, family worship, and corporate worship all have different "expectations" of behavior. Remember, it's not about what people do during worship. It's about the Spirit within worshipers.

Are you free to worship? You may choose to lift your hands and shout. You may choose to sit quietly with your eyes closed. You may clap and sway. Just allow the Spirit of God which resides in You to express to God your adoration and praise.

Father of worship, I praise You for allowing freedom in worship. You have not dictated a stiff, formal manner that we have to follow. Thank You for giving us room to express to You our love and devotion.

WHO?

Judges 12

BEST VERSES: 11-12

Now Elon the Zebulunite judged Israel after him; and he judged Israel ten years. Then Elon the Zebulunite died and was buried at Aijalon in the land of Zebulun.

What can be said about Elon, the 11th judge of Israel. Well . . . not much. These two verses are all we know, and they don't say much. But we must remember that every single word of the Bible is inspired by God. That means that these verses are significant. Our job is to discover what they mean.

Elon judged Israel. That was no easy task. And he did it for ten years. That's a long time! He must have been a leader. The Lord must have seen something in him to place him as a judge. His name was etched for eternity in God's Word. My point is no one is insignificant. We all have purpose.

TEACHING MOMENT

Our children definitely need to be taught that. So many children suffer from low self-esteem. They don't feel they matter. They don't think they have significance. They see themselves as less than others. But they aren't. God took the time to create them; therefore, they are all important.

Take them to this verse and show them that. We don't know what Elon did. We don't know if he had a wife and/or children. We don't know his age when he started ruling or when he died. All we know is he was a judge, and he died. Period. But Elon was important to the history of Israel. God placed him there for a reason.

God has placed you where you are for a reason. Do you know what that is? Do you want to know? He doesn't want to keep it a secret from you. Ask Him. Let Him show you your purpose and reason for living. Oh, how He wants to show you!

Lord God, You have placed me in this time and place for a reason. Help me to discover the full reasons why. Show me how You want to use me to shape my city, country and world.

MADE TO LOVE

John 15

BEST VERSES: 12, 17
This is My commandment, that you love one another, just as I have loved you. . . . This I command you, that you love one another.

Twice in this chapter of John's Gospel Jesus gives us a command to love one another. Why did He command this? Was it because He knew we would not choose to love each other? Well, let me ask you this. Is it hard to love others? Don't answer that.

I think we can learn a lot from our children on this subject. They know when someone loves them. They can just tell. They feel safe. They want to be with that person. They are drawn to them. I think that is exactly why children ran to Jesus and why He used them as illustrations of faith.

Back to the verse. Twice He commands "that you love one another." I hate being *commanded* to do anything. I don't mind being **asked.** Why is that? We are all stubborn about wanting to control our own actions. We need to understand what Jesus expects from us.

The words "commandment" and "command" really stress the end result of the action. So, the purpose of Jesus "commanding" us is not to control us, but instead to produce love in us and through us. He wants to use us to love others for Him. He, in fact, will love others through us. So, as we follow His orders to love one another we are in fact just being His vessels through which He loves us.

TEACHING MOMENT
Now back to your kids. How can you teach them to love one another? Just like Jesus. We can love others through Him. Love their friends. By doing this we are teaching them how to love one another. Won't you let Jesus command you to love one another so you can show your children how to do likewise? Just be obedient.

Father of love, love others through me. Give me that safe place where others can feel comfortable. Express through me the love You have for all mankind.

IN FAVOR

1 Samuel 2

BEST VERSE: 26

Now the boy Samuel was growing in stature and in favor both with the LORD and with men.

Doesn't this verse sound familiar? Luke 2:52 says, "And Jesus kept increasing in wisdom and stature, and in favor with God and men." Hmmm. Very similar. I wonder if Luke had this verse about Samuel in mind when the Holy Spirit inspired him to pen those words.

But look at the words. Both the Hebrew word for "favor" in 1 Samuel 2:26 and the Greek word for "favor" in Luke 2:52 mean "pleasing" or "beautiful" or "in favor." What does that mean? It means just want it says. Samuel and Jesus had this in common. They both pleased God and those around them. Centuries apart—man and God-man—and they both pleased the Father.

TEACHING MOMENT

These words are so good for our kids. We should be teaching them how to be "in favor." As they please their heavenly Father through obedience to His Word and His Son, they will be in favor with us and those around them. They will be pleasing to others. They won't rub people the wrong way.

When your children stray from this, we need to give them gentle reminders of what this means. It is so easy to get caught up in our own desires and plans that we forget to please God. We forget to strive to be "in favor" through obedience. It is so much easier to live in obedience if our motivation is to please the Father. I am not talking about a works mentality. I am talking about loving Him so much we can't bear to disappoint.

Are you desiring that? Do you reflect each day on how you can stay in favor with God and man? I want to encourage you today to do that. Take a look at your actions and words. Do any of them lead in a direction other than obedience? If so, stop right there. Redirect and follow Him.

Lord and Father, I do want to be in favor with You daily. I know my hope is in Christ. I rest in that. But I also want to please You through my actions. Thank You for empowering me to do just that.

IT'S NOT ALL ABOUT YOU

Deuteronomy 9

BEST VERSE: 6
Know, then, it is not because of your righteousness that the Lord your God is giving you this good land to possess, for you are a stubborn people.

Moses is preparing the people to enter the Promised Land after forty long years in the wilderness. He knew these people. He had seen the stubbornness all those years. He had begged God to not destroy them. He wanted to make sure they understood one thing—this blessing they were about to receive had nothing to do with their own righteousness.

Have you ever thought you deserved something? Maybe at work you felt you deserved that promotion over someone else. Maybe at school you knew you were better than anyone else because you had the highest GPA. We fall into the same trap of stubbornness and vanity. People haven't changed.

TEACHING MOMENT

That is why we must teach our children humility. There is nothing wrong with being proud of your accomplishments, but we must never allow our children to become boastful and arrogant of them. Everything we receive is a gift from God. It is a blessing we don't deserve. For in fact, all we deserve is hell.

That sounds harsh, I know. You can't imagine your children suffering in eternal damnation. But only the blood of Christ frees us from that certain destination. Make sure your children are aware of that gift and receive it early. Remind them over and over that only His righteousness, not theirs, will get them into heaven.

Are you banking on your goodness? Do you think if you are good enough or busy enough you will slide into your eternal reward? It's not about you. It's all about Him. He is the one we look to for our redemption.

Thank You, Lord, for saving my soul. Thank You, Lord, for making me whole. Thank You, Lord, for giving to me life more abundant, so rich and free.

NEVER TOO OLD

Exodus 7

BEST VERSE: 7

And Moses was fourscore years old, and Aaron fourscore and three years old, when they spake unto Pharaoh.

Aren't you amazed that Moses and Aaron were both in their eighties when they started this journey to lead the Hebrew children out of Egypt? I know what you are thinking. "Yeah, but they lived so much longer back then." True, but eighty is eighty, my friend. Who starts a new venture at eighty or eighty-three? No one.

But God had given them a new task which only they could do. God needed them to be the men He would use to confront Pharaoh and lead the people to the Promised Land. He chooses certain people whom He has gifted in certain ways for certain tasks at certain times.

TEACHING MOMENT

Our children need to know that God has a purpose for them in this life. They may discover that at an early age. It may not be revealed to them until they are older. But we can be certain that, if we are surrendered to Him, He has a purpose for our life here on earth.

Our jobs, as parents, is to provide the environment and the encouragement for our children to fulfill God's purpose in their lives. Are you able to see God's giftedness in your children? What strengths has He given them? What special talents do they have? God can use all of those. But what He really needs is a surrendered heart, one that is willing to follow even if they don't know where He is leading.

Are you modeling that for your child? Are you willing to drop your shepherd's staff and begin a new journey? Are you willing to confront those things in your life that hold you in bondage? Are you willing to lead others to the Promised Land?

God has a purpose for you, too. Watch for the burning bush! He wants to speak to you.

God of all ages, and I mean that literally, don't let me use my age as a reason for not serving You. Show me how to use my gifts up until the day I die.

GOOD WORDS TO HEAR

Luke 3

BEST VERSES: 21-22

Now when all the people were baptized, Jesus was also baptized, and while He was praying, heaven was opened, and the Holy Spirit descended upon Him in bodily form like a dove, and a voice came out of heaven, "You are My beloved Son, in You I am well-pleased."

JUST OBEY

I love to baptize believers. There is something joyous about lying them back in the waters and seeing the smile begin to erupt on their faces as they are coming up out of the waters. It's almost as if they are hearing God say, "You are My beloved child, in you I am well-pleased."

Now, I have yet to see a dove come down on anyone I have baptized. That would be cool though. But I know the Holy Spirit is there because, as believers, He is dwelling in them as I baptize them. So, all the elements of Christ's baptism are there—people watching (public baptism), waters to immerse, the Holy Spirit, and the Father's pleasure.

TEACHING MOMENT

The next time your children get to see a baptism at church, read them this passage. Talk about how Christ was obedient to the Father and gave us the example to follow. Jesus did NOT need baptism to save Him (neither do we for that matter). He was the Savior. He was obeying His Father in heaven and as a result, the Father showed His pleasure.

Perhaps your child is contemplating getting baptized. They have asked Christ into their heart and are ready for that step of obedience. Encourage that. Have them talk with your Pastor. But encourage that. Don't think they need to wait until they are older. Let them hear those words "I am well pleased" from the Father.

How about you? Have you followed the Lord in baptism? If not, let me encourage you today to get that done. The joy you will receive from the Lord for obeying Him in this will far outweigh any fear you feel in getting up in front of others. Trust Him and He will whisper to you too, "You are My beloved child; in you I am well-pleased."

Father God, I did not see a dove descend from heaven when I was baptized, but I still remember the day. Thank You for blessing me. Thank You for allowing me to be obedient.

FEBRUARY 27

WORD SURE SPREADS FAST

Ruth 2

BEST VERSE: 11

Boaz replied to her, "All that you have done for your mother-in-law after the death of your husband has been fully reported to me, and how you left your father and your mother and the land of your birth, and came to a people that you did not previously know."

I know you have heard of the "grapevine." You know, that invisible vine that carries news from person to person. Well, I renamed it the "kudzu vine." Kudzu grows faster than grapevines, but unlike the grapevine, kudzu only strangles and destroys what it comes into contact with. At least the grapevine produces fruit.

Well, here in Ruth we truly have a grapevine message service. The news of the good that Ruth has shown her mother-in-law has spread far and wide. Boaz, a relative of her deceased husband, has learned of Ruth's kindness, and, in return, he shows her an unexpected kindness. Finally, it seems Ruth's fortunes are turning around.

TEACHING MOMENT

Our children need to understand that our acts of kindness are seen by others either directly or indirectly. Boaz had never seen Ruth before, but her "testimony" had gone before her. Our children can learn that their testimony can touch people they have never met. And just like Ruth, that testimony may bring about blessings in the future. That wasn't Ruth's motive for showing kindness to Naomi. Neither should it be ours. But God has a way of blessing those whom bless others.

What acts of kindness can you and your children do today? Is there an elderly neighbor who needs some yard work done? Is there a project at church that you and your children could do? Ask the Lord to help you build your testimony so that it shines on Him, not you. Ask the Lord to allow you to bless someone else today. He, in turn, will bless you. Perhaps in ways and by someone you could have never imagined.

Lord, I do want to bless others. Direct me to those whom You would have me help. Let me be the one blessing and not just the blessed.

FEBRUARY 28

WHAT IS GOOD?

Joshua 21

BEST VERSE: 45
Not one of the good promises which the Lord had made to the house of Israel failed; all came to pass.

I have written several times about the promises of God and Him being a promise keeper. So, there is no need to do that again. But look at the adjective which describes the promises. It says, "good promises." I assume that is in contrast to a bad promise, but who wants that, right?

This word "good" is the Hebrew word *towb*, pronounced "tobe." But what is "good." Well, this is the same word used to describe creation. God made the light and said it is good. He made the trees and said it is good. You get the picture. Everything and anything God makes is good. That includes His promises.

TEACHING MOMENT
We have to remind our children of that, don't we? Our teaching about God must include that He is all good, no matter what He allows to come our way. His work in our lives is good.

Let me encourage you to do a word study on this word *towb*. It has so many more meanings that your child needs to know. It can mean precious, beautiful, better and best. All these words describe our God, too. He is all those things. AND since He made you and your children, they describe you, too.

Do you see yourself as *towb* in God's eyes? If you don't, you are calling God a liar. Why? Because everything that God creates is good, including you. Live like it.

Creator of all good, remind me daily of Your goodness. Whisper in my ear that I am good. Remind me that I am commanded to do good and be good because of Your goodness, not mine.

STANDING UP FOR JESUS
Matthew 26

BEST VERSES: 69-70

Now Peter was sitting outside in the courtyard, and a servant-girl came to him and said, "You too were with Jesus the Galilean." But he denied *it* before them all, saying, "I do not know what you are talking about."

Parents, if you haven't faced that moment in your child's life when they try to avoid being seen with you because it is not cool, then just wait. It is coming.

Several years ago, our family went on a 3-day cruise. It was our first and last. It's just not my wife's thing. Plus, my son got sick and well . . . it just didn't turn out great. However, . . .

They did have karaoke at night. Can you see where I am going with this? We went down to watch, and I couldn't help myself. I had to get up and sing. I decided to sing . . . are you ready . . . "Joy To the World" by Three Dog Night. Yep, I did it. My kids were teenagers, so you can imagine what they were doing. They were trying to get UNDER the table. Their body language screamed, *That's not my dad! I have never seen that man before.* Or they wanted to say, *That strange man kidnapped me!*

Peter knew the Lord intimately. He had spent three years with Him day and night. And now when He is being tried and convicted, Peter denies ever knowing Him. But Jesus understood, just like I understood my kids. Their denial of me didn't change my love for them. Peter's denial of Jesus didn't change His love for Peter.

TEACHING MOMENT

May I encourage you when your children start to "put some distance" between you and them? Let them do that safely. Give them some space. But constantly reassure them they are loved, and nothing they can do will ever change that.

O God, there is nothing I can do to cause You to leave me, I know that. But Lord, help me to not do anything to bring shame to Your name. Let my life be a beacon for others.

SEEING IS BELIEVING?

Luke 9

BEST VERSES: 7-9

Now Herod the tetrarch heard of all that was happening; and he was greatly perplexed, because it was said by some that John had risen from the dead, and by some that Elijah had appeared, and by others that one of the prophets of old had risen again. Herod said, "I myself had John beheaded; but who is this man about whom I hear such things?" And he kept trying to see Him.

Herod just never figured it out, did he? He heard all about Jesus, but he could not accept the fact that He might be the Messiah. You see, Herod knew an earthly Messiah meant an end to his rule. And he sure didn't want that. Besides he didn't want anyone meddling in his affairs (he had married his brother's wife, which was forbidden).

Seven of the saddest words in Scripture are "And he kept trying to see Him." Even when he did finally see Jesus, he didn't recognize Him for who He was. Seeing is NOT believing.

TEACHING MOMENT

Do your children believe everything they see? Today with the Internet and the limitless possibilities of computer imaging, they may see something and believe it is true. I mean it's right in front of them. It has to be real, right? We have to teach our children that seeing something does not make it true. The devil will try to deceive us. And he will definitely use the Internet and computers. It's just too easy for him now with these tools.

Our children must learn that our faith is not dependent on sight. Our faith is solely dependent on believing the Word of God. We may live to see Jesus return, but seeing Him then will not get us to heaven. We will need to have seen Him before—as our Savior and Lord. And if that is the case, we will see Him every day in those around us.

Open your eyes today! See Him! And once you see Him, live for Him. In fact, let Him be your eyes today. I promise that if you do, the world will look a lot better. You will see limitless opportunities to serve Him. Seeing is NOT believing, but *believing* IS *seeing*!

I want to believe and see deeper, O Lord. Open my heart to a stronger faith in what You want to do in and through me. Allow me to show others how to live a life pleasing to You.

SHEPHERDING

Psalms 23–24

BEST VERSES: 23:1–6

The Lord is my shepherd, I shall not want. He makes me lie down in green pastures; He leads me beside quiet waters. He restores my soul; He guides me in the paths of righteousness for His name's sake. Even though I walk through the valley of the shadow of death, I fear no evil, for You are with me; Your rod and Your staff, they comfort me. You prepare a table before me in the presence of my enemies; You have anointed my head with oil; My cup overflows. Surely goodness and lovingkindness will follow me all the days of my life, and I will dwell in the house of the Lord forever.

Did you ever memorize this psalm? Most of us who grew up in church learned this in Sunday school. It is probably, next to the 100th psalm, the most quoted one in The Book of Psalms. But have you ever stopped to really understand what the psalmist is saying here?

He is trusting completely in the guiding hand of the Shepherd. He is allowing the Lord to guard him, guide him, and graze him. The Lord is providing protection, plans and provisions. Are you allowing the Lord to do that in your life?

TEACHING MOMENT

As we raise our children, we are doing the same. We are protecting them from any harm we can. We want to keep them safe whenever possible. We are also feeding and clothing them with what they need. We are making plans for them as we teach them to obey us and God. We want their lives to be according to God's will.

As you do this "shepherding" of your little flock, won't you reflect on this psalm? Read this to them today. Show them how, just as you do these things for them, the Lord also wants to do the same for them, spiritually. As we teach them God's Word, they can see Him working in their lives.

I am thankful, Lord, that You are my Shepherd. I am safe within Your fold. You are constantly watching over me and making sure I am taken care of. Praise You!

MARCH 4

WHO WANTS SHEEP?

John 10

BEST VERSE: 11

I am the good shepherd; the good shepherd lays down His life for the sheep.

I have to admit I don't know much about shepherding sheep. I have never owned sheep, nor do I want to. All I have heard about sheep makes me want to avoid them. They aren't smart (so I'm told). They wander off. They are easy prey for predators. So why would anyone want to be a shepherd to them?

But someone has to tend the sheep. In my years of ministry, I have had the opportunity to lead others. I have seen that as a kind of shepherding. Some of the people whom I led were easy to shepherd. Others—well—let's just say they weren't as easy and leave it at that.

TEACHING MOMENT

Our children are like that. Some are easily directed and cared for, while others fight us every step of the way. But they still need to be cared for. The sheep that wanders off needs the shepherd. Our children who "wander off" need a shepherd.

Jesus said the sheep know His voice. Do your kids "know your voice"? Do they hear the caring in the words you use? Do they know when you are warning them of danger? Do they come to you when you call them? Do they long to hear your words?

Shepherding children is often a thankless task. But it is one that the Lord has given us as parents. We must guard, guide, and graze our children, just like a shepherd would for his flock. On those days when you want to give up, remember that He is the one who can show you how to shepherd. He is the Great Shepherd. He knows all the tricks. Just ask Him.

Jehovah God, so many sheep are without a shepherd. Will You put the right sheep in my flock? Will you give me the wisdom to bring others into the fold?

MARCH 5

MY STRENGTH

Psalms 19–20

BEST VERSE: 20:7
Some boast in chariots and some in horses, but we will boast in the name of the Lord, our God.

It seems there are a lot of verses on bragging and boasting. We are warned again and again about not being conceited or "stuck up." We have plenty of examples of individuals in Scripture who did just that.

But here in this verse, we are given the very thing to brag and boast about—the name of the Lord, our God. Now that is something to brag about! Why? Because He is eternal. He is never going to change. He ALWAYS wins. His name is comforting. His name is "I AM."

TEACHING MOMENT
Try this! Keep a brag book. That's right, I said *keep a brag book.* But here is the guideline. Only write down things that the Lord has done in your family. Every night at dinner ask your family what the Lord did that day. Now some days it will be so easy to name something, and other days it will be hard. It will be hard, not because the Lord hasn't done anything, but because we weren't watching.

Right now, take a moment and write down one thing the Lord has done for you in the last 24 hours. Go ahead and do it now. Reading the rest of this devotional entry can wait a moment or two. Find a blank journal book or spiral notebook or writing pad. Got it? Good. Now start your book, beginning with today's "boast." You will be amazed when you go back and read your entries. You will have forgotten a lot of these blessings. Remind your children of some of them when they are struggling. God is always at work.

Are you doubting God? It's okay. We all go through times when we feel closer to Him than at other times. Reflect on His past blessings in your life. Thank Him for being faithful to you. He loves to hear our praise. Boast in His name today!

O Lord, our God, I will boast of You today. I will brag on You to others. I will give thanks for all You have down in and through me.

RIGHTEOUS LIVING

Lamentations 1

BEST VERSE: 18A
The Lord is righteous; for I have rebelled against His command.

Have you ever told someone they need to confess their sins because the Lord knows them anyway? I have. It's true. Lamentations isn't known for its cheerful words. It is a book of . . . well . . . lamentations, thoughts of mourning and grief. And in this verse Jeremiah, the author, tells why.

It's really simple. The Lord is righteous. We rebel and receive the consequences for our disobedience. It may not happen right away, but it will. Israel and Judah had rebelled against the Lord for years and years until judgment came. But it came, and when it did, they knew why.

TEACHING MOMENT
How do we teach our children to NOT fall into this trap of rebellion? Their sin natures are bent toward disobedience against us and God. All we can really do is show them our surrender to the Lord. We have to model an obedient spirit. We have to live our lives in such a way that they want to model us and not rebel against us.

That doesn't mean we have to be perfect, but we do need to strive toward it. We need to desire to be the very image of Christ to our children. When they see mom or dad, they should see what Jesus would have looked like in the flesh. Wow! That's pretty demanding, isn't it? Yep. But you don't have to do this by yourself. Christ does it through you, if you will just surrender.

What is holding you back from representing Christ to your family? You may say, "But Carl, they know me too well." Exactly. So, they will know any righteousness is not of you. That will point them directly to Jesus. They know you can't do it by yourself. Surrender to Him now.

Lord, thank You that I can't do this on my own. I must surrender rather than rebel because You are righteous, and You demand righteous living from me. Thank You that You are my righteousness.

MARCH 7

DON'T WORRY, BE HAPPY

Psalms 43–44

BEST VERSE: 43:5
Why are you in despair, O my soul? And why are you disturbed within me? Hope in God, for I shall again praise Him, the help of my countenance and my God.

You are probably too young to remember that song, "Don't Worry, Be Happy." It has a bit of a reggae style to it and was popular quite a few years ago. I wonder if the psalmist was playing that tune on his lyre?

But, seriously, the question he asks is a good one. "Why are you in despair, O my soul?" He is chastising himself for not putting his trust in Jehovah God. He knows the answer. He knows his hope. Do you?

TEACHING MOMENT
Children, just like the rest of us, can beat themselves up about stuff. They can despair. They can get depressed. Use this psalm during that time. Show them the answer to their lowliness. It does NOT rest in someone or something. The answer is God. The answer is their faith in Christ Jesus.

Now let me ask you a question, mom and dad. Are you a depressing person? Do you worry or despair a lot? If you do, you WILL negatively affect how your child reacts. You will put a damper on their hope. They need to see you resting in Jesus. Show them how to do that.

We all get down sometimes. But we, as believers, can't stay there. The world is watching us. This hope we preach must be lived out. This hope we say we believe in must be evident in our lives to be believed by others. Trust Him today. He is the help of our countenance and our God.

Lifter of my head, I will praise You. Even in the pit of despair I will look up to You. Thank You for loving me and bringing me out.

MARCH 8

WHO ME?

Judges 6

BEST VERSE: 12
The angel of the Lord appeared to him and said to him, "The Lord is with you, O valiant warrior."

I love this story of Gideon. Here he is, beating out the grains of wheat in a wine press. He is literally hiding from the Midianites, and the Angel of the Lord (I believe this is Jesus) appeared to him and said, "The Lord is with you, O valiant warrior." Gideon probably looked over his shoulder like, *Who is He talking to? Certainly not me! I'm no valiant warrior.*

That's exactly why the Lord picked Gideon. He didn't see himself as worthy. He was a humble man from a lowly family in the tribe of Manasseh. He had no prestige or position. But God saw something in Gideon that He could use. He was obedient. God said "Go," and he went. He had some questions and even asked God to confirm some things. Obviously, that was okay with God, because He did it (see verses 36–40).

TEACHING MOMENT
What do you think the Lord is going to ask your son or daughter to do for Him? Will they be the next Gideon standing up for their nation? Will they be called upon to lead? Will they be asked to surrender their safety and security to reach a lost world? We do not know the calling the Lord has for our children, but we do know He has called us to prepare them. Gideon knew the history of his people. He knew of God's power and strength. Do your

children? Have you told them how He has worked in your life? Have you shared your confidence in the Lord with them?

As I teach each Sunday morning in our Children's Church, I know I am standing before future missionaries, doctors, lawyers, teachers, and homemakers. I want to instill in them the confidence to trust the Lord and to do whatever He asks, no matter how crazy it sounds. You may know the rest of Gideon's story. God told him to send home most of his army. He didn't need them. All God needs is our availability. He can do the rest.

Here I am, Lord, use me. Put me wherever You want. I know that is a dangerous prayer, but I mean it. I am confident that wherever You lead, I am safe.

MARCH 9

LEVEL GROUND

Psalms 25–26

BEST VERSE: 26:12
My foot stands on a level place; In the congregations I shall bless the Lord.

I love to take hikes. I don't do it a lot, but I love it. In Tennessee, where I live, there are tons of places to hike. A lot of them have hills and gorges. The views are normally breathtaking, but there is one drawback—the ground isn't level. You have to hike up and down these hills, sometimes on pretty treacherous ground.

It is much easier to walk on level ground. David knew that. He knew it was better to be sure-footed. God is like firm, level ground to us. He is always sure. He is always a firm foundation. We should do as David and set our feet on the level place that is our Lord. It is there we are able to stand against the enemy.

TEACHING MOMENT
Have you ever played "King of the Mountain" with your kids? What fun! Find a good hill and see who can stay on top the longest while the rest of the group tries to push them off. It's not a game for the faint of heart.

But this game can be used to teach this verse. It's hard to stay on top of that hill when the ground beneath your feet isn't level. It's hard to advance up that hill and try to push someone off who is above you. Childhood games can teach such great life lessons.

What hill are you trying to climb right now? What hill are you trying to defend on your own? Step down on level ground. There's a saying I love: "The ground is level at the cross." In other words, we are all equal there. Set your feet there.

Father, thank You for giving me sure feet. Thank You that I can depend on You for my support. Help me show others the value of resting on Your foundation.

BETTER CHECK WITH GOD

1 Samuel 30

BEST VERSE: 7
Then David said to Abiathar the priest, the son of Ahimelech, "Please bring me the ephod." So Abiathar brought the ephod to David.

This ephod was probably the same one Ahimelech had at Nob behind which the sword of Goliath was hidden. His son, Abiathar, had brought it with him when he joined David. Why was this ephod used to talk to God? The priest had the ephod in which contained the stones used to cast lots to hear from God. God had initiated that means of communication long ago when Aaron was the priest. David knew that, of course, and wanted to get clear direction from God before proceeding.

Think about it for a second. David and all his men had just returned to find their city destroyed and all their wives and children missing. But he stopped long enough to seek God's counsel instead of reacting out of the flesh. His men were ready to stone him, but he turned to God for guidance.

TEACHING MOMENT
We need to help our children learn this lesson. When the world seems to be falling apart all around them, that is the VERY time they need to stop and

pray. God is aware of their circumstances. He has the answer, but they must ask Him. He won't just jump in if they aren't seeking him.

Jesus tells us to seek first the kingdom of God. If we do that, He promises to add all things to us. If we seek His wisdom and truth, He will guide us in the right path. Now, that path may not be easy. David had to go fight the Amalekites for about two whole days to get his family back, but he did. He and his army followed the Lord's counsel and attacked.

Will you follow the Lord's counsel today? Will you show your children that they too must seek the Lord and then do what He says, no matter what He says? If we do that and teach them to do the same, we will find that God is ready to guide and provide.

O God, You have all the answers I need to every situation I face. Remind me today to stop and ask You for guidance. Let me see You first.

MARCH 11

ANT HILLS

Proverbs 5–6

BEST VERSES: 6:6-8
Go to the ant, O sluggard, observe her ways and be wise, which, having no chief, officer or ruler, prepares her food in the summer and gathers her provision in the harvest.

Have you ever sat and studied an ant hill? Boy, those little guys are busy. They never seem to stop. In and out, up and down. They are carrying food in and going out again to forage. We can learn a lot from them.

Too many of us are, just as the writer says, sluggards. We are lazy. We want others to wait on us. We even expect God to just mysteriously meet our needs when we call on Him. We need to examine our lives and see if we are acting like the ant or the sluggard.

TEACHING MOMENT
Are your children lazy? Do they just sit around playing video games or watching tv? Get them out of the house. Give them chores to do. Children

need to be motivated to move. Find every opportunity to get them outdoors and moving. Reward them for work they do around the house but do that carefully. You don't want them expecting to be rewarded for every chore.

Go outside and find an ant hill. Bring a magnifying glass, if you can. Let your kids see these fascinating creatures up close and personal. Spend some time watching them, and then talk about this verse. It's pretty amazing to see how God creates us to work in the same way.

So, let me ask you, are you the ant or the sluggard? Before you answer, think about it. How many hours in the day do you waste watching tv? How much time do you spend on the computer? Get up, and get moving. Ask the Lord to show you what He would have you do with your time.

Lord, forgive me of idleness. I want to spend my time honoring You and working for Your kingdom. I know You are coming soon, and I want to be found busy.

MARCH 12

NAP TIME

Genesis 2

BEST VERSES: 2–3
By the seventh day God completed His work which He had done, and He rested on the seventh day from all His work which He had done. Then God blessed the seventh day and sanctified it, because in it He rested from all His work which God had created and made.

When I married my wife, Chris, and we would visit my family in South Georgia, she hated Sunday afternoons at my parents' house. Why? Because after church and a typically big Sunday lunch, do you know what we did? We took naps. Chris didn't grow up like that, and she hated that everyone was snoozing while she was left by herself in the land of the conscious. But now, after over thirty years of marriage, where do I normally find her on Sunday afternoons? You got it—taking a nap.

God rested! Did He need rest? No! He is God. He was giving us an example. We need to stop each week and recharge our batteries. We need time to refresh our bodies and our souls. Do we have to take a nap one day a week? Of course not. But finding some form of rest will do us a lot of good.

TEACHING MOMENT

Nap time is not too hard to teach our younger children. Now when they get a little older, they don't want to take that nap. But here is where we teach them the importance of rest. Some kids go until they drop. That's not necessarily good. One part of taking that nap is discipline. Knowing your limits. Taking care of yourself. Hey, the good part is you can "model" this for them by napping yourself. Now, if you will excuse me, I think I am going to...zzzzzzz.

Have you taken time to rest? Make that your New Year's resolution that you will begin to take some time each week on the Lord's day to rest. I promise it will be the best resolution you have ever made and kept.

Father, You have told us to rest on Your day. We need to rest our bodies but also refresh our souls. Help me to teach my children the importance of resting—resting in You.

MARCH 13

SALVAGEABLE

Matthew 1

BEST VERSE: 5

Salmon was the father of Boaz by Rahab, Boaz was the father of Obed by Ruth, and Obed the father of Jesse.

The first part of Matthew gives us the genealogy of Jesus. You may find that boring, but I think it is so interesting. I have been trying to research my family tree, so anytime I see a genealogy I try to learn something.

This verse caught my eye today because of the women mentioned. Do you see it? King David's father was Jesse. But look who his great grandmother was—Ruth, the Moabite. And David's great, great grandmother was Rahab, the harlot from Jericho. Wow! Tell me God can't use you! If the God of the universe used a harlot and a Moabite in the line of Jesus, He can use anyone He wants.

This is a great story to share with your kids. You may not want to go into great detail about Rahab's career choice, but you can definitely talk about them being pagans whom God called into His family. Your children need to know that God can use them, just as they are. He has a plan for their lives. They just have to yield to Him.

Perhaps your son is farsighted. So what? God can use that. Maybe your daughter is short. Big deal! God can use that. It does not matter what "deficiency" the world may say your child has. God can take them and use them for greatness. Do you really think Rahab and Ruth knew the Messiah would come through them? I don't think so.

Are you allowing the Lord to use you, mom and dad? Are you allowing Him to take your shortcomings and make them strengths? Are you bowing your will to His? Stop making excuses and let Him use you. He will!

Lord, use me just like I am. I am Yours to put where You want. No matter what others say about me, You have a purpose for me.

MARCH 14

BOY, YOU SMELL

John 11

BEST VERSE: 39B

Martha, the sister of the deceased, said to Him, "Lord, by this time there will be a stench, for he has been *dead* four days."

My wife has a very sensitive nose. If I walk outside for a second and walk back in the house, she will say, "You smell. Have you been outside?" I mean, come on, I was outside for like a minute. I kid her that she should have worked at a perfume factory. She has the best olfactory senses in the world.

But even I could have smelled Lazarus. He had been dead four days inside a sealed tomb. If you have ever smelled a dead body, well, let's just say you won't soon forget it. But Jesus wanted to make sure that everyone knew Lazarus was dead. Some Jews believed the spirit "hung around" for three days after death. Jesus waited four days on purpose.

Have your children ever come in the house after a long day in the yard playing and smelled to high heaven? What a perfect time to talk about this story. "Johnny, you smell like Lazarus!" "Who is that, Mom?" Then you can tell him the story and how Jesus raised him from the dead.

Another cool thing about the story to tell them is that Jesus called Lazarus by name. He didn't want every stinking corpse in the cemetery to wake up. That would have been quite a sight. No, He called the one He was seeking. He calls us by name too. Even when we are stinking, He calls us by name. Pretty cool, huh?

I know I have more "stinking" days than "smell good" days. I tend to let my flesh win more than it should. I let my own desires control me, when I know my spirit should. I don't know about you, but I had rather smell good than stink any day.

Father, will you take this old stinking corpse and raise it afresh today? I praise You for saving me and giving me the power to walk with You. Let my aroma be yours and not my flesh.

MARCH 15

HANGED MAN

Deuteronomy 21

BEST VERSES: 22-23
And if a man has committed a crime punishable by death and he is put to death, and you hang him on a tree, his body shall not remain all night on the tree, but you shall bury him the same day, for a hanged man is cursed by God. You shall not defile your land that the Lord your God is giving you for an inheritance.

Right here in Deuteronomy we find a fulfillment of Christ. He became accursed for us. He hung on a tree (the cross) to bear the sins of the entire world. Isn't it interesting also, that Jesus was taken off the cross and buried the same day, just as the verse says above?

Jesus came for one purpose—to pay the ransom for the human race. He knew the price before He ever left Glory. He knew the penalty for sin because

He is the one who wrote the Law. He knew when He hung on that cross His Father in Heaven would see Him as accursed. But He came anyway. Why? Because He loves us and wanted us to have access to the kingdom of God.

TEACHING MOMENT

This is a truth that our children must learn. We, as parents, need to show them the power of paying a debt for someone else. I am sure you will have the opportunity to do that at some point, if you haven't already. Perhaps your son has broken something belonging to someone else and needs to replace it. He doesn't have the money, so you step in and pay the debt for him. There you go—a simple picture of what Christ did for us.

While that example doesn't capture the magnitude of what Christ did, most children can understand the "forgiveness" of a debt which they do not have the ability to pay. We also need to show them the joy in which it must be done. Jesus did not die on the cross begrudgingly. He came willingly. He wanted to die for us.

How about you? For whom have you sacrificed? I mean, really sacrificed? Are you willing to let go of something you hold dear for the sake of someone else? Are you willing to lay it down?

God, I know You love a sacrificial heart. You love seeing us dying to ourselves and giving of ourselves to others. I want to please You, Father.

MARCH 16

KINDNESS REJECTED

2 Samuel 10

BEST VERSE: 2

Then David said, "I will show kindness to Hanun the son of Nahash, just as his father showed kindness to me."

No one really knows the story behind Nahash's kindness to David. Scripture does not tell us. We do know that Nahash was Saul's enemy, so many speculate he was kind to David since "the enemy of my enemy is my friend," or so they say.

Regardless of the reason the kindness was shown, David feels obligated to repay the kindness toward Nahash's son, but the son rejects it and even "spits in the face" of David by humiliating David's servants he had sent. Not cool! There are lessons to be learned here.

TEACHING MOMENT

Our children need to learn two things from this lesson. First, they should repay kindness shown. When someone blesses them, they should find a way to repay that. It's just the right thing to do. A thank you card is appropriate or some other way to show their gratitude.

Secondly, don't spurn a kindness shown from anyone, even from someone you "think" is your enemy. You don't know their motive. Perhaps the Lord is working on them. This act of kindness may be of the Lord. As believers, we need to accept this act as Christ would. Now, don't be gullible, but be loving.

Is there someone to whom you need to show a kindness? Someone maybe who has blessed you lately and you failed to thank them? Our children are watching how we respond to others. What better way to teach them these lessons from David than for them to see us do the same.

Now, if the other person turns your kindness away, don't put together an army and attack them. Let's leave that to David. The Lord knows your motive. He will defend you. Trust Him to do that. You just need to be obedient to follow the Lord's direction toward others.

Father, help me to be a blessing to someone today. I truly thank you for others You put in my life to bless me.

GOD, ARE YOU SURE?

Genesis 39

BEST VERSE: 23B
. . . and whatever he did, the Lord made to prosper.

Do you think Joseph wondered why he was suffering so much? Sold into slavery by his brothers, bought by Potiphar to be his slave, falsely accused by Potiphar's wife and then put in prison for a crime he didn't commit. The Bible does not say that Joseph yelled or screamed at any of this. He had no power to demand anything. He was helpless in the face of all his accusers. But God. . . .

God had a bigger plan than Joseph was made aware. Through all these events, God was placing Joseph right where He wanted him. He had to go through all these events to be in the position years from then to save His chosen people.

TEACHING MOMENT

Do your children ever ask you why they have to go through bad times in their lives? The loss of a friend or a breakup with a boyfriend or girlfriend can cause heartache and pain. Your children will probably come to you in tears, wanting you to comfort them. This story is perfect to explain God's sovereignty.

God has a perfect plan for your child. That plan may take them through some difficult times. But He is faithful to bring them through, just like He did Joseph. Joseph couldn't see the future, but he trusted the one who could.

Do you trust the Father with your child's future? Do you trust Him with yours? Do you trust Him with today? If we can trust Him for eternity, why can't we trust Him in our daily challenges? If we can trust Him for our salvation, why can't we trust Him with everyday decisions?

Let the Lord lead you through the pits, slavery, and prisons of your life. Perhaps He is preparing you to rescue your people!

PASS THE SALT PLEASE

Matthew 5

BEST VERSE: 13

You are the salt of the earth; but if the salt has become tasteless, how can it be made salty again? It is no longer good for anything, except to be thrown out and trampled underfoot by men.

I don't know about you, but I can't get by without salt. Food without salt is just, well, blah. Every year when I travel to Uganda and Kenya, I always carry little packets of salt and pepper to liven up the food. Sometimes I can find salt there, but normally I can't, or it's all clogged up with humidity and therefore, useless.

But you know what? I should be more concerned with my salty life. Does my Christian walk give flavor to those around me? Does my lifestyle "taste good" to others. Do I make people want more of Jesus?

Sure, I know we can live without salt. But we can't live without Christ, not really *live*. We may survive. We may even appear successful in the eyes of the world. But when it all comes down to it, a salt-free life is not worth anything eternally.

TEACHING MOMENT

Why not cook your next meal for your kids and leave out the salt? Don't have any on the table. Make sure the food is bland and REALLY NEEDS SALT to be good. What a perfect way to apply this verse. I promise they won't soon forget the lesson.

Won't you be salt in the world?

Thank You, Lord, for making me salty. Help me to be so salty that those around me crave the Living Water.

REWARDED

Joshua 19

BEST VERSE: 49

When they finished apportioning the land for inheritance by its borders, the sons of Israel gave an inheritance in their midst to Joshua the son of Nun.

Over forty years had passed since Joshua walked the land of Canaan with the other spies. Joshua 19:49 shows him finally getting his reward. Notice what the verse says: "the sons of Israel gave an inheritance in their midst to Joshua the son of Nun." They recognized Joshua as their leader and wanted to bless him.

Don't you think Joshua thought this day would never come? He had been waiting and waiting. He was probably tired of waiting. Yet the day had finally come. He had been faithful to the Lord as Moses' servant and now as the leader of the children of Israel. God said, "Rest."

TEACHING MOMENT

One thing our children today don't seem to understand is sometimes you have to wait to get what you truly want or deserve. Our society seems to expect instant gratification. They want it now. They want it immediately. We have to teach our children to wait. You've heard the expression "Good things come to those who wait." Well, it's true. And we have the most to wait for—eternal life.

The next time your child(ren) can't wait for something, use this story about Joshua to teach them about patience. This is not an easy task, but it is one that is so needed. What you teach them now about patience will help them later.

Now, how about you? Are you patient? Are you willing to wait? Do you believe God has a blessing for you, if you are faithful? He wants to bless you, but sometimes that blessing is delayed. You may not see that blessing this side of eternity, but it's coming.

Remember, Joshua waited over forty years for what God had promised him. All during that time he was faithful. We never see him complain. He just did what God asked him. Will you?

I can wait, O Lord. My eternal reward will come one day, but while I am here, help me to live each day in service to You.

PROMISE KEEPER

2 Samuel 21

BEST VERSE: 7

But the king spared Mephibosheth, the son of Jonathan the son of Saul, because of the oath of the Lord which was between them, between David and Saul's son Jonathan.

How many times have you heard your children making promises to their friends? Remember the pinkie swear? Kids promise things all the time. They promise to never stop being someone's friend (until a better friend comes along). They promise to clean their room (until they get busy outside playing). They promise to do their homework (but fall asleep before it is finished).

Promises are meant to be kept, not broken. David had promised Jonathan that he would protect his family. And here in this passage he had to choose which descendants of Saul to turn over to the Gibeonites for them to kill in order to stop the famine going on in Israel. Tough choice, but he kept his promise to protect Jonathan's son.

TEACHING MOMENT

How about you, mom and dad? Have you made promises to your children that you have not kept? Have you promised to take them to the ballpark, but haven't? Have you promised to go with them to the movies, but just haven't gotten around to it? They are watching and will model your promise keeping skills.

Our Father in heaven will always keep His promises. He promises to never leave us or forsake us. He promised to send us His Holy Spirit, and He did. He promises to love us with an everlasting love. Aren't you glad that He is a promise keeper?

I want to be a promise keeper, Jesus. Stop me from making rash vows without any intention of keeping them. Let my "yes" be "yes" and my "no" be "no" (James 5:12).

HEDGES

Psalms 15–16

BEST VERSE: 16:1
Preserve me, O God, for I take refuge in You.

I love a nice hedge or bush. In fact, I have planted or maintained several through all my moves. One, in particular, reminds me of this verse, though. When we lived in Florida, our first house had an ugly utility box in the right front corner of the lot, right next to the street. So, I decided to plant something around it so it would be hidden. I wanted a nice flowering hedge of some sort, so I picked a bougainvillea.

Do you know anything about bougainvilleas? Well, they grow pretty fast and have beautiful flowers. However, they also have large thorns which can tear you up. What began as a flowering hedge to hide something became a flowering tormentor that "protected" that box. You see, that word "preserve" in our verse can be translated "put a hedge about."

TEACHING MOMENT
We can build hedges to hide or protect. We need to pray a hedge around our children to keep them from harm or evil influences. Have you ever prayed that? "Lord, please put a hedge of protection around little _____." We need to do that. We need to ask the Lord to protect their hearts.

But we also need to teach our children to pray that themselves. They need to learn how to pray for spiritual wisdom and understanding. There is no better "hedge of protection" than God's wisdom and understanding. If they have the mind of God they will make good decisions.

How are you doing, mom and dad? Are you praying that for yourselves? We can get attacked and brought down. We need to be praying that for ourselves each day. Temptations are great. We must guard our hearts. No, we must pray for God to guard our hearts with His hedge of protection.

Lord, I want You to plant huge, spiritual bougainvilleas around me to keep the enemy away. Keep them far away. Let them now even get close.

DECEIT BEGATS DECEIT

Genesis 38

BEST VERSE: 15
When Judah saw her, he thought she was a harlot, for she had covered her face.

The 38th chapter of Genesis is an interesting read (for adults). When you read it, you can scratch your head and say, "Why would the Lord put this in Scripture?" But we know that every word is inspired by the Holy Spirit and has a message for us. So, what is the message of this chapter? It is a story filled with deceit, lies, and sin.

Judah's original lie against Tamar (promising her his youngest son) gave Tamar a "reason" to deceive Judah. Judah's decision to visit a harlot (sin) led to shame and humiliation for both him and Tamar. What a "made for tv movie"! But do you know who one of the sons became? Perez, who was the twin brother of Zerah, is in the direct line of King David and thus, also in the lineage of Jesus. He was NO mistake.

TEACHING MOMENT
Let me say upfront, this is a hard story to tell your children. You might want to hold this one for when they are older. They may have questions you don't want to answer right now. But it's in the Word, so be prepared. For me, it is clear. God does not make any mistakes. The mistakes WE make can be turned around and made into blessings.

Perez played a key role in the tribe of Judah. As I said earlier, he was a descendant in the messianic lineage. You can't get more important than that. All children are a blessing, whether they are planned or not. God can use each child to be a blessing for others.

Tell your kids that. Tell them they are a blessing. Tell them God has a special plan for them. Remind your children over and over again that God does NOT make junk. They have a purpose for being here.

Creator of all life, thank you for creating me in Your image. Show me how to show others their purpose in life. Help me point my children to Your plan for them.

MARCH 23

PITCHING THAT TENT

John 1

BEST VERSE: 10
And the Word became flesh, and dwelt among us. . . .

Recently we had a father/son campout at the church I serve. We had been planning this since the previous fall, but it was postponed twice due to weather. However, the third time was the charm, as the saying goes. We had absolutely perfect weather.

I got there early to set things up and had the privilege to watch each group of dads and sons arrive and begin to put up their tents. We had a total of 15 or 16 tents, and I believe each one was different. Some were pitched using those little flexible poles that are connected with an elastic cord inside. Others used the larger poles that connect. Some had room dividers inside the tent, and others were just one open tent. We had large ones that could sleep 6-8 and small ones like mine that was really meant for one.

Pitching a tent is a skill that every dad should teach his son though. Most boys love to get out in the woods and camp. Knowing what kind of tent to buy and how to put it up will be a skill dads can pass down to their sons and will last a lifetime.

Did you know that the word "dwelt" in John 1:10 means to pitch a tent? Jesus came to earth and pitched His tent among us. He lived among us. And now through His Holy Spirit, He pitches His tent IN us. The beauty of that is His "tent" fits everyone. It is big enough for one or big enough for millions.

Now, here is the good part. Once Jesus pitches His tent IN us, He never takes it down. He is with us forever. He never gets tired of us, packs up His tent, and leaves. He never says, "Okay Carl, I've had enough of this living in you thing. Time for me to go home." Nope, He is here to stay.

TEACHING MOMENT
Dads, if you haven't done so already, won't you teach your sons or daughters how to pitch their tents with Jesus? It is much easier than pitching that real tent. Show them how to invite Jesus to dwell within them. That is something that will last this lifetime and the next.

O God of Jacob, when I am unsettled, settle me. Help me to set up camp and stay close to You. Pitch Your tent in me today.

MARCH 24

CHOOSE YOUR LEADERS WISELY

Judges 9

BEST VERSE: 14
Finally all the trees said to the bramble, "You come, reign over us!"

Abimelech had convinced the people to proclaim him as their leader. He was the illegitimate son of Gideon, who lived in Shechem. The people chose him over Gideon's sons and lived to regret that decision. This quote in verse 14 is the voice of Jotham, the only son who survived Abimelech's murderous tirade of his other 69 brothers. It was prophetic. Abimelech was a bramble who brought destruction on Shechem.

So, what does this mean for us? Choose your leaders carefully. Many people promise great things. They tell us to just elect them, and they will bring prosperity. . . .pick them, and they will lead us to success. There are no guarantees to prosperity, no matter who is holding office. With that in mind, whether it be a local political election or selecting leaders for a community group, it is far more important to choose leaders who exemplify Christ's teachings.

Your children may grow up and run for an office. They may be elected as class president in school. They may even be elected to Congress or as President. Teach them to represent well. Teach them to live by God's standards. Teach them to lead well. You just never know how God may use them.

They may never run for office, but they will have the opportunity to vote for others. Teach them to vote for people who stand for good. Show them who you are voting for and why. I have a couple of "line in the sand" issues when I vote. One of them is a candidate's view on life. I cannot vote for anyone who is for abortion. I know God would not be pleased with that.

How do you decide your leaders? What guidelines do you use? We have the best "litmus test" around—God's Word. Use it to guide you whom to elect. Do your part and trust God to put in power those whom He has selected to lead.

O God, I pray for our local and national leaders today. I pray they will seek Your face today. I pray for their safety and good health.

MARCH 25

THIS LITTLE LIGHT OF MINE

Mark 4

BEST VERSE: 21
And He was saying to them, "A lamp is not brought to be put under a basket, is it, or under a bed? Is it not brought to be put on the lampstand?"

TEACHING MOMENT

What a perfect verse to share with our kids! This is a verse that is so easily played out with your children. Go into a room with a lamp and a basket (or something else) that will cover the lamp. Turn on the lamp and then turn off the room light. Now cover the lamp with the basket. They will see very quickly how dark the room gets with the lamp not being allowed to shine its light. Even if a little of the light shines through, they will get the message.

Now tell them how in our lives the light of Jesus needs to shine so others can see it. We need to let it shine brightly. We do NOT need to hide our light. Not only is it easier to see in a well-lit room, but it may prevent someone from stumbling. Our "Jesus light" can also help someone in a dark world and perhaps keep them from stumbling.

After you have done this with your child, the hard part begins. YOU have to live it. YOU must let YOUR light shine. Your child needs to see YOU shining YOUR light in dark places. When you are in the store and someone is not kind to you, let your light shine. When you are in traffic and someone cuts you off, let your light shine. When you see someone asking for help, let your light shine.

You see, roleplaying is one thing, living it is so much more! Now go shine your light!

Father of lights, shine through me. Let Your light shine so brightly in me that others see You and not me. This light of mine is only bright if I keep You up front.

MARCH 26

INSULATED BUT NOT ISOLATED

John 17

BEST VERSES: 15–16
I do not ask You to take them out of the world, but to keep them from the evil **one**. They are not of the world, even as I am not of the world.

This world is not our home. As believers, we know that. It is a temporary place—a place we are just visiting. Our real home is heaven. But it is the only home we have right now, so we need to make the most of it. Jesus knew that. He said as much when He said, "I do not ask You to take them out of the world, but to keep them from the evil one."

Now understand something. If God wanted, He could instantly take us to heaven when we are saved. We could say, "I believe," and instantly be there. As cool as that may seem, He wants us to stay here and spread the good news. And because He does, He protects us from the evil one (Satan), who wants nothing more than to tear us down.

TEACHING MOMENT

I love hearing children's descriptions of heaven. They are beautiful, simple, and creative. We should talk to our children about heaven. But we need to spend more time teaching them how to live here on this earth. They need to know that Jesus said these words about being here. John 17 is a great chapter about that.

Take some time and read this to them. And I mean, take some time. There is so much in this chapter. But it is so good. It is so reassuring. It can embolden your children to live for Jesus, knowing He is cheering them on.

I want to live with the Word of God insulating me from the fiery darts of Satan. There is NOTHING Satan can do to me, unless the Lord allows it. God's Word protects my mind and spirit. It gives me the strength to carry on when I think I can't make it another day. The Word allows me to walk into any room equipped to share the good news. It's not because of me. It's all because of Him.

Father, You are my protector. I know that and believe that. I trust You to be my insulator. Keep me from isolating myself from the lost who so desperately need to hear from You.

MARCH 27

DO YOU SEE A STRANGER?

Matthew 25

BEST VERSE: 40
The King will answer and say to them, "Truly I say to you, to the extent that you did it to one of these brothers of Mine, *even* the least *of them*, you did it to Me."

Are you ever driving in town with your children and come across people at the intersections holding signs asking for money or food? What do your children ask you? What is your answer? Do you roll down the window and give them a few dollars? Do you give them a gift card to McDonald's or somewhere else? Just what do you do?

I have to admit that I have become a bit cynical about these people. I have heard from someone who used to do that how many of these individuals are simply conning people. They aren't homeless or hungry. They just want someone to give them something. However, that does not excuse me from acting when I feel the Spirit move.

TEACHING MOMENT

Recently I was cleaning out my daughter's truck for her and found a couple of baggies that contain gloves, crackers, hand wipes, toothpaste and a toothbrush, and a few other items. I asked her what they were for. She said she gives them to people she sees at those intersections when she feels the Spirit leading her. Boy, I was ashamed of myself for my own cynicism and thoughtlessness. My girl had taught me a lesson.

Will you let your children's tender hearts convict you? When they see someone in need and want to help, let them. Let them be the one Jesus refers to in the verse we read when He said "you did it to Me."

Lord, help my cynical spirit. Let me respond when the Spirit tells me and not try to rationalize my gifts. I want to see them as You do—as a lost child needing redemption.

MARCH 28

DID YOU SEE THAT?

Exodus 24

BEST VERSES: 9—10

Then Moses went up with Aaron, Nadab and Abihu, and seventy of the elders of Israel, and they saw the God of Israel; and under His feet there appeared to be a pavement of sapphire, as clear as the sky itself.

Can you imagine for a second what went through the minds of these men as they gazed upon God? I am not surprised that Moses and Aaron were allowed to see Him, but the rest? They must have been scared to death. They were probably fearful they would be struck down by just looking. But they weren't.

Who were these seventy elders? Were these the men Moses had chosen to help judge the people? Were these trusted men who had proven themselves? They aren't named, but it doesn't matter. God obviously trusted these men for Him to reveal Himself to them in this way. They were counted worthy to be in the very presence of the God of Israel.

TEACHING MOMENT

Have you ever been somewhere with your children and observed a truly amazing sight? Perhaps it was an incredible sunset or sunrise. Maybe it was the view from the top of a mountain. Maybe it was something else in nature that took your breath away. That would be a great time to share this verse and explain how these men must have felt.

Seeing an incredible sight here on earth today can't compare with seeing God. But your children need to know that they can enter the very presence of God every day as they pray. He is listening and invites them to come to Him. There is no fear. There is no trepidation. We come because we know He loves us and wants to be with us.

Have you visited God today? Have you looked upon His presence? Are you longing to see His face as you lift your voice in prayer? He says, "Come."

Father, I see You all around me. I long to see You fully. I praise You for the exhibitions of Your presence all around me.

MARCH 29

IT MAKES SENSE TO ME!

Judges 21

BEST VERSE: 25

In those days there was no king in Israel; everyone did what was right in his own eyes.

To me, Judges 19—21 contains one of the most interesting stories in the Old Testament. The actions of all the characters (the Levite, the concubine, the men of Gibeah, the army) really don't make sense. Their actions do not line up with Scripture.

But the final verse of chapter 21, which is quoted above, sums it up. Everyone did what was right in his own eyes. If that is your philosophy for life, then you are your own master, and it doesn't matter what anyone thinks about you, even God.

TEACHING MOMENT

Moms and dads, teach your children that good and evil exist in this world. No matter where they go or what they do, God's Word will remain constant. It will continue to point them in the right direction and help them discern between what is good and what is evil. The world will tell them differently. Right in one place may be wrong somewhere else, and vice versa. But good and evil are always good and evil according to God's Word.

The participants in the events of Judges 19—21 decided upon themselves what made sense. They did things according to what they thought best. Many lives were lost in this story. I counted over sixty-five thousand. Our actions, when governed by our own ideas, can be costly. However, when we allow the Lord to lead, we can trust the outcome. He always knows best.

Are you trusting God for the direction in your life, or are you deciding your own path? Have you asked the Lord for the wisdom you need to teach your children, or are you relying on a worldly philosophy? There really is only one right way. That's the Lord's way.

Father, even though I want to do it my way, will You change my heart. Help me surrender to Your will. I want to honor You.

MARCH 30

SHEDDING TEARS

Genesis 23

BEST VERSE: 2

Sarah died in Kiriath-arba (that is, Hebron) in the land of Canaan; and Abraham went in to mourn for Sarah and to weep for her.

Why do we men think we can't cry? Me? I cry during TV commercials. Remember the Folger's coffee commercial when the young man comes home to surprise his family? He sneaks in and makes a pot of coffee.

When his mom comes down and sees him, I am bawling. It's okay to shed tears. There are times when tears are so needed.

Abraham had just lost his wife. She died at 127 years old. They had been married a long time. Did his tears mean he didn't trust God anymore? Of course not. He was a man missing his wife. He was faced with burying her in a foreign land among strangers. He was hurting. He was grieving. He was crying.

TEACHING MOMENT

Do me a favor. When your child is crying over something, don't tell them to stop crying. I know, I know. Kids cry over nothing. But when we tell them to "dry those tears" it can send the wrong message. They may think they can't cry about anything.

Take a moment and share this verse with them. Explain how even grownups cry sometimes. Even Jesus cried when a friend died (John 11:35). Tears can be a healing thing too. It can make them feel better if not "overdone." Hey, you can even cry with them. What a great lesson!

Are you too hard-hearted to cry? Or are you like me, a big crybaby? Let the tears flow. Let them heal your heart. Don't be afraid to grieve or shed that tear. The Lord will soothe your heart.

O Lord, don't let me believe the lies of the world. I don't have to "get tough" and "dry the tears." Let me feel the freedom to cry when I need to. I know You will dry every tear one day.

MARCH 31

WHO REALLY OWNS THIS STUFF?

Matthew 22

BEST VERSES: 15–22

Then the Pharisees went and plotted together how they might trap Him in what He said. And they sent their disciples to Him, along with the Herodians, saying, "Teacher, we know that You are truthful and teach the way of God in truth, and defer to no one; for You are not partial to any. Tell us then, what do You think? Is it lawful to give a poll-tax to Caesar, or not?" But Jesus perceived their malice, and said, "Why are you testing Me, you hypocrites? Show Me the coin used for the poll-tax." And they brought Him a denarius. And He said to them, "Whose likeness and inscription is this?" They said to Him, "Caesar's." Then He said to them, "Then render to Caesar the things that are Caesar's; and to God the things that are God's." And hearing this, they were amazed, and leaving Him, they went away.

Moms and dads, most people read this passage and focus on giving to Caesar what is Caesar's. Not me. I focused on giving God what is His. Agree? So, the question has to be asked—What is His?

TEACHING MOMENT

We need to teach our children early that everything we have belongs to Him. Our very breath is a gift from God, which He gives us liberally. The clothes on our back, the food on our table, and the toys we give them—all come from Him. When our children learn this early, they are more likely to respect what they have and also share with others.

Our world is so focused on getting all it can that we fail to teach that everything belongs to Him. We hold all our possessions with open hands so that we can release them to Him or someone else. Won't you help your child to learn this basic truth of stewardship today? It will be a lifelong lesson for them which you can begin now.

God, You provide us with everything. Give me Your eyes to know who to bless. Remind me daily of your blessings!

DON'T BE FOOLISH

1 Samuel 25

BEST VERSE: 25

Please do not let my lord pay attention to this worthless man, Nabal, for as his name is, so is he. Nabal is his name and folly is with him; but I your maidservant did not see the young men of my lord whom you sent.

How could such an intelligent, beautiful woman like Abigail (verse 3 describes her that way) marry a foolish man like Nabal? Even his name meant foolish or disgrace. Now, here she is trying to cover for him by sending gifts to David to avoid bloodshed.

As Christian parents, we want our children to marry someone who loves Jesus. We want their spouse to be wise and discerning. We want them to be protective and loyal. I am willing to bet that Nabal was none of these. And here was Abigail, seemingly stuck in this marriage to a "fool."

TEACHING MOMENT

How do we protect our children from making a similar mistake in their choice for a life mate? Well, this story might be a good one to share. We don't know all the details of how she came to be married to Nabal. Perhaps, as was common to that time, it was an arranged marriage. Perhaps, when he was younger, he swept her off her feet. However, it happened, here she was.

Our guidance will only go so far when we counsel our children in this area. But it is still our responsibility to speak up and advise. The Lord expects us to give wise counsel to our children. The best counsel we can give, however, is to be the kind of husband or wife the Lord desires for our spouse and model that for our children. When they see you living out a godly marriage, they will be more open to being drawn to a godly spouse.

So, don't be a Nabal. Be wise, for your future son-in-law's or daughter-in-law's sake.

Lord, let my life be an example for my children. May I treat my wife as You would—with honor and respect. Let me direct my children toward the one You have for them.

DELAYED REWARD

1 Samuel 27

BEST VERSE: 6
So Achish gave him Ziklag that day; therefore Ziklag has belonged to the kings of Judah to this day.

Do you know where Ziklag was? It was in the region of Gath in the land of the Philistines. "Big deal, Carl. Why do you mention that?" Maybe this verse will give you a hint. "Then a champion came out from the armies of the Philistines named Goliath, from Gath, whose height was six cubits and a span." That's 1 Samuel 17:4.

Don't you get it? David was given a city in the home region of Goliath which remained the possession of the kings of Judah forever. At this point, David had never gotten a reward for killing Goliath. But now, the king of Gath, gives him a city. He had to have known who David was. Interesting.

TEACHING MOMENT
Our children must learn that they will not always see a reward for doing the right thing or the holy thing. Sometimes, in fact most of the time, the reward is delayed. It is NOT about the reward. It's about pleasing the Lord.

We are way too quick to reward our kids. We bribe them with prizes, or we entice them with trinkets. We are held hostage by the fear of their behavior if they don't get what they want when they want it. Stop that. Teach them to wait. That is a worthy skill to learn.

But, are you just as guilty? Do you demand instant gratification? Do you expect to be recognized and rewarded the moment you do the right thing? Stop that too. Let your reward be pleasing the one who made you. That should give you joy.

O Great Rewarder, teach me to wait. Teach me to find my joy in just pleasing You. Help me show my children how wonderful that is.

A MISUNDERSTANDING

Joshua 22

BEST VERSE: 34
The sons of Reuben and the sons of Gad called the altar *Witness*; "For," *they said*, "it is a witness between us that the Lord is God."

Isn't it amazing how fast we can jump to conclusions? For some people that is the only exercise they get. In this chapter, the tribes of Reuben, Gad, and the half tribe of Manasseh have crossed the Jordan back to the land which was given to them. They build an altar, not for sacrifices, but for a symbol to future generations that they are part of the Israelite nation.

But the other tribes hear about it and think they are setting up their own altar. So, they take off to confront and wage war, if necessary. The altar was called "Witness," which in Hebrew is *ed*. An altar called Ed. Pardon me, but I just think that is funny.

TEACHING MOMENT

I promise you that your children are going to be the cause of or the victim of misunderstandings. There is just no way to avoid it. People see and hear what they want. Teaching our children to deal with these situations is an important skill to master. How should they react when they are falsely accused?

Peace and calm must reign. They should ask themselves if they have indeed wronged someone. If they are living to please the Lord, they may not be in the wrong. But sometimes, no matter what they do, people will get upset. Tell your children to continue to love and obey the Lord. Tell them to let Christ fight the battles for them. That's the lesson they need to learn.

Are you dealing with false accusations? I've dealt with that in the past. Sometimes, though, I have actually wronged someone and didn't know it until I was confronted. I am thankful for accountability.

O Lord, thank You for showing me when I sin against others. Protect me when I am doing good and am accused by those who would do me harm. And thank You for letting me be an example to others.

ABANDONED?

1 Samuel 12

BEST VERSE: 22

For the LORD will not abandon His people on account of His great name, because the LORD has been pleased to make you a people for Himself.

In this chapter of 1 Samuel, Samuel is establishing Saul as the first king of Israel. He lays out the conditions for God's blessing on the king and the people. But here in this verse we find a truth that holds true even today. It says, "the Lord will not abandon His people on account of His great name,"

Did you catch that? If we are His people, He will never abandon us. Back then it meant following the Lord and obeying His commands. Today it means the same, but through the Lord Jesus Christ. Don't let anyone tell you that you can find God in many places or religions. There is only one way to be His people—through Jesus.

TEACHING MOMENT

One of my greatest fears today is the bombardment on our children of the inclusiveness of all beliefs and lifestyles. God has standards, even today. We can't let our children believe that basically anything goes, as long as you say you love God. That is not it. It's not just about loving God. It's about total surrender to Him and His Will for your life.

Our children need to see us totally surrendered to Him. They need to hear us asking God for direction in the family decisions and then following whatever it is He says to do. My children observed my wife and I seeking the Lord in our ministry moves. There were some opportunities that God allowed to enter our lives that, after praying and seeking His Will, were obviously not the right moves for us. Saying "no" to a great opportunity isn't easy, but it's right.

Do you believe God will NOT abandon you? He won't if you are His. Do you hold that truth today? If you aren't, then there is only one thing you can do—turn to Him. Allow Him to come in and be the source of your strength. Let Him be your King.

Father, I know as your child You will never leave me or forsake me. Remind me today to look to You for each step I take and then take it, no matter where it leads.

GOD'S IN CONTROL

Daniel 2

BEST VERSE: 21

It is He who changes the times and the epochs; He removes kings and establishes kings; He gives wisdom to wise men and knowledge to men of understanding.

Isn't it comforting to know that no matter who gets elected to a political office or who God allows to be your boss, He's got it all under control? Oh, you didn't know that? You don't believe that? Then you must be very miserable.

If there is one passage in Daniel that speaks through the ages it is this verse. God's sovereignty screams through this verse. His ability to shape the world and direct men is apparent right here. Daniel served four pagan kings while in captivity, but he did it faithfully. If he can do that, why can't we submit to those God has placed over us?

TEACHING MOMENT

Our children must learn submission. Part of the job we have as parents is to make sure they understand authority. As parents, we are their authority as long as they live under our roof. In fact, until they are out on their own providing for themselves, they fall under our authority. We have the right and the responsibility to teach them that.

Now I don't mean we are slave drivers or taskmasters. But we are preparing our children to submit so that when they are adults, they will learn that all authority is God-ordained and for their benefit. This applies to government, careers, and home.

Are you a submissive person to the authorities in your life? Do you realize God has placed them over you to prepare you for His service? If you haven't faced this reality, now is a good time to confess your rebellious spirit and submit to God's authority in your life first and then submit to those He has placed over you. Will you do that?

As Your children, we are always under Your roof. We can thank You for having the great pleasure of submitting to You. It's for our protection and Your purpose in our lives! Give us godly wisdom to know that our children imitate us and watch whether we submit or not.

APRIL 6

TREASURES OR TRAPS?

Matthew 6

BEST VERSES: 19–21

Do not store up for yourselves treasures on earth, where moth and rust destroy, and where thieves break in and steal. But store up for yourselves treasures in heaven, where neither moth nor rust destroys, and where thieves do not break in or steal; for where your treasure is, there your heart will be also.

This passage from the mouth of the Lord Jesus is a fitting follow up from yesterday's passage about Lot. Lot had done this exact thing. Lot had put his focus on earthly treasures.

Jesus warns us here that all those earthly things we hold so dear will one day be destroyed by moth or rust or they will be stolen by a thief. Now that's encouraging, isn't it?

Why do we strive for "things"? Why do we long to get more stuff? Why can't we be satisfied with what the Lord provides? I have seen people with more than they could ever use and others with just the day's provisions. The "things" did not determine their joy. That only comes from within when we allow Jesus to rule and reign in our lives.

What are these "treasures in heaven"? I am sure they are things that please the Father, and they are things, when we get to heaven, that we will lay down at His feet. After all, everything we have been given here on earth actually does belong to Him, right?

Mom and Dad, be careful how you show your children the importance of earthly possessions. The lessons they learn now about "things" will impact them and their future families. Not getting the new gaming system is not going to destroy them. Not getting that new pair of shoes or that new baseball glove will not scar them for life.

Focus your heart on heavenly things and take your eyes off the world!

Father, You are the provider of all things. Thank You for giving to me just what I need and sometimes even those things I desire. You are an incredible God!

APRIL 7

DO YOU REMEMBER?

Joshua 24

BEST VERSES: 26–27

And Joshua wrote these words in the book of the law of God; and he took a large stone and set it up there under the oak that was by the sanctuary of the Lord. Joshua said to all the people, "Behold, this stone shall be for a witness against us, for it has heard all the words of the Lord which He spoke to us; thus, it shall be for a witness against you, so that you do not deny your God."

Joshua has just finished talking to the people about all that God has done for them. He is giving them a charge to be faithful to Him, and the people vow to do just that. So, to remind them, Joshua sets up this big ole rock at Shechem. He wants something physical which they can refer to and remember the vow they made to follow Jehovah.

TEACHING MOMENT

Have you ever given anyone something to remember you by? Do you buy souvenirs when you are on vacation so you can remember the feelings and good times you had? Your children need those "souvenirs" of childhood. What can you put in their hands to remind them that they belong to your family? Why don't you and your kids think of something that represents your family and make something they can keep?

More importantly, what can you and your children come up with to remind you all of the Lord? A Christian heritage is so important for later in life. Maybe you have a family verse. Maybe when you presented them before the church (you may call it Baby Dedication) to vow that you would bring them up to honor the Lord, you chose a verse for them. Why not get that verse put on a plaque and put it in their room? Refer to it when they are old enough to understand. When they leave home, it goes with them. It can be "something to remember you by."

Memories of salvation and spiritual growth are important, Lord. I realize that. Help me make memories for my family. Help me establish some family traditions around You that we can look back on later and smile.

APRIL 8

JUST ASK

John 16

BEST VERSE: 24
Until now you have asked for nothing in My name; ask and you will receive, so that your joy may be made full.

How many times as parents do our children ask us for something? Within reason we are happy to do it. Dads, we are especially vulnerable to that little girl who has us wrapped around her little finger, right? And moms, either son or daughter gets you, right?

Is Jesus saying here to ask for ANYTHING? Do you think He meant to give us permission to ask for anything we want, and He would be obligated to give it? I don't think so. You always have to look at Scripture, not only in context to the verse you are reading but to the Bible as a whole. Jesus says in the previous verse if we ask the Father for something *in His name*, He would give it to us. So, for what do you ask your Father?

We only ask the Father for things that we know will please Him. He wants to bless us, but only with things that are going to make us more like His Son. If we ask for things *in the name of Jesus* (which means we know Jesus would approve of it) then the Father will gladly give it to us. That's what the verse says. It doesn't say He will make us rich or powerful. Don't read into the verse.

TEACHING MOMENT

So, when you teach your children to pray, always pray in agreement with Jesus. If Jesus is pleased with your request, I promise you the Father will be too. When you have a loved one who is in need of a physical touch, guide your children to pray, believing God can heal, but also accepting God's will in the situation. When you have a financial need in your family, guide your children to pray, believing He is your provision while accepting the fact that He may use others to meet that need.

Prayer is powerful, and we often underestimate the power of the "ask." Ask Him. He is always listening. After all, don't you want your joy to be complete?

Lord God, You answer all prayers. I know that. Sometimes I don't like the way you answer, but I will accept Your Will. Thank You for allowing me to come before You anytime, anywhere.

APRIL 9

IS IT PARTY TIME?

Genesis 45

BEST VERSE: 16

Now when the news was heard in Pharaoh's house that Joseph's brothers had come, it pleased Pharaoh and his servants.

This may seem like a strange verse to pick out, but something about this intrigued me. Look at what it says. Pharaoh and his servants were pleased when they heard his brothers had come. Hmmm. . . .

Now this is TOTALLY reading between the lines, but it appears to me that they must have heard Joseph's story about his brothers selling him into slavery. He had probably told them how many brothers he had. He probably told them about his father and mother. Now, out of nowhere, they appear.

And it says Pharaoh and his people were pleased. Why? Why should they care about Joseph's family? Don't you rejoice with your friends when they receive good news? Joseph had obviously endeared himself to Pharaoh and his servants. They rejoiced with him. They were happy for him.

TEACHING MOMENT

The next time you hear of some good news about a family member or a family friend, bring out this story. Explain to your children that, just like Joseph's friends celebrated with him, we celebrate with our friends and family. Not because we just want an excuse to party, but because our love for our friends and family is built upon years of "doing life" with them. We celebrate because we know their story. We celebrate because we have probably also cried with them and know how they may have suffered in the past.

Do you rejoice with others? Or are you jealous of them? I think we can learn a lesson here. Rejoice when others rejoice, and weep when they weep. That sure sounds familiar, doesn't it?

I rejoice that I am in Your family, Lord. You help me rejoice with others. Thank You for the joy of knowing You as my Father.

APRIL 10

WHO'S ON YOUR THRONE?

Exodus 37

BEST VERSES: 7-9

He made two cherubim of gold; he made them of hammered work at the two ends of the mercy seat; one cherub at the one end and one cherub at the other end; he made the cherubim *of one piece* with the mercy seat at the two ends. The cherubim had *their* wings spread upward, covering the mercy seat with their wings, with their faces toward each other; the faces of the cherubim were toward the mercy seat.

Have you ever wondered why the Lord told Moses to make the ark the way He did? Maybe it's just me, but I have always wondered about the cherubim. Why were they placed on the lid? Why are they facing each other? I found one explanation that I think you will like. "Because the Lord's presence was in the space above the Ark (Leviticus 16:2; Psalm 80:1), and Moses spoke to God there (Numbers 7:89), it was sometimes said that God was enthroned between the cherubim (1 Samuel 4:4; 2 Samuel 6:2)" – (from gotquestions.com).

So, the cherubim are bowing before the enthroned God on the mercy seat. That led me to ask the question, "Who do I have on my throne?" Do I bow before a holy God each and every day? Or do I put myself or someone else on that throne?

TEACHING MOMENT

It is our responsibility as parents to teach our children who to put on their thrones. We should be constantly pointing them to Jesus. When they begin to elevate some celebrity or sports figure, point out that they are just flesh and blood and subject to failures. When they think their whole world revolves around that boyfriend or girlfriend, remind them that Jesus is the King whom will never desert them.

Our children naturally are drawn to people of power. But it is so dangerous to allow them to do that without knowing the reality of everyone's frailty in this world. Even parents can let children down, right?

So, who do you have on your throne today? Are you taking the position of the cherubim and bowing before Him today? Are you in a perpetual bow before Him, just as those two cherubim are? We should be for only He deserves our worship and praise!

You, O Lord, are the only God. You are the only One on the throne of my life. Praise You for reigning over me.

COUNT THEM

Joshua 12

BEST VERSES: 1A, 24B

Now these are the kings of the land whom the sons of Israel defeated, . . . in all, thirty-one kings.

Thirty-one kings! That's a lot of kings. That's a lot of kingdoms. But God gave them victory over each and every one. Why do you think king number 30 or 31 didn't just try to make peace? Why did they all choose to fight? Because God had determined that they all had to be defeated and removed from the land. He wanted the children of Israel to have complete control.

Isn't it the same with us? God does not want us to live among those who will cause us harm. He will not allow His children to be led astray by those who blaspheme His name. He gives us a way out. He tells us how to insulate ourselves against such attacks. Sadly, we choose to embrace the world's lifestyles and rationalize it as being culturally sensitive.

TEACHING MOMENT

There is probably no greater lesson to teach your children than to live sanctified. Now, you can't tell them to be sanctified and go your way. No! You have to model sanctified living. You have to choose God's way and not the world's. That may mean appearing "intolerant" or "old fashioned" to them. That's okay.

You have probably heard the saying, "If you don't stand for anything, you will stand for nothing." That adage, although not biblical, does agree with Scripture. We have to stand for truth. We must defend the faith. And when we do, our children see that. They will learn to be bold in their witness.

Do you stand boldly in your community? Do you refuse to bow down to cultural pressure? We do not have to be antagonistic, but we do have to be true to the Word. Don't compromise your faith. Stand for truth.

Thank You, Lord, for giving me the courage to stand. Thank you for having my back when I face the enemy. I know You are still fighting our battles.

BLESS YOU

Deuteronomy 33

BEST VERSE: 1

Now this is the blessing with which Moses the man of God blessed the sons of Israel before his death.

Isn't it sad that the only time most of us ever hear those words "bless you" is after we sneeze? It's such a—well—blessing to hear those words. In my experience, it seems Christians are the least likely to "bless" someone when we should be the most diligent at it. Blessing someone invokes *God's blessing* on them, not *ours*. We are praying God's protection and presence. What's NOT good about that?

Here in this chapter, the next 28 verses are Moses' final blessing on the tribes of Israel. He goes through each tribe and blesses them. Some get one sentence, and others get several. The length of the blessing isn't the important thing. It's the blessing being done that is key.

TEACHING MOMENT

Have you ever blessed your child? You don't have to be ordained to bless them. You don't have to take them to the Pastor for that. You can do it as often as you desire. Let me encourage you to do that. I would often pray for my children before school, asking for protection and provision (especially on test day).

Blessing your child, speaking truth to them from God's word, is a huge encourager to your children. When they hear Mom or Dad praying a blessing on them, they know that you and God are both on the same team rooting for them. They know that you have them on your mind. They realize how much you desire God's direction in their lives.

If you aren't in the habit of blessing your children, let me encourage you to do that today. Make it a routine. Let them hear your heart for them according to God's will. I promise you will be blessed too.

Father, today I ask Your blessings on my brother or sister who is reading this right now. Give them good health. Meet their physical, emotional and spiritual needs today. Protect them from those who would want to harm them and give them peace.

APRIL 13

UNDESERVING

2 Samuel 7

BEST VERSE: 18
Then David the king went in and sat before the LORD, and he said, "Who am I, O LORD God, and what is my house, that You have brought me this far?"

All David wanted to do was build the Lord God a permanent home. He had called Nathan (the prophet) in and said to him that he wanted to build a house for God since He was still in a tent. David recognized that all that had occurred in his life was the direct result of God directing and blessing him. Now here he was living in a beautiful home and reigning as king of Israel. He wanted to give something back to God.

He wasn't expecting to hear through Nathan that the Lord was granting his household kingship forever. Even those words prophesied the reign of Jesus, who was of the tribe of Judah. David felt unworthy and undeserving of such an honor. "Who am I . . . and what is my house, that you have brought me this far?"

Do you ever feel unworthy of God's blessings? Look around you. Look at all the Lord has blessed you with. When I return home after spending time in other countries, I feel so unworthy of the things the Lord has blessed me with. I do not deserve any of them. I am so blessed.

TEACHING MOMENT
Our children must be taught, however, to recognize these blessings. They grow up with them and simply take them for granted. They have always had a computer or a cell phone or a television or air conditioning. They just assume those things will always be. We have to teach them that all those

things are fine, but they all are a result of a loving God who has blessed your family.

God doesn't need anything from us. His existence and glory aren't dependent on our recognition of Him. But when we acknowledge Him and His goodness in our lives, He is pleased. Don't you and your children want to please the Father? He desires to bless you. But don't demand it, and don't even expect it when you think you need it. Simply trust Him, and He will bless you in ways you could never expect.

Father, I am unworthy of anything You could possibly bless me with. Your blessings overwhelm me. Thank You for Your undeserved kindness to me and my family.

APRIL 14

READY OR NOT, HERE I COME

Matthew 24

BEST VERSES: 42–44

Therefore be on the alert, for you do not know which day your Lord is coming. But be sure of this, that if the head of the house had known at what time of the night the thief was coming, he would have been on the alert and would not have allowed his house to be broken into. For this reason you also must be ready; for the Son of Man is coming at an hour when you do not think *He will*.

Do you remember playing "Hide and Seek" as a child? Maybe you taught your children to play that game with their siblings or friends. I can still remember playing that in our yard in South Georgia. One of us would be picked to be "It," and the rest would run and hide somewhere as "It" counted to 100. Then "It" would holler, "Ready or not, here I come." My heart would be pounding from the excitement, hoping "It" would not find me.

TEACHING MOMENT

Our children need to know that Jesus has already hollered, "Ready or not, here I come." We see right here in the Scriptures that He is coming "at an hour when you do not think *He will*." Are your children ready? Are you ready?

We should not frighten our children with this news. That is not how God works. But we also should not hide the fact that He is coming. And when He comes, He will come to take all His children home to heaven. That is a good thing. He comes and tags us, not as "It," but as "His." Unlike the game of Hide and Seek, we WANT to be found by Him when He comes. We want to be carried home.

Point your children toward home. Prepare them to watch for His coming. Let them know that they are loved and cherished by a heavenly Father who just wants them home for eternity. Ready or not, here He comes!

O God, I know You are IT! You are counting down to the end of days, and I want You to find me faithful. I want to be found ready. Help me live each day as if it is my last.

ARE YOU READY?

Daniel 12

BEST VERSES: 1-2

Now at that time Michael, the great prince who stands guard over the sons of your people, will arise. And there will be a time of distress such as never occurred since there was a nation until that time; and at that time your people, everyone who is found written in the book, will be rescued. Many of those who sleep in the dust of the ground will awake, these to everlasting life, but the others to disgrace and everlasting contempt.

Is your name in the book? I attended a wedding recently, and as I entered the building there was a guest book for me to sign. Now that book had multiple blank lines for all the guests to sign their names and addresses, so the bride and groom would know who attended. But signing that book did not give me the right to enter. I had already been invited to attend.

The difference in that book and the one mentioned in our passage today is I will not be granted permission to even enter heaven unless my name is ALREADY written in the book. I have to have a reservation in advance. I am not worried, though. I know my name is in the book and my check-in date has been predetermined. I am ready.

I am sure at some point in the next days or weeks you will have the chance to sign something while you are with your kids. Why not take that opportunity to share this verse? Talk about how when you accepted Christ (or, if your child is a believer, when they did) your name was written down in the Lamb's Book of Life. It was signed with permanent marker. No one or nothing can erase your name.

Kids like security. They need it to thrive. They need it to grow in a healthy way, both physically and emotionally. More importantly, they need eternal security. Having the knowledge they are secure in Christ and that nothing can change that gives them (and us) peace. They are safe! They are promised an eternal home. Is there really anything any better? I don't think so.

As hard as daily living is, what a great assurance to know in my heart that I am eternally secure in Christ Jesus. Our children need to hear early on how they can receive this new birth into a living hope. Help me share the good news with them so they can learn "rest."

APRIL 16

THE FIRST BUBBA

Genesis 10

BEST VERSES: 8–9

Now Cush became the father of Nimrod; he became a mighty one on the earth. He was a mighty hunter before the LORD; therefore it is said, "Like Nimrod a mighty hunter before the LORD."

Being a hunter, these verses naturally caught my attention. I love to hunt. I love to be in the outdoors. I will try just about any kind of hunting. There is just something about it. Maybe I should change my name to Nimrod.

But Nimrod wasn't just a hunter. He was a "mighty one." He is believed to have been the first major leader after the flood. In fact, if you read on in Genesis 10, you will see he established several cities, including the famous Nineveh (remember Jonah?). My point is this—you never know what your children will become.

You've heard people tell their children, "You can become anything you want if you try hard enough." Well, that's just not true. There is no way I could play in the NBA or in the NFL. I just don't have the size or strength. Instead, we should say, "You can become whatever God intends for you to become, if you trust Him and follow Him." That is the truth. Our kids need to hear that.

Encouraging our children to pursue their passion is important. But we should not encourage them to hold on to a passion that is just not achievable. That leads to constant disappointment and hopelessness. We do not want that for our children, do we?

Have you achieved God's goal for your life? Do you know He has directed in one way, but you have pursued in another direction? Stop and turn around. Let Him show you what He wants for the remainder of your life. He will strengthen you to do it.

O Holy Father, help me to trust You with each and every day. Point me toward the path You know is best for me. Teach me to follow.

APRIL 17

SHUT THAT DOOR!!!

Genesis 7

BEST VERSE: 16
Those that entered, male and female of all flesh, entered as God had commanded him; and the Lord closed it behind him.

After all those years building the ark, don't you think Noah knew how to close the door? He wouldn't have built a door he couldn't handle. This wasn't some ordinary door, though. This was a door that had to be sealed to keep out the water for all those days they would be afloat. Who was going to seal it from the outside if Noah and his family were inside? Certainly not those who were doomed to drown.

So, God took ahold of the door and "closed it behind him." God said, "I got this, Noah. You go on inside and get the animals all settled." You know, He still does that today. He tells us, "I've got this. Rest in Me."

TEACHING MOMENT

Do you tell your children a thousand times a day, "Shut that door!"? My mama used to holler at us if we ran outside without closing the door and leaving it slightly ajar. "I know you weren't born in a barn!"

The next time you have to remind them to close the door (and I am sure it won't be long), pull out this verse. We need to take every opportunity to point them to Scripture, even if it is the "open-door opportunity." God will secure us in His Son in the same way He secured Noah and his family in the ark. He will rescue us from destruction, if we will just trust Him.

Are you trusting? Are you allowing God to "close the door" for you? Let Him. He can handle things a whole lot better than you, I promise. His reach is longer, and His arms are stronger.

Father God, You are the One to seal me in Your Son. When I start to grab the handle of the door, stop me. Remind me You are in control of the whole situation.

APRIL 18

BE PREPARED

1 Samuel 17

BEST VERSE: 40

He took his stick in his hand and chose for himself five smooth stones from the brook, and put them in the shepherd's bag which he had, even in *his* pouch, and his sling was in his hand; and he approached the Philistine.

The question is often asked, "Why did David choose five stones?" The answer is quite simple. He wanted to be loaded for action. David was a shepherd and was skilled in the use of the sling. He had probably killed animals that attacked his father's sheep using that same sling and some stones. But a giant? One stone? Even if he did kill him with the one stone, what were the chances that the rest of the Philistines would attack anyway?

There is also the theory that Goliath had four brothers. There are four other giants mentioned in Scripture, and they could have been related to

Goliath. We don't know if they were there at the battle, but they could have been. So, what can we learn from this story?

TEACHING MOMENT

Giants are everywhere. I don't mean real, live giants who stand nine feet tall. I mean we face giants every day. Your children need to know how to use the sling and the stones (not literally, of course). Don't you bet David's father, Jesse, taught him to use that sling? We have the responsibility to teach our children to defend themselves spiritually.

How is that done? By discipling them in God's Word. We need to make them disciplemakers. They should be able to face ANY battle with the confidence that their aim is true, and they can fell any giant that crosses their path with His Word. Are you preparing them with the Word? Are you teaching them the skills necessary to bring down the giants?

Are *you* prepared? Or do you run and hide when you face giants? Do you fear and tremble like the Israelite army did in the presence of Goliath? Even King Saul was willing to allow a young David to go face the giant rather than facing Goliath himself. "Here, take my armor. But I'm not going!"

As they say today, "Buck up, buttercup!" It's time to face the giants. But don't think you can do it without the power of God in your life. You must rely on Him to fight for you, just like David told Goliath.

Thank you, Lord, for giving me the confidence through your Son, Jesus Christ, to face any and all giants who may come my way. You are the one who guides the stone.

APRIL 19

DON'T ASK ME!

Genesis 3

BEST VERSE: 9

Then the Lord said to Cain, "Where is Abel your brother?" And he said, "I do not know. Am I my brother's keeper?"

How many times have you said this? We don't want to be responsible for someone else, do we? We misuse this verse though and don't really understand the context when we say that.

Cain had just killed his brother. God knew that and knew where Abel was. He was simply trying to get Cain to admit his sin. But, just like us, he denied any wrongdoing. Aren't we just like that? Don't we deny our faults when confronted?

But this verse has deeper meaning also. We, as believers, are our brother's keeper. We have a responsibility to watch after our fellow believers. We have a responsibility to help them when they need it. We have a command to be like Jesus to a lost and dying world.

TEACHING MOMENT

Our children have to be taught to "watch out" for others, especially their siblings. We are not raising children, we are raising "child raisers." Learning how to care for others will prepare them for parenthood. Give them responsibility without all the pressure. They aren't parenting someone, but they are learning how to care for others.

Won't you look around you today and see who you can be your "brother's keeper" to? I promise if you look, He will provide someone.

Father, remind me today that I am responsible for others. Help me see them as You see them—redeemable and reconcilable.

APRIL 20

FOLLOWING ORDERS
Joshua 11

BEST VERSE: 23
So Joshua took the whole land, according to all that the LORD had spoken to Moses, and Joshua gave it for an inheritance to Israel according to their divisions by their tribes. Thus the land had rest from war.

We don't know exactly how long it took Joshua and the army to accomplish this task. They fought a lot of battles. We only have a record of one defeat, at Ai. Pretty impressive. In fact, the loss of life by the Israelites was minimal compared to the pagan nations. God had promised through Moses that they would have a "land flowing with milk and honey" if only they would obey him. They did, and now they had the land.

Do you believe God when He gives you a promise? Let me challenge you to google "promises of God" and claim them. Now, I am not talking about "name it and claim it" or "blab it and grab it" theology. I am simply pointing you to the promises of God through the Scriptures. Just don't forget—you have to keep your part. You have to obey.

TEACHING MOMENT

Promises! Promises! They can either build a relationship or tear it down. Don't let your children make silly promises you know they can't keep. It is your responsibility as a parent to teach them this. The best way to teach them this is through God's Word. Show them the promises God made to His people and how He kept His promise. Rash and silly promises do nothing to build character or reputation.

You can also make some promises to them which require some input from them. This will model God's promises to us that require our obedience. Of course, the biggest promise God makes is salvation, and that promise requires us to surrender our lives and hearts to Him. You can't promise salvation, but you make other reasonable promises. But you must keep the promise contingent on your children's feedback if they fulfill their end of the deal. Remember, you are always teaching.

Regarding promises God has made that are contingent on your feedback, what are you NOT obeying right now? God wants to bless you. Don't let your disobedience be the reason He doesn't.

God of all promises, I praise You for being the faithful keeper of Your Word. Teach me through my obedience to rest in Your promises. Help me show others the truth of Your Word.

APRIL 21

DO AS I DO

Matthew 23

BEST VERSES: 1-3

Then Jesus spoke to the crowds and to His disciples, saying: "The scribes and the Pharisees have seated themselves in the chair of Moses; therefore all that they tell you, do and observe, but do not do according to their deeds; for they say things and do not do them."

How many times did your parents say, "Do as I say, and not as I do"? Well, I heard that a few times. I know parents who drink but tell their kids not to. They smoke but tell their kids not to. Now, I am not judging you if you drink or smoke. That is between you and the Lord. I am just saying that our actions speak much louder than our words to our kids.

In this passage Jesus is pointing out the Scribes and Pharisees who "have seated themselves in the chair of Moses." What does that mean? Moses's chair? He was referring to the place where people came to have Moses judge them or give them advice. Are you sitting in such a place of judgment now? Are you sitting in judgment over your kids, all while you are doing the very thing for which you are judging them?

TEACHING MOMENT

May I encourage you today to be a model of the very behavior you desire in your children? If you want them to be kind to their siblings, then be kind to your husband or wife or that stranger you meet in line at the grocery store. If you want them to keep their room clean, then keep your bedroom tidy. You get the drift. Do, don't just say! Don't be a Pharisee. Be real to your kids.

Father, let me be a doer. I want others to see me doing the very things I am teaching. Help me to die to myself and allow You to live in and through me.

APRIL 22

BETWEEN A ROCK AND A HARD PLACE

1 Samuel 23

BEST VERSE: 28

So Saul returned from pursuing David and went to meet the Philistines; therefore they called that place the Rock of Escape.

David was trapped! Saul's army was surrounding him in the wilderness of Maon. He was sure to be captured and killed. Finally, Saul would catch his man. But . . . God.

God, yes God, orchestrated a Philistine attack to draw Saul away, allowing David to escape. Don't ever think there is no escape. If you are in

God's will and depending on Him, He will deliver. It may not be in the way you thought, but He will come through. I bet David never thought those wretched Philistines would deliver him from death.

TEACHING MOMENT

This would be a great acting-out story for your kids. Get some toy soldiers and build some hills. Study 1 Samuel 23 and some background information of the area mentioned in the chapter. Map out what was going on. Let your children see just how hopeless it appeared for David.

Our children need to understand that hopelessness in the eyes of men does not equal the same thing to God. He is hope. He brings hope. He gives hope. We don't hope in things or circumstances. We hope in Him.

Where is your hope placed today? In whom do you hope? I pray you are hoping in the God of Hope, because if you hope in anything else, you are sure to be disappointed. Look to Him who never sees anything or anyone as hopeless.

Let your children hope, not in you, but the Christ who lives in you. Let them see you hoping in Him, not in your job or family. We have to show our children that hope is not something. It is someone.

Lord, let Your hope flood my spirit today through the presence of Your Holy Spirit. Help me pour that hope out on others. Use me to give hope to others. Let me be a fountain of hope today!

APRIL 23

STANDING GUARD

Exodus 33

BEST VERSE: 11B
When Moses returned to the camp, his servant Joshua, the son of Nun, a young man, would not depart from the tent.

Moses had established the tent of meeting outside the camp. That is where he went to meet with the Lord. This was before the actual tabernacle was built. It was a special place, a place that should be protected as holy. So, who went with Moses there? None other than Joshua, son of Nun.

But he didn't just go with Moses and stand guard while he was in the tent talking to the Lord. When Moses would return to the camp, with his face shining from being in the presence of the Lord, Joshua would remain behind, standing guard at the tent of meeting. We see no indication that he grumbled or complained. He was loyal and dedicated. He was willing to serve, even if it meant guarding a tent. This was the same Joshua who had led the army in their first battle. He was a warrior, but here he was just standing there.

TEACHING MOMENT

Do your children ever complain of the small chores they have to do? Who likes doing those things? I used to have to go around the house and empty all the trash cans and then take the trash out. That may have seen like a small chore, but just imagine what would happen if no one did that. Your children need to see that there are no small chores, just seemingly small ones.

We need to teach them that everything we do as part of the family is important. Everything we do as part of the family of God is also important. Picking up trash in the pews after a service may seem a little thing, but it has to be done. Being loyal to the small tasks prepares us for the larger tasks to come.

What "small" task are you complaining about today? Do you feel undervalued? How do you think Joshua felt just standing next to the tent? But he knew he was doing something important. He was protecting the people from trying to "sneak a peek" at God. Whatever you do today, do it with excellence. You serve a master who demands loyalty and loves unconditionally.

Lord, thank You for the task You give me to serve You. Remind me each day how important my "chores" for You are.

A FIRST CRUISE

Exodus 2

BEST VERSE: 3

But when she could hide him no longer, she got him a wicker basket and covered it over with tar and pitch. Then she put the child into it and set *it* among the reeds by the bank of the Nile.

Back in 2005 our family took a cruise to the Bahamas. It wasn't a great experience due to my son getting sick and my wife not really liking being out to sea. But we wanted to do it together. Mark that off the bucket list.

Moses's first river cruise was short lived. Miriam, his sister, put his little wicker basket boat in the Nile where it was found by Pharaoh's daughter. His cruise turned out pretty good, considering the other outcome—certain death. Sometimes what may sound like a crazy plan is EXACTLY what the Lord plans for us.

TEACHING MOMENT

I promise you there will be days when your children will question some of your plans for them. "Why do I have to wear this dress, Mommy?" "Why do I have to go to school?" Ask them what they think Miriam was thinking when her parents told her to put Moses in that wicker basket boat and put him in the Nile with the crocodiles.

What Miriam learned (and what your kids can learn) is parents have to trust the Lord for guidance that sometimes does not make any sense. But He is faithful. We must trust Him to follow through on the plans He has made and has asked us to obey. That kind of faith only comes through trusting.

What are you struggling with right now? What has the Lord asked you to do? Why aren't you believing Him? He is always true to His word, and He will guide you through. Trust Him. Lean on Him. Believe His Word!

Father, I believe. Help my unbelief. I want to act on Your Word without questioning. Let me be one to show others the joy of trusting You.

THIS LITTLE LIGHT OF MINE

Exodus 27

BEST VERSE: 20

You shall charge the sons of Israel, that they bring you clear oil of beaten olives for the light, to make a lamp burn continually.

This chapter in Exodus in today's daily reading is all about setting up the tabernacle. God is a God of details. But what struck me today was verse 20 of chapter 27. God is a God of light also, and His light will "burn continually."

Can you imagine the nation of Israel in the desert seeing the glow of the light all night, every night? A constant reminder of God's presence. A reassuring "night light" for all to see. It's the same today. His light burns in and through us. We are His light in a dark world. Our light needs to be tended to daily to make sure all can see it.

TEACHING MOMENT

Kids love fire and matches, don't they? What kid doesn't love to build a fire outside and watch it glow? Of course, they want to play in the fire and roast marshmallows. I do too. But take this opportunity to talk about the light of your fire compared to God's. Your fire and its light will go out. God's light is eternal. Your firelight has to have wood or some other fuel to burn. God's light comes from God Himself.

Our children need to know that they can ALWAYS depend on the light of God. When their world seems dark, His light can brighten their way. When they allow His light to shine in and through them, they can draw others to Him. Isn't that the purpose of "our little light"?

I pray you will allow your light to shine brightly. I pray you will let His light be your light. Shine for Him and Him only.

Father of light, there is no variation or shifting shadow in You (James 1:17). Your light draws out all my darkness. Praise You for lighting my path.

REGRETS

Joshua 16

BEST VERSE: 10
But they did not drive out the Canaanites who lived in Gezer, so the Canaanites live in the midst of Ephraim to this day, and they became forced laborers.

Have you ever not done something you were told to do? How many times did you live to regret that? Probably every time. The Israelites were told to wipe out the people of the Promised Land. The Lord did not want anyone negatively influencing His chosen children. He wanted them to be focused on Him and not lured away by pagan gods.

God gives us pretty clear directions too. He tells us to not be "yoked" with unbelievers. We are told to avoid evil. It is not very complicated. But it is necessary. We can't "wallow with the pigs and not get mud on us," as my uncle used to say. We have to stay pure and undefiled.

TEACHING MOMENT
The next time you have a great rainstorm, let your kids out to play in it (as long as there is no lightning). But tell them they can't step in any mud puddles. What do you think is going to happen? Just as soon as you turn your head, little Johnny is going to be right in the middle of that puddle.

Show him how dirty he is now. He probably won't care. As you are cleaning him up, talk to him about this story. Just as they were told to avoid evil and to get rid of the pagans, Johnny was told to avoid the mud. But they didn't do that, and he didn't do that. The Israelites lack of obedience had longer-lasting consequences. Getting dirty is temporary, but your children can still learn from it.

Don't have regrets about not doing what you should have done. Do it now. Do it the first time. Don't wait. You never know the consequences that may come your way from simply not following directions.

Father, I know Your Word is true and always points me in the right direction. Help me be more ready to respond when You ask me. Let me lead others in obedience.

TESTING

Judges 3

BEST VERSE: 4

They were for testing Israel, to find out if they would obey the commandments of the Lord, which He had commanded their fathers through Moses.

God's commandments were clear. Get rid of all the pagan nations that lived within the borders of the Promised Land. He even drove some out Himself through supernatural means, but He left some just to see if His people would obey Him.

God knew their hearts. They had already begun to intermarry and worship pagan gods. God desired their obedience, but He wasn't going to force them. They had to obey willingly, just like we have to today. However, if disobedience is chosen, consequences will come. They experienced it, and so will we.

TEACHING MOMENT

Children need to learn that there are always consequences for any decision they make. They can choose to obey and be blessed or disobey and be disciplined. It's their choice. Give it to them. But make sure they are fully aware of the consequences.

Not following through with the consequences is the worst thing we can do as parents. You may be thinking, *But Carl, they didn't mean to disobey.* Are you sure about that? Don't get pulled into those big, ole puppy dog eyes. Be firm but loving.

What do you prefer—blessings or discipline? I don't know about you, but I choose blessing. That means I have to obey my heavenly Father even when I think I want my way. Notice I said "think." I don't always know what is best. I know you find that hard to believe, but I don't. But He always knows best.

Heavenly Father, hold me accountable for my actions. That sounds funny to say, but I mean it. Let me rest in Your knowledge of what is best for me.

LIARS LIE

Genesis 27

BEST VERSE: 24

And he said, "Are you really my son Esau?" And he said, "I am."

Man, what a liar! Lying to his own daddy! And not just lying, but stealing too. He stole his brother's blessing. And to top it all off, his mother was in on it. We talk about dysfunctional families today, but this one takes the cake.

Jacob is the one God chose to birth the twelve tribes of Israel. There was nothing worthy in him. God just chose him. Jacob didn't deserve to be used by God, but God used him anyway. What a lesson for us today and for our children.

TEACHING MOMENT

Some parents give up on their kids when they make mistakes. Some write them off. God never does. The next time your child lies to you, read them this story. Explain how lying is bad and should never be a part of a believer's life. But God can forgive that, just like any other sin.

Explain to your children that God has a plan for their lives. They probably have NO idea what that is now. I bet Jacob never thought he would be the father of Israel, that his name would be changed to Israel, that he would end up in Egypt, and that one of his sons would literally rescue the family. You just never know how God can use a liar.

What are you running from? Are you like Jacob, running from an angry brother you have deceived? Whom have you dishonored? Go to the Lord. Let Him forgive you of your transgressions. Let Him point you in the right direction. Let Him show you the way.

Father of all nations, forgive me. Let me see Your will rather than my own. Give me the wisdom to guide those whom you have placed under my leadership.

ARE YOU KIDDING ME?

Genesis 17

BEST VERSE: 17

Then Abraham fell on his face and laughed, and said in his heart, "Will a child be born to a man one hundred years old? And will Sarah, who is ninety years old, bear a child?"

I love a good joke. I especially love one when the person telling it has the gift of telling jokes. Do you know what I mean? My brother-in-law had that gift. He could, as they say, really spin a yarn. I bet Abraham was thinking, "Man, this guy can really tell a joke. Come on! Really? Ninety-nine years old? Having a child? That's funny enough, but by Sarah? No way! She has never been able to get pregnant."

Listen, dear brother and sister, do not doubt what God can do. If the Lord had desired to have Sarah birth an elephant, that would have happened. He created everything. Orchestrating a child between Sarah and Abraham was no huge task for Him.

TEACHING MOMENT

How do you get this concept of making the impossible possible across to your children? How can you explain to your children that God can do anything? Our belief that He can or can't has nothing to do with it. Abraham laughed. Later, Sarah laughed. But it still happened. God had a plan, and it involved their future son, Isaac.

Now Abraham and Sarah had to do their part (as they obviously did), but God was the one who designed the plan. Our children need to understand that God has a perfect plan designed for them. They just need to listen and obey. They need to leave all the "heavy lifting" up to Him. He wants to use them, but He won't make them His unwilling servants. He desires willful obedience.

How about you? Are you fighting against God or with Him? I find myself way too often fighting against Him. It is so easy to fool myself into thinking I am not. Listen to Him today and allow Him to have His perfect Will in your life. It's much easier that way!

O God, You are a big God. Your Word is true, and I can trust it with my life. No word from You is impossible. You call us all to different tasks. I will listen and obey.

A CHANGE OF TUNE

Genesis 44

BEST VERSE: 18
Then Judah approached him, and said, "Oh my lord, may your servant please speak a word in my lord's ears, and do not be angry with your servant; for you are equal to Pharaoh."

I am sure you have heard that expression, "he sure changed his tune." Someone totally flips their thinking. They were adamant about one thing, and then they believe the opposite. Judah had changed his tune. Why do I say that? Judah was the one who had suggested years earlier to his brothers to sell Joseph into slavery. It was his idea. Now he stands before the second most powerful man in Egypt, begging for mercy.

I bet when Joseph finally revealed himself to his brothers, Judah was shaking in his boots (or should I say sandals?). Judah's remorse, however, was not for what he had done to Joseph. His grief was directed at how losing their youngest brother Benjamin would affect their father. This was what touched Joseph, I believe.

TEACHING MOMENT
How do you get your children to show concern for someone else? Some kids are just made that way. They show mercy and compassion for others even as toddlers. Others, not so much. They could care less about how someone else feels. All they think about is themselves. We see that about Judah in other passages. But here he shows true love for his father.

There is really only one way for your child to "change their tune." They have to be reborn with the Spirit of God. They must receive a new heart from the Lord. They must ask Jesus to be their Lord and Savior. Have you been praying for that? Have you been plugging the gospel every time you get a chance?

How about you, Mom and Dad? Have you had a "change of tune" about your relationships? Are you willing to die to yourself for the sake of your spouse? Will you? Would you? Can you? No, you can't! But with Jesus all things are possible.

Father of Mercy, give me the mercy I need to give to others. It is not easy sometimes to show that to others, but I know I need to. Help me be merciful as You have shown me mercy.

GOD'S MATH

Deuteronomy 20

BEST VERSE: 1

When you go out to battle against your enemies and see horses and chariots *and* people more numerous than you, do not be afraid of them; for the Lord your God, who brought you up from the land of Egypt, is with you.

Moses is giving the people instructions for when they would enter the Promised Land and begin to possess the land. He knew they would encounter armies much bigger than their own. But Moses also knew that God counted differently than man. After all the Trinity is proof: 1+1+1=1.

God wasn't concerned about the size of any pagan army. He could just speak and wipe them off the face of the earth. He did create the world by just speaking, after all. So, Moses is trying to ease any apprehensions that might have existed. Trust God. He's got this.

TEACHING MOMENT

Your children are going to face things (if they haven't already) that seem insurmountable. They will make every excuse in the world why they can't win or pass or survive. Read them this verse. Remind them that the Hebrew children faced a task that seemed impossible. But God. . . .

Your children may doubt the power of God in their lives. If they are believers, they possess the power of the Holy Spirit who can and will guard them and protect them. He will guide them into making the right decisions—if they will just trust Him.

Are you trusting Him? Are you allowing the Holy Spirit to dictate your marching orders? He will not only give you good directions, but He will also personally escort you there. That's pretty cool.

I want to live in power. I do not want to limit what You can do. I know You don't care about the number or size of my problems. You've got this!

WHAT A GREAT PROBLEM!

Exodus 36

BEST VERSES: 6B-7

. . . Thus the people were restrained from bringing any more. For the material they had was sufficient and more than enough for all the work, to perform it.

How often is that the case? You need supplies for a project, and you receive more than you need. Most of the time we are trying to figure out how to stretch what we have to get the job done. Not this time. Moses issued the call for donations for the tabernacle and then had to say, "Stop! We've got enough."

How does this happen? Why doesn't this happen all the time? Well, there is only one answer, which we see earlier in 35:21, "Everyone whose heart stirred him and everyone whose spirit moved him came and brought the Lord's contribution for the work of the tent of meeting and for all its service and for the holy garments." Who do you think stirred their hearts?

TEACHING MOMENT

How do you teach this to your kids? How do you explain the Lord stirring your heart? Once again, we see it is better caught than taught. As the Lord stirs your heart to do something, make sure your kids understand that. Talk to them about your prayers regarding this and how the Lord has directed you. Explain how you have responded to His leading.

There are some things in the faith walk that words can't explain. But your kids can watch and learn. They can hear your prayers for direction from the Lord and then watch as you respond to His leading. Let them be right there in the middle of it. And then they can share in the blessing. They can learn to rejoice in a stirred heart.

What are you wrestling with right now? Are there things the Lord is "stirring" you to do? Don't wait. Do as He leads. I promise the blessing will follow.

Stirrer of hearts, move in me. Stir my heart to respond to Your call. Help me stir others through my obedience to You.

FAMILIAR VOICE

Genesis 46

BEST VERSES: 1-2

So Israel set out with all that he had, and came to Beersheba, and offered sacrifices to the God of his father Isaac. God spoke to Israel in visions of the night and said, "Jacob, Jacob." And he said, "Here I am."

As far as we know from Scripture, it had been a while since the Lord had spoken to Jacob (Israel) in a dream or any other way. Do you remember Jacob's dream at Bethel when he fled from Esau? God had promised to make him a great nation and to bring him back home. Well, here's the same voice speaking to him again. This time the Lord says, "Go to Egypt."

I can't help but wonder why there was this gap in time of God speaking to Jacob. Did Jacob get comfortable back in Canaan? Did he get distracted with his family and flocks? Did his grief over Rachel and Joseph drown out the voice of God? We don't know. But when God spoke to him again, he recognized His voice. Sweet!

TEACHING MOMENT

If you ever go out of town for work, do you call home and speak to your children? Of course, you do. Who wouldn't do that? I bet the second they hear your voice, they know it's you, right? Today we have FaceTime and Skype so they can see your face too, but they know your voice. Why? Because you talk to them when you are home.

We need to teach our children to recognize the voice of the Lord. We need to talk to them about listening to His call on their lives. When they feel that draw of the Spirit toward God, they need to be able to recognize it is the Lord. That's only possible if they know what He sounds like. What is that? Love! Truth! Obedience! Just! Holy!

Do you struggle hearing God? Many of us do. But most of the time it is because we are too busy listening to other things. We get bombarded by life's pressures and don't hear what He is trying to tell us. He will NOT force us to listen, but He is always calling.

O Lord, I know Your voice. It always points me towards truth. It always agrees with the Word. Help me help others recognize and respond to Your call on their lives, especially my children.

BEWARE OF FALLING ROCK

Joshua 2

BEST VERSE: 15
Then she let them down by a rope through the window, for her house was on the city wall, so that she was living on the wall.

A lot of people miss the point that when the walls of Jericho fell, one section didn't. Rahab's home stood safe and sound. Rock and timbers and gates were falling around her, but she was (please excuse the pun) rock solid. The two spies had promised her safety if she tied the scarlet thread out her window.

Now, you have to remember that the spies had no idea of the plan of attack on Jericho. They assumed it would be a normal siege. "Mark your window, Rahab, so we won't come into your home and kill you." They didn't know her home would be the only one standing on the wall when they came into the city.

TEACHING MOMENT
This would be a great story to teach your kids using building blocks or Legos®. (You may want to hold off explaining the harlot part until later.) Build a wall of a city; designate one section as Rahab's, and then act out the battle—with all the walls falling down. I bet when you do that it will be hard to avoid knocking down that section.

God tore down this massive wall around Jericho as He promised, but He also honored the promise of the two spies to keep Rahab safe. The point for your children is this. If we are obedient, even if the world seems to be falling down around us, we are safe in God's promises. We may get a little dusty and shake a little, but we are safe.

Is your life shaking all around you right now? Do you feel like the walls are collapsing? Turn to Him. Place your life firmly in His powerful hands. He can protect you. He loves His children and will only allow what is going to make you more like Him to touch your life.

Lord, when everything seems to be exploding around me, remind me to stop and pray. I don't need to tie a scarlet thread outside my window for You to know where I am. I place my family in Your capable, strong hands.

MAY 5

HOW DO YOU LOVE?

John 13

BEST VERSE: 35
By this all men will know that you are My disciples, if you have love for one another.

What a simple yet powerful statement from the lips of our Lord. Have you ever stopped to think about what He is saying here? He is saying that others (all men) will know (know through experience [*ginōskō*]) that you follow and believe in Him (become disciples) by loving (*agapē*) each other.

I think it's curious that Jesus didn't say, "other believers will know." He said all men, lost or saved. How does a lost person know you are a disciple? By the love you show. We are not told to just love *those who love us*. We are told to love *everyone*. Why? Because He did, so much so that He laid down His life for them.

TEACHING MOMENT
Do your children know how to show love? I don't mean just to you or their family. I mean to everyone. How do we teach them to love everyone without putting themselves at risk or in danger? How can a child express Christ's love to a stranger? Just watch them. Children can surprise you. They can love people we would not even look at. They can accept a stranger when we turn our backs.

We are facing so many threats in our world today to the Christian way of life. We are challenged on our standards and deeply held beliefs. Even in that, we must love. I heard recently of a refugee from Iraq who said she was thankful for ISIS. What! How? She said if ISIS had not come to her country and forced her to leave, she would have never heard about Jesus. She is now burdened for ISIS that they too could find Christ.

Will you encourage your children to love others so the world will know they are Christ's followers? Will you love that way yourself? Will you pray for the Lord to put someone who is very unlovable in your path today so you can love that person?

I don't want to love those who hate me, God. But You command me to be Jesus to them, which means I have to love them. Love them through me.

MAY 6

HELPING HANDS

Exodus 17

BEST VERSES: 11-12
So it came about when Moses held his hand up, that Israel prevailed, and when he let his hand down, Amalek prevailed. But Moses' hands were heavy. Then they took a stone and put it under him, and he sat on it; and Aaron and Hur supported his hands, one on one side and one on the other. Thus his hands were steady until the sun set.

Don't you just love this story? I don't mean the battle and the victory. I mean Aaron and Hur coming to the aid of Moses. Nowhere does it say that Moses asked for their help. They saw Moses struggling and the obvious effect it had on the army, so they jumped in. They rolled a rock over to Moses, sat him down, and lifted his hands. Teamwork!

Don't you want people around you like that? I do. I need other men in my life who will step in and help when they see me struggling. Men, myself included, don't ask for help too easily. We think we can do it ourselves. But when we try and are failing, we aren't the only ones who suffer. Our wives and our children do, too.

Teaching our children to rely on others can be tricky. We don't want them to be moochers and depend on others for everything. We don't want them to be lone rangers and never ask for help. There's a delicate balance that is best taught by modeling this for them. Make sure they know when others come to your aid. Make sure they hear you thank them too.

Teamwork among believers is so crucial to a healthy church and church family. Being able to call on someone when we are in a pinch is a wonderful gift. Your children will do well to learn this early in life. They can learn it by being that person for someone else, too.

Father, You are the ultimate team builder. Show me those around me I can depend upon. Help me lean on them. And let me be that for someone else when they are in need.

MAY 7

THOSE WHO KNOW ME BEST

Mark 6

BEST VERSE: 4

Jesus said to them, "A prophet is not without honor except in his hometown and among his *own* relatives and in his *own* household."

Boy, isn't that the truth? Those who know us best can be the most critical. But here is Jesus, the Son of God, who was PERFECT, and He wasn't honored or respected by his hometown, relatives, or household. Why would we expect to be treated differently?

TEACHING MOMENT

Before you jump ahead of me, let me make my point. Just because we don't expect to be treated this way does not give us the excuse to "let our hair down" around those who know us best. We have to teach our children that we need to be just as loving, holy, and Christ-like at home as we would be at church or around strangers. Unfortunately, we tend to act very unlike Christ at home sometimes. We would never behave at church like we do at home. What is that teaching our kids?

I am as guilty as the next person, so I am not pointing fingers. But I am thankful that the Holy Spirit convicts me when I speak harshly or act unkind towards my wife or children. This happened just recently. I didn't really do anything, but the perception from my wife was I was angry. I had to apologize and ask her forgiveness for the way I had portrayed myself to her. Sometimes we inflict hurt and don't even know it. We still have to make that right.

Moms and dads, let me encourage you today to put Jesus first in your home. Be Jesus to your family above all others. That will teach your children more about living the Christ life than any words you use.

Lord, You have blessed me with a wonderful family. Forgive me of my harshness with them. Remind me today that those closest to me deserve my best. I need to treat them best first.

BEAUTIFUL NAME, WONDERFUL NAME

Judges 13

BEST VERSES: 17–18
Manoah said to the angel of the LORD, "What is your name, so that when your words come **to pass,** we may honor you?" But the angel of the LORD said to him, "Why do you ask my name, seeing it is wonderful?"

Philip Bliss wrote a hymn in 1874 entitled "Wonderful Words of Life." The chorus reads, "Beautiful words, wonderful words, wonderful words of life." I couldn't help but think of this hymn when I read these verses. The Angel of the Lord (Jesus in the OT) appears to Manoah and his wife and when asked his name, says, "It is wonderful."

Truly the name of Jesus is wonderful. His name is above all names. His name carries with it the reminder that His birth, life, death and resurrection changed human history. Even the calendar is based on his life.

TEACHING MOMENT
When you picked out a name for your child, did you research its meaning? I bet you did. My first name, Carl, means strong and manly. That fits me

exactly. Ha ha. Seriously, that name was my maternal grandfather's name. I am proud to carry it, even though I never knew him. Do your children know why they were named what they were named? They should know that.

But more importantly, we want our children to carry the name of Jesus wherever they go. They should be known as a Christ-follower. When people think of them, they should think of Jesus. How can you as parents help them to do that? By carrying the name of Jesus yourself. *You* need to be known that way. People should see the "Wonderful Name" emblazoned on our foreheads (you know what I mean).

Look at the words of the last verse of that hymn: "Sweetly echo the gospel call, Wonderful words of life; Offer pardon and peace to all, Wonderful words of life; Jesus, only Savior, Sanctify us forever." Amen!

Your name is Wonderful! O God, wondrous God, show me Your wonder in the everyday things. Let me see Your splendor all around.

MAY 9

WAITING ON GOD
1 Samuel 24

BEST VERSE: 10
Behold, this day your eyes have seen that the Lord had given you today into my hand in the cave, and some said to kill you, but *my eye* had pity on you; and I said, "I will not stretch out my hand against my lord, for he is the Lord's anointed."

I am not sure I could have done what David did. Saul was relentlessly pursuing David to kill him. If given the opportunity to kill David, Saul would have not blinked an eye. He saw David as a threat to his throne, so he wanted him dead and gone.

Now, here in this cave, with the support of his men, David has the chance to stop running and claim what God had already promised him—the throne of Israel. How tempting is that? Surely, the Lord had provided this opportunity. Right? Wrong!

Your children will be faced with many life and death choices. Now, I don't mean that literally. But every choice they make in life is a matter of spiritual life and death, beginning with the choice to receive the Lord Jesus as Savior. Every other decision they make is built on that one. What will please the Master?

David had to make a quick decision. If he didn't, one of his men would have probably slain Saul for David. But David, I'm sure, consulted the Lord in that cave and was reminded that only God establishes kings and kingdoms. God would place David on the throne when it was time. God wasn't through preparing David for the throne.

Children want to make quick decisions. We need to slow them down sometimes and let those choices marinate for a while. We need to teach them to ask the Lord what will give Him honor and then do that, no matter how crazy it seems.

Are you seeking the Lord in your daily decisions? Are you asking Him to help you make not only the right choice, but also the godly choice? David could have killed Saul in that cave, and no one would have objected (well maybe Saul). Even Saul's son, Jonathan would have approved. But David did the godly thing. He let God's anointed leave unharmed.

Help me make the godly choice today, O Lord. I want to do what You want, even if others think I should make another choice. God, give me Your peace in the midst of the decision-making process.

MAY 10

REPUTATION

Daniel 6

BEST VERSE: 16
Then the king gave orders, and Daniel was brought in and cast into the lions' den. The king spoke and said to Daniel, "Your God whom you constantly serve will Himself deliver you."

Do you realize Darius was a pagan? As far as we know from Scripture, He wasn't a worshiper of Jehovah. But he recognized the power of Jehovah in the life of Daniel. Not only that, but he even believed, I think, that Jehovah could deliver Daniel from the lions' den.

Do pagans around you recognize the power of God in your life? What will God allow to come into your life to point unbelievers to Him? How will you respond when these trials come? Will you complain and waste the opportunity to be a witness?

TEACHING MOMENT

Our children must be taught that, as believers in Christ, they represent a holy and righteous God to a lost world. They may be the only representative of Jesus their friends may see. So, all they do should point to Him. I am not saying they have to be perfect, but they need to be very aware of how the lost world sees Jesus through them.

Little things like lying about another friend, cheating on a test, or being disobedient to parents (not that any of these are little) while in the presence of a lost friend can ruin any opportunity they may have to witness to that person later. If they are no different than the lost world, then why should their lost friend change?

It is my prayer today that you will live a life of reputation. People will know whom you represent. People will acknowledge Jesus because of what they saw Him do through your life. Amen?

Father, help me teach my children to always represent You, especially to the lost. Let my life give them that example.

MAY 11

GOOD HEARING

Psalms 5–6

BEST VERSE: 6:9
The Lord has heard my supplication, the Lord receives my prayer.

The older I get the more I appreciate good hearing. I have lost some hearing of high tones in my left ear which can be so aggravating. But I am so thankful that I can still hear. I have friends who can't hear at all and others who need to wear hearing aids.

But the thing I am most thankful for is that I know my God has perfect hearing. He is always listening for me. His hearing is absolute. He can hear me and everyone else in the world who calls on Him. When someone calls on Him for salvation, He is quick to send His Holy Spirit. When one of His children needs assistance, He is there, listening and directing His angels to respond accordingly. He doesn't always answer in the way we want, but He does listen.

TEACHING MOMENT

Has your child ever said, "Dad, are you listening to me?" I used to get that from mine. If I am reading or watching television, I have to redirect my hearing. I cannot focus on a conversation and read or watch something. I bet your children can't either. What a perfect time to use this verse. Remind them that God is always listening. He is always attentive.

We need to teach our children to talk to God, knowing that He is listening. When they begin their prayers, He is already waiting to hear them. As they pray, He is preparing to answer. He has the ability to multi-task, unlike the rest of us.

Will you allow the Lord to hear from you today? Will you speak to Him like He is sitting right next to you? Open your heart to Him today. He wants to hear your needs. He wants to hear your struggles. He wants to work in your life. But you have to let Him.

Lord, I give it all to You today! Bend Your ear towards earth to hear my heartfelt prayers and supplications. I know You are waiting.

THAT'S MINE

Genesis 25

BEST VERSE: 26A
Afterward his brother came forth with his hand holding on to Esau's heel, so his name was called Jacob.

What a name! Grabber! How would you like that name? It's no wonder the two boys didn't get along too well. Every time Jacob's name was called, he was reminded of the birth story. "Don't you remember, Esau, how your brother was holding on to your foot when you were born?" I bet that story got old.

But God has a plan for everything He does and allows. God chose Jacob to be the line through which the nation of Israel would be birthed and eventually through which the Messiah would come. God makes no mistakes. We may think we have it all figured out, but we will see, in the end, that He knows best.

TEACHING MOMENT
Do your children "grab" for stuff? Do they always seem to want what the other child has? I've seen it a lot. If you put two two-year-olds in the same room with a dozen toys, it won't take long until they are fighting over the same toy. "Mine, mine, mine!" We "grab" the stuff we think we have to have.

Teaching our children contentment is hard work. The world is working against us all the time. But when they learn to receive with gratitude and accept what they have, they will have learned a great life lesson. Now, there's nothing wrong with ambition and achievement. It just shouldn't come against the rights of others.

What are you "grabbing" for? Do you eye what somebody else has and desire it? Let the Lord be your desire. Let Him show you what you need. After all, He desires the best for you.

My God and Savior, I know You want the best for me. But sometimes it is just hard to wait as others all around me seem to have all they desire. Help me to rest in You and teach others to do the same.

BOY, THAT SMELLS GOOD

Luke 7

BEST VERSE: 50
And He said to the woman, "Your faith has saved you; go in peace."

Can you imagine the smell that was in the room? If you have ever spilled some cologne or perfume, you know how it fills the room with the aroma. The people, no matter where they were sitting or standing, eventually got a whiff of that perfume. AND whenever Jesus left the room and walked past them, they could smell it. Sweet smell!

But the beautiful thing about that smell is not the scent, but the memory. They had heard Jesus tell her that her sins were forgiven and that her faith had saved her. I dare to say that everyone, even Simon (who questioned the action), had a flashback to this event the next time they smelled that perfume.

TEACHING MOMENT
Moms and dads, don't you just love the smell of your children after they get out of the bath and are wrapped in that towel, still warm from the bath waters? My wife loved to smell our babies. There is still something about a clean newborn's smell that is so fresh.

The next time you give your boy or girl a bath, tell them this story and compare it to the freshness we have in Christ through our salvation. We are washed clean, pure and spotless! We have a fresh new scent that simply exudes Jesus! What a great smell!

Unfortunately, we let sin back in, and that fresh scent is soon forgotten. Go back to the cleansing waters of Christ. Let him cleanse you once again and let the aroma of Christ linger in the air as you pass others.

Father, let Your sweet aroma bathe over me so everyone smells You on me. Let me be used to draw others to You. You are the sweetest fragrance I could ever wear.

STUCK!

Psalms 39–40

BEST VERSES: 40:1–2

I waited patiently for the Lord; and He inclined to me and heard my cry. He brought me up out of the pit of destruction, out of the miry clay, and He set my feet upon a rock making my footsteps firm.

A few years ago, I was hunting in a swampy area that required me to walk through several inches of water to get to my tree stand. I had really intended to get some new hunting boots, but just had not gotten around to it. The boots I was wearing were kind of water proof, but not completely. I managed to get to my stand with damp but not horribly wet feet. Thankfully, it wasn't a cold day.

The problem came as I started to exit the woods at dark. I had not realized when I walked in (in the light) that there were several muddy areas along my path. As I walked out, I accidentally got off the path and into one of those areas of mud. Not only did I get my feet very wet, but I was trudging along in several inches of thick, clingy mud. I was so thankful to finally reach solid ground, thoroughly exhausted.

TEACHING MOMENT

What a fun verse to share with your kids the next time you get to play in the mud outside. Most kids love mud. Take a walk with them through it. Compare how different your walking is in the mud and on grass. Let them feel the tug and pull of the mud on their feet.

Now you can tell them how sin does the same thing to our spirits. It pulls us down. It bogs us down. It makes walking with Christ so hard. But Jesus is our firm foundation upon which we can walk confidently. As we keep our feet on the solid ground, we can navigate the paths He has set before us. We must allow Him to show us the safest path to follow through the swamps of life.

How about you today? Are you tired of pulling your feet out of the mud? Are you tired of walking through the mud of life? Are you tired of cleaning all that mud off your shoes? Then walk with Jesus. Even if He leads you into a swamp, He is there to pull you through!

Lord, I get stuck often, but it is almost always when I'm off the path. Keep me focused on following You. I know You will never lead me astray.

REMOVE THE MUZZLE

Deuteronomy 25

BEST VERSE: 4
You shall not muzzle the ox while he is threshing.

You may read this passage and ask yourself, "What does this even mean?" Well, back in those days, they used animals to thresh the grain. They would lay the stalks of wheat or barley on the ground, usually in a prepared place. Then they would walk their ox or donkey or some heavy animal over it to break the grain from the stalk and husk. Muzzling the animal was cruel since it needed to eat too. Moses was saying to take care of the animal you have asked to make your work easier.

This verse has been applied for centuries to those who serve in ministry. Basically, don't starve your pastors to death by paying them very little while they feed you the Word. Make sure they are taken care of by the church. A pastor should not be concerned with how he can provide for his family. His only concern should be caring for his flock.

TEACHING MOMENT
You may be thinking, *Okay Carl, how are you going to use this verse to apply to our children today?* Don't you believe every passage has something to say to us? Of course, it does. Find out a need your pastor has right now. Then take your children along to meet that need. He may need new tires on his vehicle. Arrange to get his keys from his wife or secretary and take your kids with you to get new tires put on his car.

Maybe he has a financial need. Get your kids involved in giving him a special love offering. Do it quietly so you don't bring attention to yourself or your kids. Teach your kids that giving can be a special blessing when you can do it secretly or anonymously. Whatever you do to bless your pastor, do it with your kids. They won't soon forget it.

I guarantee there is at least one need in your pastor's life that you can meet this week. It may be a simple gift card to a restaurant or mowing his lawn. Do it. Bless him. Don't muzzle the ox when he is threshing.

Father, I thank You for the Pastors in my life who have fed me. Show me ways in which I can be a blessing to him and his family today.

NO POVERTY

Deuteronomy 15

BEST VERSE: 4

However, there will be no poor among you, since the Lᴏʀᴅ will surely bless you in the land which the Lᴏʀᴅ your God is giving you as an inheritance to possess.

Read that verse again. Can you imagine no poverty? Can you imagine a society where everyone has enough to eat? How about clothes to wear or shelter over their heads? I drive down the streets of Chattanooga, Tennessee, where I live every day. And every day I see people out begging for food. I see homeless people living under bridges or in the woods behind a shopping center. Why?

I truly believe it is because we do not honor our God. If we all worshiped the one true God, and I mean everyone, then there would be no one in need. I know that sounds like a pipe dream. But why would the Lord tell Moses to say this to the people as they were entering the Promised Land? Do you think God was lying to them? Of course not. But they had to do their part and obey Him.

TEACHING MOMENT

The next time you are out with your children and you see those on the street asking for a handout, bring up this verse. Because we live in a fallen world, sin has consequences. Some sins lead to poverty. Talk to your children how they can follow the Lord's leading in helping those less fortunate. No one is promised wealth and prosperity. But all who turn to Him are promised to have their needs (not wants) met.

You may be thinking, *Now wait, Carl, that sounds like pie-in-the-sky promises. God doesn't promise that.* Really? Didn't Jesus say the Father knows the number of hairs on your head? Doesn't He clothe you better than the lilies? God knows our needs and will meet those according to His perfect plan.

Are you stressing out over finances right now? Have you turned that over to Him? Let Him have your debit card. (I would have said checkbook but no one has those anymore.) Ask the Lord to meet that need you have and then thank Him for meeting it. Finally, as you are able, help meet that need of someone else. That may be just the way God is meeting that need they are praying for.

Lord, thank You for being the God of all, not just the rich and well off. You care for the lowest of the low. Show me how to help meet the needs of others.

MAY 17

I GOTTA LOVE WHO?

Luke 6

BEST VERSE: 27
But I say to you who hear, love your enemies, do good to those who hate you.

Luke 6:20–38 is Luke's version of The Beatitudes. Let me encourage you to read the entire passage. But for simplicity's sake, I decided to just list verse 27 of this passage. If we can teach our children to love their enemies, well, then they can handle just about anything, right?

Do you have any enemies? I mean, do you have people in your life who truly hate you? Enemies want to destroy you. They want to see you hurt and bleeding. They would prefer you not exist. Pretty harsh!

I don't think I have any real enemies in my life right now. Even people who may not like me don't wish me physical harm. That was not always the case. I remember there was one boy in my school who was always trying to "one up" me. We competed aggressively for prestige and position. (This was in my days before Christ). We had more than one fight trying to be the bigger man.

I wonder what could have happened if I had known the Lord then and shown him love rather than anger. If I had done good to him rather than harm, he and I both may have been better at the very thing we were trying to achieve.

TEACHING MOMENT

Our children need to see you love those who "hate" you. Maybe you have a neighbor who is hard to get along with. Bake them some cookies or mow their lawn. Show your children that we can love anyone—if we let Jesus do the loving. Why? Because He loves them. He died for them. The least we can do is show them His love.

Love is not possible, Lord, unless it's Your love. I want to love others, so help me love them through You. Give me Your supernatural agap love for everyone.

SOON AND VERY SOON

Mark 13

BEST VERSE: 37
What I say to you I say to all, "Be on the alert!"

There is NO doubt about it—Jesus is coming again! Are you ready? Here in Mark 13, He warns His disciples about the time. The chapter ends with these four words: BE ON THE ALERT! Actually, in in the Greek it just one word, *gregoreō*, which means "stay awake."

Have you ever been so tired you literally could not stay awake? I mean, you could sleep standing up. That happens when we don't get enough rest or when we have been working long hours. But here I truly believe Jesus is warning them about sleepiness from boredom or sloth. We must be ready at all times.

How do you teach your children to watch for Jesus? You don't want them to be worried about His return. As a believer, we welcome His return. It is nothing to be feared. But we do need to be ready. What does that mean? It means we do all we can to serve Him and tell others about Him every day.

I bet your children have friends who are lost. Help them share Jesus with them. Help them find a way to invite them to church or to your home for Bible study. Teach your children how to share the gospel with someone. That's being alert! That's staying awake.

Are you doing the same? Are you being alert? With whom have you shared the good news lately? Are you practicing what you are preaching? If Jesus came back this instant, would He find you sharing about Him or denying Him?

Father, help me to be alert today. Give me keen eyes to watch for others in order to share Your message. Help me to bring as many as I can to meet You.

MAY 19

FAMILY AND FRIENDS

Proverbs 7–8

BEST VERSE: 7:4

Say to wisdom, "You are my sister," and call insight your intimate friend.

One day while reading this passage and noticing that Solomon used these two analogies, I took a step back to ponder. I understand the part about calling insight my intimate friend. An intimate friend is one you can rely on. You know them deeply, and they know you. You can call on them anytime for help. That's insight.

But calling wisdom my sister? What does that mean? I have two sisters. I love them both. A brother defends his sister. He stands up for her. He wants no harm to come to her. That's how we should treat wisdom. We should protect it and do nothing to hurt it. We should love wisdom.

If you are blessed with boys and girls, you know the love/hate relationship that exists between brothers and sisters. One minute they are hugging or playing well together. The next they are ready to kill each other. Our job as parents is to teach them how to treat each other, because they will always be family.

Read this verse to them and ask them to tell you what they think it means. Do you think your little Johnny is going to equate wisdom with his sister Susie? Probably not. Do you think Susie is going to consider Johnny her intimate friend? My guess is no. But because God uses these pictures in His Word, we know it is possible.

Who is your intimate friend? I hope it is insight. Who is your sister? I pray it is wisdom. We all need that in our lives. If you are lacking wisdom and insight right now about something, turn to the one who can give it to you.

Thank You, Lord, for giving me wisdom and insight. Let me see these as my sister and intimate friend. Let me hold them close and turn to them daily.

MAY 20

SETTLING FOR SICKNESS

John 5

BEST VERSE: 6

When Jesus saw him lying there, and knew that he had already been a long time in that condition, He said to him, "Do you wish to get well?"

Have you ever known anyone who just liked to tell you about their ailments? My paternal grandmother would wax eloquent about her body aches and illnesses. You never wanted to call her and ask, "How are you doing, M'aam-maw?" You were guaranteed a lengthy description if you did.

Some people like the attention they get from being sick. They really have gotten used to being sick and are quite comfortable with it. Although Jesus knew what this man was thinking, He still asked him that question, "Do you wish to get well?" Jesus was prepared to heal, but only if the man wished it.

TEACHING MOMENT

Don't let your children settle into a bad place. We need to encourage them to step out of the "funk," if they are in one. We need to show them how to press forward and succeed. But they will only do that if we show them the true source of their strength. Jesus still wants us today to "pick up our pallet and walk." Whatever is holding us down needs to be laid aside.

It's interesting in this story that although the healed man was questioned and even berated for carrying the pallet on the Sabbath day, he kept walking. He was going home, a new man, a walking man. Our children will face ridicule for trusting in Jesus. They need to be taught to continue and just ignore the criticism of those who want to keep them down (crippled).

What is holding you down? Do you feel crippled and unable to reach the healing waters? You don't need to pursue a magical potion. All you need is Him. He can cleanse you and heal you of anything that is holding you down. Trust Him. Now, I must warn you. He heals in various ways. He just wants us to trust Him. He will do the rest—His way.

Thank you, Lord, for picking me up and showing me the way. Thank you for telling me to pick up my pallet, the thing I have gotten used to, and start walking.

MAY 21

BONDSERVANT

Exodus 21

BEST VERSE: 6

. . . then his master shall bring him to God, then he shall bring him to the door or the doorpost. And his master shall pierce his ear with an awl; and he shall serve him permanently.

Read verses 1–6 again, and then come back to this devotion . . . Get the picture? This man has chosen to NOT leave his master. He has chosen to serve him indefinitely. And, as a result, he is marked with a piercing through his ear. Everyone who saw that piercing would know that he had chosen his master over freedom.

I have heard a lot of messages on being a bondservant. I have heard a lot of sermons on this exact passage, or at least the topic being used as a reference. But I don't think I have ever heard focus on the piercing as a visible sign to everyone around them. We have the same mark on us as followers of Christ. No, not a piercing. But we have been stamped with His seal on our hearts. Everyone should know we have chosen the Master.

TEACHING MOMENT

So, go out to your garage and get an awl. Take your child to the door post, and pierce. . . . I am just kidding! DON'T do that! But you do need to talk to your children about standing out in the crowd as a follower of Christ. They may not have a physical mark on their body that shows they are a Christian, but people should know.

Ask your daughter how people can know she loves Jesus. I bet you get answers like this: loving others, doing good things, obeying parents, and so forth. These are all great ways. But what is the most important way others can know? By doing His will ALL THE TIME! That's what Jesus did, and so should we.

Are you a bondservant of the Lord Jesus Christ? Are you pierced through with surrender to His will? Forsaking all others, you choose to follow Him? He will keep you and defend you, like any good master. Yet there is no master more worthy of your service.

Master, I will follow. I will do as You desire at all times. Keep me close to Your side so I may observe You and serve You.

MAY 22

FAILING ISN'T FAILING

Exodus 4

BEST VERSES: 10-13

Then Moses said to the Lord, "Please, Lord, I have never been eloquent, neither recently nor in time past, nor since You have spoken to Your servant; for I am slow of speech and slow of tongue." The Lord said to him, "Who has made man's mouth? Or who makes him mute or deaf, or seeing or blind? Is it not I, the Lord? Now then go, and I, even I, will be with your mouth, and teach you what you are to say." But he said, "Please, Lord, now send the message by whomever You will."

As parents we hear all kinds of excuses from our children. You give them a chore to do, and normally we hear, "Oh Mom (insert whine here), I don't want to do that now." I can just hear my own kids in their younger years.

Moses kept giving the Lord excuses why He should not send him to free His people. He didn't understand that it wasn't about his abilities. It was totally the Lord's abilities, which are limitless.

TEACHING MOMENT
When your children say they cannot do something, remind them that in Christ all things are possible. If you don't try, you will never do it. Failing isn't failing if you try. Did you read that right? Yes. As long as we do our very best and trust the Lord with the outcome, we cannot fail. It's all on Him. And we know that He will never let us down.

I am thankful, Lord, for the ability to try. Help me try my best every time. Help me to rely on You for my strength and then give it my all.

MAY 23

UNITY

Judges 20

BEST VERSE: 1
Then all the sons of Israel from Dan to Beersheba, including the land of Gilead, came out, and the congregation assembled as one man to the LORD at Mizpah.

We read in Judges 19 and 20 that a great evil had been done to one of the sons of Israel, and the entire nation came together to hear and reply. I am reminded of our national response after September 11, 2001. The entire nation came together to mourn and then respond to a great evil which had been done to us. Probably for the first time since Pearl Harbor, the nation responded as one.

Why does it take tragedy to bring us together? Think about it. Families wait until a funeral to get together. People reach out when they hear someone has been in a car accident or has fallen ill. Why do we wait until something bad happens to unify? God wants us to come together now!

TEACHING MOMENT

Our children must be taught the importance of family. We need each other. Some families do a great job of being together. Others don't. The next time your family has a get-together or a family reunion read them this verse. Depending on how old they are, read them the entirety of Judges 19-20. It is a difficult passage for children, but one we can learn from.

As children grow and move away it gets more difficult to stay connected. Don't let distance be an issue. With the advantages today of technology, distance is not a hindrance. You can still stay connected. Unity—it's important for nations, but it is also important for families.

Is your family unified? Do you have "squabbles" that have been left unsettled? Make them right today. Reach out to those whom you have been separated from because of hurt feelings or something else. Above all, we Christians must set the example of unity in our families. We must show the world how to live.

Father, I want to make the wrong right. I choose to "Be the wrong one, if necessary." I only want to please You.

MAY 24

MAJESTY

Psalms 7-8

BEST VERSE: 8:1
O Lord, our Lord, how majestic is Your name in all the earth, who have displayed Your splendor above the heavens!

As I write this thought today, I am sitting at a table in the dining hall at a church kids' camp. It's quiet right now, since all the kids are still sleeping. (Do you know how nice that is?) But all around me are hills, trees, and birds starting to sing. There's a mist rising from the valleys. All I can think of is how majestic this world is in its beauty. God did real good!

But as majestic as the scene is, it pales in comparison to the majesty of our God. We cannot even begin to describe it. No man has ever observed His true majesty. We can only imagine at how it must look. Aren't you excited to be able to do that one day?

TEACHING MOMENT

Our children are often overwhelmed at new sights and sounds. Here at camp, many of the children are experiencing camp for the first time. Watching them transform from nervous, shaky campers on the first day to care-free, totally involved campers by the end of the week is awesome. They can learn so much so quickly.

Teaching our children about the majesty of God is best done by pointing out all those things around us that our Father has made. The complexities of nature and our bodies are great ways to talk about His majesty and His greatness. Only a majestic God and a great God could have made all we see.

Our children need to know that a majestic God is also magnificent, dignified, illustrious, full of splendor, and full of grandeur. Those are just a few of the words to describe Him. Why not take the time to explain each of those words and how they relate to our heavenly Father? There is no way to fully explain Him, but it's a start. As the song says, "Majesty, Worship His majesty."

You are a majestic God, O Lord. I praise Your name today. I magnify You above all.

MAY 25

STOP ROCKING THE BOAT

Luke 8

BEST VERSES: 22–25

Now on one of those days Jesus and His disciples got into a boat, and He said to them, "Let us go over to the other side of the lake." So they launched out. But as they were sailing along He fell asleep; and a fierce gale of wind descended on the lake, and they began to be swamped and to be in danger.

They came to Jesus and woke Him up, saying, "Master, Master, we are perishing!" And He got up and rebuked the wind and the surging waves, and they stopped, and it became calm. And He said to them, "Where is your faith?" They were fearful and amazed, saying to one another, "Who then is this, that He commands even the winds and the water, and they obey Him?"

Don't you just love the fact that it was Jesus' idea to go across the lake? And being God, He knew a storm would come. So why in the world would He put the lives of the disciples in danger? Simple answer—they weren't in danger because they were with the Master. Jesus wasn't worried about the wind and waves. Shoot, if the boat had sunk, He could have just walked to shore and taken all the disciples with Him. He chose, however, to let the winds and waves come, and He asked them, "Where is your faith?"

TEACHING MOMENT

When was the last harrowing storm you went through? Did your children know about it? Were they aware of the wind and waves lashing against your family's boat or house? Were they (and you) afraid of sinking, drowning, or being swept away by the wind? What did you say to them? What did you hear the Lord saying to you?

Just as He did with the disciples, the Lord will sometimes lead us into or allow us to enter storms. But just like in this passage, He is in control. He has the ability to calm the storm. Your children need to see your faith in the midst of the storm. God may allow a storm just for that purpose. As we teach our children to trust the Lord in the storm, our own faith grows.

So, be still my child. Stop rocking the boat. Let Jesus calm you or the storm. Either way, He's got this.

In the fiercest storms, I will trust You, Jesus. I know Your strong, right hand will deliver me. I simply have to reach out and take it.

REST

Judges 5

BEST VERSE: 31C
And the land was undisturbed for forty years.

This probably seems like a strange verse to use for today's devotional reading. It is the last part of the last verse in Judges 5, which is the "Song of Deborah" after they had defeated the army of Jabin, king of Hazor in Canaan. You really should read Judges 4 and 5 to get the full picture. But the story ends with this short phrase, "And the land was undisturbed for forty years."

I was thinking about my country, America. We have been at war with terrorism since 2001—18 years at this book's press time. How sweet would it be if we could have forty years of peace? Doesn't that sound great? No young men or women would be sent into harm's way. No deaths due to battle. Billions of dollars could be used for other purposes.

Don't hear me wrong. I am not against the war on terror. We have to defend ourselves, and we have to fight against evil. I guess I am just a little jealous of the forty years of peace Israel experienced here.

TEACHING MOMENT
This might be a little challenging to teach your kids. But hey, how about this? The next time your children get into one of those knock down-drag out fights that only siblings can get into, pull this verse out. Tell them, "I wish I could have forty minutes of peace in this house!"

Seriously, our children do need to learn to experience peace. That only comes from obedience to God and resting in Him. The Israelites' peace came after obeying God and listening to Deborah, the judge at the time. That is definitely a lesson worth learning.

Are you at peace today? Or are you reaping the turmoil of disobedience like the Israelites were under Jabin? Aren't you tired of fighting? Won't you allow the Lord to direct your steps toward peace?

He wants to give you rest. He desires that for you. He wants to lead you beside still waters. Take His hand. He will lead!

MEMORY STONES

1 Samuel 7

BEST VERSE: 12

Then Samuel took a stone and set it between Mizpah and Shen, and named it Ebenezer, saying, "Thus far the Lord has helped us."

Isn't it interesting the number of times in the Scriptures when stones were used to mark an occasion? Jacob and his vision of heaven, Joshua crossing the Jordan, plus many more.

Here we see Samuel, the great prophet, marking a great victory over the Philistines with a stone, which he named "Thus far the Lord has helped us." That got me to thinking about the moments in my life when the Lord has helped me. Did I "mark" those times with a stone of remembrance, or have I completely forgotten His blessings?

I can think of times in my family when God provided money just when we needed it. There was the time we needed a washing machine, and a friend provided one. There was another time when we were in a car accident, which could have been tragic—only to escape with minor injuries.

TEACHING MOMENT

Moms and dads, may I encourage you to take the time to mark those times in your family's life when it is apparent the Lord stepped in? Why don't you spend some time today and reflect on those times? Why don't you get your children to help you come up with some creative way to "mark" those times? How about creating a "memory board" on which you can list each time God does something to help your family?

However, you choose to mark those special God times in your family, make sure your children understand it was God, not you or someone else who did this. Point them to the One Who is their true source of help.

Lord God, You have done so much for me. Help me remember those events and mark them as special. Help me share those God events as evidence of You working in and through me and my family.

FINDERS KEEPERS, LOSERS WEEPERS

Deuteronomy 22

BEST VERSES: 1–3

You shall not see your countryman's ox or his sheep straying away, and pay no attention to them; you shall certainly bring them back to your countryman. If your countryman is not near you, or if you do not know him, then you shall bring it home to your house, and it shall remain with you until your countryman looks for it; then you shall restore it to him. Thus you shall do with his donkey, and you shall do the same with his garment, and you shall do likewise with anything lost by your countryman, which he has lost and you have found. You are not allowed to neglect them.

I remember saying that when I was a child. "Finders keepers, losers weepers!" Boy, it felt good to find something really cool outside while playing or to find some money on the ground. I thought I had really scored something. It was even sweeter if it belonged to one of my siblings, and I had always eyed it.

TEACHING MOMENT

But this passage in Deuteronomy tells us we should NOT keep items we find belonging to someone else, especially if we know whose belongings they are. What a great lesson for our children to learn. We should look out for the belongings of others. We should hold on to them to keep them safe and then return them when they ask about it.

This, of course, goes directly against our flesh. We want, want, want! We see something and we want it, sometimes even when it belongs to someone else. Teaching our children to control the desires of the flesh at an early age will bid them well later in life. When they get a job, and are tempted to take something at work that is just "lying there," it could be the end of a career or worse. You've heard it said a hundred times, "Honesty is the best policy." What a perfect passage to teach your children. Isn't the Word just awesome?

Help me Lord, to look out for others. Let me be the first to return a lost item or to pick up something I know belongs to someone else to keep it safe. Remind me I represent You.

CRYING WON'T LAST

Psalms 29–30

BEST VERSE: 30:5B
Weeping may last for the night, but a shout of joy comes in the morning.

Let me be quick to say that I know that grief is real. I have lost both my parents, an infant child, and scores of close friends. I am a weeper. I cry easily, and when these loved ones passed, I wept for them openly. I am not ashamed to cry.

But I also know, as a follower of Christ, just as David knew so long ago that "joy comes in the morning." You could even say as Christians that joy comes in the MOURNING. Isn't that great? No matter how deep the grief, His joy goes deeper.

TEACHING MOMENT

Many parents want to shield their children from grief. They seem to think they are sparing them from harm. Listen to me carefully. Teach them how to grieve. When they lose a pet, cry with them. When a grandparent dies, help them grieve. When a close friend moves away, let them cry on your shoulder.

But then, point them to Jesus. Teach them that through the lowest moments in life, Jesus is always there. He will be there to hold them and love them. He will hug them tighter than you ever could. Teaching proper grief is important for your child. Don't shield them. Embrace the grief, knowing joy is coming.

Perhaps you are suffering grief today. Perhaps you have not let the passing of a loved one go. Let it go today. Revel in the joy of Jesus. Live your life to bring joy to others by the very way you handle grief. Point them heavenward.

Because of Your joy, Lord, I can face the losses of life. I know You know the depth of my sorrow and can bring me to the brink of joy. I praise You because of that.

AHHH, THAT NEW SMELL

Lamentations 3

BEST VERSES: 22–23

The LORD's lovingkindnesses indeed never cease, for His compassions never fail. They are new every morning; great is Your faithfulness.

Don't you just love the smell of something new? Have you ever gone to a car dealership just to sit in the new cars and smell their interior? I know, that sounds weird, right? But you should try it sometime. Now, I can't afford a new vehicle, but it is nice to just smell the new sometimes.

How about the smell of a fresh new day? Walking outside early in the morning and taking a whiff of dew and other scents reminds us of the promise of a brand new day. All things new. Brand new start. Just like the lovingkindness of God. That also is new every day.

TEACHING MOMENT

Has your son come home lately in a funk? Had a bad day at school or on the soccer field and feels like life is just over? Read him these verses. Maybe your daughter just had a fight with her best friend and feels her life is in shambles. Read these verses to her. As bad as it seems, God promises us a brand-new beginning each and every day.

What can you do to help your children truly experience renewal? Don't get into the same old spiritual morning routines with them. What do I mean by that? I mean mix it up. One morning pray with them for their friends. The next morning read a passage of Scripture about family. Another morning, sing your devotion. Just keep it fresh.

Are you in a funk yourself? Do you need a reminder that God sends us His compassion daily? (Go sit in that new car and think of the newness of God). God wants to "freshen" you up. And through His Spirit, He can.

Father of all, show me your lovingkindness and compassion today in a way I have not experienced lately. Let me "smell" the newness of faith today.

LIKE A DOG

Judges 7

BEST VERSE: 7

The LORD said to Gideon, "I will deliver you with the 300 men who lapped and will give the Midianites into your hands; so let all the *other* people go, each man to his home."

Don't you just love this story of Gideon and how the Lord chose the men who would fight with him? He starts out with twenty-two thousand men and ends up with three hundred. Three hundred! Now that's a huge RIF (Reduction in Force). There would be no mistaking the fact that it would be God who delivered Israel and not their huge army.

But God uses how they drank to weed many out. Those who knelt at the water (9,700) were sent home. Only those who lapped the water with their tongue, like a dog (300), were chosen. So, being looked at like a dog was a good thing here. I just find that strange.

TEACHING MOMENT

Of course, the lesson for our children in this verse is obvious. Drink like a dog. No, just kidding. The lesson is to allow the Lord to decide how you fight your battles. God has a bigger plan than yours. He can see the end result; we can't. In fact, He can see the outcome, however we choose to obey. But He wants to direct us in His way.

This is a fun verse to act out with your kids. They will probably think you are silly and maybe a little crazy as you show them how these three hundred lapped their water. But they will remember the verse. Just make sure you make the application that goes with it.

So, are you lapping or kneeling? Are you allowing the Lord to direct you and choose you? Are you alert for the enemies around you, or are you looking down and unaware? These are great questions to get you thinking about your circumstance.

Do you think Gideon was concerned about the Lord's tactics? Perhaps, but the Lord gave him specific instructions for the battle. He basically said to Gideon, "Do it my way, and you will be victorious." He is still saying that today.

Will you follow the Lord, no matter how illogical it sounds? Will you trust Him in the battle?

'CAUSE I SAID SO

Genesis 15

BEST VERSE: 6

Then he believed in the LORD; and He reckoned it to him as righteousness.

If you haven't read the whole story of Abraham (Abram at this point) lately, you really need to. It is quite an interesting story of God's faithfulness and man's faith. I mean, just look at this verse. Abram believed God, and God declared him righteous. For something he had done? No! Because he believed Him.

God promised Abram a son, one which he wouldn't see for many years. It seemed impossible. Abram didn't understand how God would do it. He just believed He would do it. Simple faith. God said it, so that settles it.

TEACHING MOMENT

What a great lesson for our kids. Mom and Dad, we need to show our kids how to trust. They learn this by watching us. If all they ever hear and see is us fretting and worrying, how will they learn to trust. We take them to prayer with us and give it over to the Lord. We let Him take our burdens and trust He will see us through.

It is a joy to pray with our children over things that they are concerned about. Let me encourage you to get them a prayer journal. When they pray for something write down the date and the request. When God answers, and He will, mark down how He answered and the date. This will be a treasure one day to read.

Are you trusting today? Are you believing as Abram did? He will declare you righteous also as you believe on the name of Jesus and trust Him with your life. The Lord will work great things in your life as you trust Him to work.

O Lord, trusting is hard sometimes. I want to see immediate results. Help me rest in You and allow You to work in Your perfect time. Let me be the example of faith for my children.

GOOD INTENTIONS

2 Samuel 6

BEST VERSE: 9

So David was afraid of the Lᴏʀᴅ that day; and he said, "How can the ark of the Lᴏʀᴅ come to me?"

This is one of the most misunderstood stories in the Old Testament. David is bringing the ark of the covenant to Jerusalem when Uzzah is killed for touching the ark while trying to keep it from falling. David didn't understand this. Why would God kill a man for protecting the ark? David had not researched or been told that the proper way to transport the ark was NOT on a cart. It should have been carried on two poles by four men, men of a certain tribe of Israel.

David was always so careful to follow the Lord's directions. We see that over and over in his stories. But this time, in his zest to worship and glorify God, he failed to seek it. Sometimes worship can be misdirected, can't it?

TEACHING MOMENT

We need to teach our children that there is a right way and a wrong way to worship. I am not talking about the type of music or the clothes we wear (well, maybe a little). I am talking about what we bring attention to in worship. We should never worship in such a way that people look at us rather than the Lord. We should not be a distraction to others. All they should see is Jesus.

In these days of "wide-open" worship services where it seems anything is accepted, we need to be careful to teach our children that reverence is still needed. David failed to show reverence to God by the way he instructed the men to carry the ark. That may sound simple and maybe a little stupid to some. But God demands reverence and expects His children to follow His instructions.

As you go to worship this week, think about how you are worshiping. As you celebrate the Savior, are you pointing others to Him? Do you worship in such a way that others are drawn to Jesus? Don't let anything you do or say point them toward you.

I will show You the reverence due You, God. I will honor You who deserves all praise and glory.

VENGEANCE IS MINE

2 Samuel 16

BEST VERSE: 10
But the king said, "What have I to do with you, O sons of Zeruiah? If he curses, and if the LORD has told him, 'Curse David,' then who shall say, 'Why have you done so?'"

The problem with vengeance is it doesn't belong to us. Just look at this story. Shimei comes out and starts cursing David as he is leaving Jerusalem, fleeing from Absalom. David's mighty men want to cut off Shimei's head, but David says, "No, the Lord will take care of him." Well, he doesn't exactly say that. He really says he trusts the Lord to do what he should do with Shimei and himself.

Not me! I want vengeance. I want to get payback. How about you? We think we have the "right" to defend ourselves against harsh words or ill treatment. I am NOT saying we should be a doormat for others. I am saying, though, that we need to trust the Lord to defend us. Perhaps that person who is giving you such a hard time has been put there by God to build your faith.

TEACHING MOMENT
There is no other way to teach our kids this truth than by living it out ourselves. We can preach it to them until we are blue in the face, but until they see someone else actually doing it, they don't believe it can be done. And remember, you can't do it. Only Christ in you can do it.

Others are going to turn against your children. They will have friends who call them names or try to ridicule or embarrass them. If they learn now how to handle that, they will be so much further down that road of maturity. The Lord will only allow to come into our lives what He knows we can handle. We have to trust that.

Are you trusting Him today to be your defender? Or are you taking up your sword against those who mistreat you? Ask yourself what Christ would do. Would He lash out at that person or would He love them? I am not saying it will be easy, but it is what He asks us to do.

I will be the first to step up to defend the weak and vulnerable. But I am also quick to try to defend myself. It is not easy to just "take it" when you know you have done nothing wrong. Let God handle it. He has a big enough back to shoulder the burden.

Father, help me to let You defend me against my enemies. Give me the wisdom to rest in You.

JUNE 4

RETRIBUTION

Joshua 13

BEST VERSE: 22
The sons of Israel also killed Balaam the son of Beor, the diviner, with the sword among the rest of their slain.

God finally brought judgment on Balaam for his sin. Everyone loves the story of the talking donkey, but that is NOT the point of the story. Balaam basically sold out his ministry. He knew better than to go but kept listening to the invitation until he went.

How many times have you said "no" to sin but finally relented after the constant temptation? I can walk past a coconut cake once, but if it's still there every time I walk past, I will eventually succumb to the temptation. I just can't help myself, or can I?

TEACHING MOMENT
Do you children blame their failings, their sins, on the devil? You know, the devil made me do it. Do they blame their siblings? How about the school?

They can always blame someone else for their sin. We must point out that everyone has a choice. They choose to sin.

But we know we have a way of escape in Jesus. He will show us the way out of this tempting situation, if we will just go to Him. That's what we have to teach our children. They cannot rely on their own power and strength. That will NEVER work. They have to rely on Him.

If Balaam had relied on the Lord, he would have never gone to see the Israelites. He would have stayed put. What will you do? When you face that temptation to sin, go to the Lord. No, run to the Lord. He will show you the way of escape.

My Rescuer, I know I can depend on You for deliverance. Help me to stop and listen to You for clear directions. Thank You!

JUNE 5

GOD IS!

Genesis 1

BEST VERSE: 1
In the beginning God created the heavens and the earth.

This verse may seem like a simple little verse with absolutely no meaning except that God did something. Oh, it is so much more.

Do you understand that this verse and the verses that follow establish Who God is and what He has done and will continue to do? Belief in this verse is the bedrock of our faith in His Word. If we can't believe that God literally made the earth in six days and then rested, why should we believe anything else that is written in this book?

TEACHING MOMENT
We need to teach our children that the God they pray to and worship on Sundays is the same God who created everything there is. There is no "Big Bang" or "slimy ooze" from which we all came. They have to learn to trust the God of Creation, not just the God of Sunday School.

Do not believe the lies of the world. Cast all your doubts out the window. Believe what He says! He loves you and has made you in His image. Hallelujah!

Father, Creator of all, thank you for creating me in Your image. Thank You for allowing me to see You create in others the desire to follow You. You are an amazing God!

JUNE 6

NEW NAME

Genesis 32

BEST VERSES: 27-28
So he said to him, "What is your name?" And he said, "Jacob." He said, "Your name shall no longer be Jacob, but Israel; for you have striven with God and with men and have prevailed."

People change their names today for various reasons. Women normally take their husband's last name when they get married. Some want to make a statement to the world. Others want to hide their identity. Children take the last name of the family who adopts them. But we see here that God changed Jacob's name to send a message to everyone about how Jacob had prevailed. One definition of this name is "triumphant with God." I really like that.

If God changed your name, what would it be? "Constantly begging"? How about "Scared of his shadow"? Or maybe this one suits you, "Doubting Thomas." I would want mine to be "Faithful One" or "Highly Favored."

TEACHING MOMENT
Most parents give their children names for a reason. Some are family names and some just appeal to them. Have your children ever asked why you named them what you did? Why not use this story to talk about names? What a great way to share this wonderful passage about Jacob's name change to Israel and what that means.

Don't you want your children to be "triumphant with God"? What parent doesn't want that? We long to see them secure in their faith and trusting Him for all things. We don't want to see them turn their backs on Jesus or have lifelong doubts about who He is. We need to point them to the name above all names—Jesus. After all, His name does mean Savior.

Name above all names, You are the One I want to be named after. Give me Your name! Let others see Your name emblazoned on my disposition and countenance daily.

JUNE 7

BZZZZZZZ
Exodus 23

BEST VERSE: 28
I will send hornets ahead of you so that they will drive out the Hivites, the Canaanites, and the Hittites before you.

This verse just proves that God will use anything to accomplish His Will. He has used frogs and gnats, hailstones and bloody water. He even used a donkey. And here, He tells Moses He will use hornets to drive the heathen nations out.

Have you ever been chased and stung by bees or yellow jackets or hornets? It's pretty terrifying and painful. For some it can be downright deadly if they are allergic. Don't be surprised what God might use to get your attention, as He shows you His plan for your life.

TEACHING MOMENT
I bet you and your children have watched bees gather pollen or you've seen a wasp nest or a hornet's nest. Refer your children to this verse the next time you observe something like that. Talk about how God can use the smallest thing to accomplish His will and bless His children. I bet your kids will find it kind of funny to think about throngs of people being driven out of their homes and off their lands to make room for God's people. Why not let them draw a picture of that?

The humor of the scene isn't the main thing, though. It's the fact that God will work ahead of us to prepare the way. Your children need to learn that. They need to trust that God will do amazing things for us, if we just trust Him.

Are you trusting? Are you allowing Him to drive out your enemies, or are you taking them on yourself? Let Him work, while you enjoy the show. He will tell you when He wants you to step in, I promise.

Father of all creation, thank You that You will use all of Your creation to show me who You are. Use me, Lord, to show others Your way. And help me trust You to take care of my "enemies."

JUNE 8

THAT'S JUST NOT FAIR!

Joshua 17

BEST VERSE: 14
Then the sons of Joseph spoke to Joshua, saying, "Why have you given me only one lot and one portion for an inheritance, since I am a numerous people whom the LORD has thus far blessed?"

How many times have you heard your children say, "That's not fair, Mom!" Perhaps their sibling got an extra dollar in their allowance for doing an extra chore. Or maybe their brother was taken for an ice cream cone because they had cleaned their room without being asked.

Our kids see everything! And they don't like it if they think they are being cheated "their fair share." This passage today talks about how the sons of Joseph were complaining to Joshua because they thought they deserved more than they were given. While other tribes had conquered their portion of land and taken possession, these folks were reluctant because the enemies they faced had iron chariots. They were afraid to take them on. They had forgotten one huge thing—God was fighting on their side! Also, the land was already their land. They just had to claim it.

TEACHING MOMENT

I love what Joshua did. He was a good parent to them. He said, "If you want it, go get it." He didn't do it for them. He told them it was their job to possess the land. We parents can take a lesson here. Stop doing everything for your kids. They must learn to do those things on their own. They must experience "the fight" sometimes. They must feel the tiredness in their bones after completing a chore. They need to see how a task looks after THEY complete it. Stop enabling your children just because one whines and says, "Mommy (Daddy) I don't know how!" You have shown her a hundred times. She knows how.

Don't you want strong, independent children? Don't you want them to be able to stand on their own two feet? Don't you want them to make good decisions? Then teach them life's not fair. But God is! He will always do what's best for them. Allow them to build that trust and faith in God by stepping out sometimes. They will always succeed if they are trusting the Father.

O God, push me to do more for You. Don't allow me to whine and complain. Help me stretch my abilities to honor You.

JUNE 9

A FORGOTTEN WEAPON

1 Samuel 21

BEST VERSES: 8–9

David said to Ahimelech, "Now is there not a spear or a sword on hand? For I brought neither my sword nor my weapons with me, because the king's matter was urgent." Then the priest said, "The sword of Goliath the Philistine, whom you killed in the valley of Elah, behold, it is wrapped in a cloth behind the ephod; if you would take it for yourself, take *it*. For there is no other except it here." And David said, "There is none like it; give it to me."

Of all things to find in Nob! Goliath's sword! The last time we saw it was when David had killed Goliath and put it in "his tent." So how did the priest get it and hide it in Nob? That question is one we will have to ask the Lord one day. Scholars debate how it got there. Perhaps David dedicated it to the Lord after the battle with Goliath. Some even say the cloth it was wrapped in was Goliath's battle robe or cloak.

So, what secret power did this sword hold? None, except to remind David of God's faithfulness to give him the power to kill a giant when he was just a lad. Well, that might have been enough for me! Can you imagine how David felt when he once again held that sword in his hands? Can you imagine the memories that flooded his mind when he saw that sword? The thoughts of the day of his salvation from Goliath at the hands of the Lord would have been coursing through his mind.

TEACHING MOMENT

Your children are going to face times when they feel like there is no hope. They are going to forget all those times when God has rescued them. They may even doubt their salvation. They need reminders! They need something to refresh their minds of God's faithfulness. What can you put back, like the priest did with Goliath's sword, to present to them on those days?

Perhaps it will be a picture of the day they followed Christ in believer's baptism. Perhaps it will be a small wooden cross they made in VBS the year they asked Christ into their heart. Perhaps it will be the AWANA award they received for memorizing all those scriptures. Whatever it is, be prepared to hand it over to them. God will remind them of His faithfulness, but sometimes that memory needs a jolt.

Lord, thank You for the reminders of victories. Thank You for jogging my memory when it gets dull. I am forever grateful for Your faithfulness to me, despite my unfaithfulness.

JUNE 10

A REASON FOR EVERYTHING

Exodus 29

BEST VERSE: 46

They shall know that I am the LORD their God who brought them out of the land of Egypt, that I might dwell among them; I am the Lord their God.

When is the last time you read Exodus? When you get into the chapters with the descriptions about the tabernacle and the clothing, your eyes start to glaze over, right? You start thinking, *Okay God, do I really need to know that Aaron and his sons had to wear certain undergarments? Really?*

This verse today struck me though. The Lord gives the reason for all the detail with these words. He wanted to make sure they knew He was God and He dwelt among them. Wow! Now tell me, who doesn't want to be reminded of that?

TEACHING MOMENT

So, the challenge is how can we use this verse with our kids. Easy! Take a look around you. Challenge your kids to find things in nature or in your home that reminds them of the Lord. Since God is everywhere and everything exists because of Him, that should be fun. Make a list of everything they name. It doesn't matter how silly it may sound. God reveals Himself to people in different ways.

Maybe your son sees God in that toad he has been playing with. Perhaps your daughter sees Him in the flower she picked just for you. Explore with your children why and how they see God in the items they named. Later on, when they feel God is not around, remind them of the list. Show them how close He really is.

May I challenge you today to take a fresh look around yourself. Discover God in your everyday surroundings. Let His image burn into your mind in the things that you have overlooked lately. He wants to be near you. Let Him!

Everywhere I look, O Lord, You are there! Surprise me today with Your presence.

JUNE 11

FEAR = WISDOM

Proverbs 1–2

BEST VERSE: 1:7
The fear of the Lord is the beginning of knowledge; fools despise wisdom and instruction.

I distinctly remember writing this verse down in a letter to my older brother, Tim, when he was away at college. I had just gotten saved the summer before my senior year of high school. Tim was going into his senior year of college, and I was concerned for his salvation. I had been a very negative influence on him and wanted to make up for it by pointing him to Christ.

Solomon begins his proverbs with these words in verse 7 of chapter 1. Here is the wisest man who ever lived, up to that point, telling us true wisdom comes from a healthy fear of God.

The meaning of the word "fear" in this verse is more akin to the word "awe." We need to keep in mind what an awesome, glorious God we serve.

TEACHING MOMENT

Children have a hard time understanding "awe." When we talk about fearing the Lord, their little minds think about being scared. They fear the dark. They fear the boogie man. They may even fear broccoli. So, try not to use the word "fear" when describing this.

Respect is a good word to use. Adore is good also. But awe is the best. How to define awe to a child. Watch a beautiful sunset. Look at a mountain dappled in fall colors. Look at the ocean waves continually breaking. And then think of the one who made it all. Now that's awe.

Have you lost your awe of God? Get it back. Look at Him with a whole new respect. Recognize His majesty. Consider all He has done. Be in awe!

Lord, You truly are an awesome God. You are indescribable. You are beyond description. And You still love me. Now that is truly awesome.

JUNE 12

SHUT YOUR MOUTH!!!

Mark 15

BEST VERSE: 5
But Jesus made no further answer; so, Pilate was amazed.

I have to tell you—I hate being falsely accused. I immediately jump into defensive mode and begin to formulate my response while the other person is still talking. I don't even wait for an invitation to respond. I quickly start talking.

I need to stop and do what Jesus did in this passage. When He was being falsely accused by the religious leaders, He just stopped talking. Why? He was innocent! He had NEVER done anything wrong. (I can't say that.) But it would not have mattered what He said, anyway. They were intent on killing Him. He was just in their way.

I am not saying that it is wrong to defend ourselves. But we need to listen to our accuser's words. Perhaps their accusation is really a cry for help. Perhaps they need us to correct a misperception so they can return to fellowship with us and God. We can actually be a healing balm for them—if we would just take a moment to listen.

TEACHING MOMENT

What can we teach our children from this passage? Simple! Shut your mouth! Now, I don't mean that in a cruel way. I mean we need to teach them to guard their words carefully. If they haven't been accused of something they didn't do yet, they will. Someone will point a finger at them and declare to the world that they are the guilty ones when in fact they are innocent. But just like Jesus, they too can keep silent. Wait! Be patient. Let the right time come to respond. Jesus will give them the words to say when it is time—not before.

Now Mom and Dad, can you practice that today? Can you "shut your mouth?" Let Jesus be your defender against your accuser. He will!

O God, it is so hard for me to keep my mouth shut sometimes, especially when I know I am right. Help me to guard my words very carefully and only speak truth.

JUNE 13

HOUSE GUESTS

Luke 19

BEST VERSE: 10
For the Son of Man has come to seek and to save that which was lost.

"Zacchaeus was a wee little man,
And a wee little man was he;
He climbed up in a sycamore tree, for the Lord he wanted to see."

Do you remember that song you learned in Sunday School? I sure do. I always thought it was funny. I have rarely seen a grown man climb a tree (unless he was deer hunting). So, to think about Zacchaeus, in his New Testament garb, climbing a tree in a crowd to see Jesus, well, that just tickles me.

He obviously had thrown all pride and decorum out the window. After all, he was a hated tax collector. He probably carried himself pretty pompously as he walked around town. He may have acted cocky and proud to try to compensate for his lack of height. But something happened to Zacchaeus when Jesus stopped, looked up at him and said, "Hey, you up there! Zacchaeus, come down! I'm going to your house to eat."

TEACHING MOMENT

Our children need to know that Jesus is waiting for them to look at Him. The moment they decide to look toward Jesus, with eagerness and anticipation—like Zacchaeus, He says to them, "Hey, I want to fellowship with you. Come to me." But they have to make eye (and heart) contact with Him first.

Aren't you thankful we don't have to climb trees to get a glimpse of Jesus? Anytime, any day, we can have fellowship with Him through the Holy Spirit. In fact, Jesus longs for fellowship with us. He wants us to invite Him into every part of our life. And when we do, we will be just like Zacchaeus. We will want to give all we have to Him and others. Because, just like Zacchaeus, we will discover that He is all we really need.

The song continues,

"And as the Savior passed that way,
He looked up in the tree,
And he said, 'Zacchaeus, you come down,
For I'm going to your house today.
For I'm going to your house today.'"

Won't you and your children invite Jesus to your house today?

Father, You are always welcome in my home. In fact, my home is not a real home if You are not in it. Come in, Lord!

FOLLOW THE LIGHT

2 Samuel 22

BEST VERSE: 29

For You are my lamp, O LORD; and the Lord illumines my darkness.

I sometimes go out on the lake to fish early in the morning or stay out on the lake until dark. If you are on the lake in a boat from dusk to dawn, you are required to have a bow light and a stern light illuminated. This allows other boats to see you and avoid a collision. Believe me, when you are on the water when it's dark, it's really dark. You want those lights on.

Those lights protect me. They show others where I am, thereby protecting them. In a similar way, the light of Jesus in me that I allow to shine, shows others where I am. It can also draw others to Jesus (the light), thus showing them protection and guidance. But I have to keep my light lit and shining for others to see. Therein lies the problem.

TEACHING MOMENT

Guiding our children with the light of Christ is really not that difficult, if we keep the light shining. Christ will do the rest. We have to keep shining the light. Jesus does the drawing. That's His job. WE ARE NOT THE LIGHT. We are simply vessels of the light.

How do we shine the light then? By keeping all things in our life that could hide the light out of the way. If I hung my hat or jacket on my boat lights, they would still be on, but no one could see them. If I cover my "Jesus light" with worries of this world and ungodly pursuits, I still possess the light of salvation, but no one can see it.

Won't you today take a look at how you are shining the light of Jesus in your life. Do you only "turn it on" when other lights are around? Do you dim it when you are in the company of friends who aren't believers? Or do you lift it high for all to see, no matter how the light is received. Light will drive away darkness—every time.

O Father of lights, will you help me today to lift my light so a dark world will know where I stand and be drawn to Your Son Who can give them light?

THE TRUTH AND NOTHING BUT THE TRUTH

Luke 1

BEST VERSES: 1-4

Inasmuch as many have undertaken to compile an account of the things accomplished among us, just as they were handed down to us by those who from the beginning were eyewitnesses and servants of the word, it seemed fitting for me as well, having investigated everything carefully from the beginning, to write *it* out for you in consecutive order, most excellent Theophilus; so that you may know the exact truth about the things you have been taught.

Don't you just love to read books to your kids? I still remember my mom holding my little sister and I and reading to us. She encouraged us to read. We would spend hours at the local library (yes, they had those back then) reading and checking out books to bring home. They even had a program where you could compete with other kids on the number of books you read over the summer. I still love to read.

Luke is writing a story for Theophilus. But it's not just any book. He is telling him "the exact truth." He wanted to make sure that he got the whole story and not just some rumors of what happened. Boy, isn't that important! I can just picture Theophilus when he got this letter from Dr. Luke. He probably read it straight through without stopping. He hung on every word. He devoured this inspired Word of God penned by Luke.

Is that how you read these familiar passages? Luke is one of those books of the Bible that we probably have read hundreds of times. We are familiar with the stories, maybe too familiar. Do you understand that it is still "the exact truth"? The words penned by Luke through the inspiration of the Holy Spirit are still the real story. Not make believe, not fable, not fairy tale. Luke's account is real, and events happened just as Luke wrote about them.

TEACHING MOMENT

As you read God's Word to your children, make sure you point out the truth that is in every word. Every word! No matter how unbelievable the miracles may seem or how astonishing the story being told may appear, it is THE TRUTH, and nothing but the truth.

Word of Life, show me the truth in Your Word each time I read it. Teach me deep truths to change my life. Thank You for the written Word which lights my path.

JUNE 16

REJOICE IN THE LORD

Matthew 13

BEST VERSE: 44

The kingdom of heaven is like a treasure hidden in the field, which a man found and hid again; and from joy over it he goes and sells all that he has and buys that field.

Just how much joy do you have? Are you sold out for Jesus? Today's verse gives us a glimpse of just how joyous we should be as believers in Christ. We should be willing to give up everything for the kingdom.

I have known a lot of Christians in my life, but I have found very few who were willing to give "all" for Christ. Most of us simply accept Christ, get plugged into a church, and somewhat trudge along. We don't get too excited. If we did, we might be accused of being over-zealous.

My wife and daughter give me a hard time about how I start moving and "dancing" when I hear music. They claim I only have one move. I just can't help it. When I hear music that I like, my legs and arms, heck, my whole body, starts moving.

TEACHING MOMENT

Teaching children to rejoice is never hard. Just put them in a room with other kids, turn on some music, and step back and watch. Every Sunday in our Children's Church program, we have our praise and worship time. When a song is played that is "moving," the kids come alive. In fact, sometimes we have to actually calm them down a bit. After all, *we are Baptist.* ☺

But our kids will learn to rejoice more sincerely as they observe us doing the same. I am not advocating anything crazy. I am just suggesting that you allow the Lord to show you how to "move." Does the love of Christ get you moving? Are you willing to sell "all" to spread the good news of the Savior?

Lord, You gave us the gift of dance. Your Word even talks about it. Free me to celebrate You as I move in worship.

JUNE 17

SO THAT'S WHY WE DID THAT!

Exodus 38

BEST VERSE: 21
This is the number of the things for the tabernacle, the tabernacle of the testimony, as they were numbered according to the command of Moses, for the service of the Levites, by the hand of Ithamar the son of Aaron the priest.

Where did all this stuff come from? These people were slaves in Egypt just a short while ago. Where would they have gotten gold, silver, fine fabric, and gems? Well, God had a plan.

Do you remember this? Exodus 12:35–36 reads, "Now the sons of Israel had done according to the word of Moses, for they had requested from the Egyptians articles of silver and articles of gold, and clothing; and the LORD had given the people favor in the sight of the Egyptians, so that they let them have their request. Thus they plundered the Egyptians."

TEACHING MOMENT
What a great lesson for our kids. God tells us to do things for a purpose. We may not understand why, but we need to just follow His instructions. Do you think the Hebrews knew why God asked them to get all that stuff from the Egyptians? No! But now they have all that to give to build the tabernacle.

Just like your kids don't understand sometimes why you ask them to do things, God does the same. Teaching our kids that lesson will take them far. Later in life, when they have obeyed the Lord in the small things, God may just show them why He asked them to do that certain thing. How cool is that?

How about you? Are you still wondering why God has asked you to do something? Hang on! He just may show you why! And if He does, you are going to see the big picture. I bet those Hebrews were so excited to be able to give. Now it all made sense.

Father, thank You for giving me direction even when I don't understand why. Help me obey. Help me be the example for others.

JUNE 18

NO MORE MANNA

Joshua 5

BEST VERSE: 12

The manna ceased on the day after they had eaten some of the produce of the land, so that the sons of Israel no longer had manna, but they ate some of the yield of the land of Canaan during that year.

For forty years, the Lord fed the children of Israel manna from heaven. The day, the very day, they ate produce in the Promised Land, the manna stopped. I wonder how many of them went out the next morning looking for it. Even though they were probably tired of "manna stew," I bet they still looked for manna for days.

God sustained them for forty years with this manna. They would not soon forget that. What would the women do with all those manna recipes? But now it was time for real food. Can you imagine their gratitude for their awakening taste buds? The kids who had been born in the wilderness had only heard about this kind of food.

TEACHING MOMENT

Try this experiment with your kids. Cook something for dinner they have NEVER had before. When they come to the table and ask what it is, tell them it is a surprise. After you coax them into eating it, tell them it is going to replace their favorite food. You will never cook their favorite food again. It's gone forever.

After they quit crying, read them this passage and explain that kids back then may have felt the same way. Then you can tell them you were kidding about their favorite food. Making a verse personal can often make it stick in their minds.

Can you relate to this verse? Have you gotten so accustomed to the normal that you can't appreciate the better stuff from God? Our "manna" may be okay, but God has so much more for us if we will just enter our "Promised Land." He wants to bless us.

Provider of all, thank You for giving me all I need. Thank You for giving me more than I deserve, often more than I expect. You are too good to me.

JUNE 19

MERCY

Exodus 13

BEST VERSE: 17
Now when Pharaoh had let the people go, God did not lead them by the way of the land of the Philistines, even though it was near; for God said, "The people might change their minds when they see war, and return to Egypt."

God decided to protect the people leaving Egypt by sparing them from having to fight and battle as they left their bondage. He knew they would have plenty of fighting ahead. So, He decided to give them a reprieve from war.

Interestingly enough, the first battle they faced was at the Red Sea when the Egyptian army was upon them. They feared for their lives. But they didn't have to lift one finger. God destroyed the advancing army in the waters of the sea. Not one Jewish soul was lost, not one sheep or cow, nothing!

TEACHING MOMENT
When our children are younger, we fight their battles for them. We defend them and protect them. But as they grow older, they have to learn to fight for themselves. They have to learn to rely on the Lord's strength rather than mom or dad's wrath. Why?

If we do not prepare our children to fight their battles, with the Lord, they will never achieve the purposes God has for their lives. Hard times build faith. Battles help us learn wisdom. We have the responsibility to teach them how to stand up for truth and righteousness. Otherwise, they will be led astray by that friend or professor who seeks to lure them away from the Lord.

How are you doing in your battles? Are you relying on someone else besides the Lord? Are you trying to do it in your own strength? Let the Lord be your pillar of fire by night and pillar of clouds by day. He stands ready to defend you, but He will ask you to be a part of the fight. Put on your armor today and report for duty, soldier of the cross!

God, praise You for mercy in my life. You spare me unknown grief and misery more times than I am aware. You, indeed, are the God of mercy.

JUNE 20

MAMA'S BOY

John 19

BEST VERSES: 26–27
When Jesus then saw His mother, and the disciple whom He loved standing nearby, He said to His mother, "Woman, behold, your son!" Then He said to the disciple, "Behold, your mother!" From that hour the disciple took her into his own *household.*"

Even in death Jesus looked down and had compassion on His earthly mother. She knew all about Him. She knew about Him before He even came to earth. The angel had told her. Now here she is in John 19, looking at Him on the cross knowing the purpose of His death. And out of all the people He could see from the cross, He looks at her.

He could feel her pain. They had that special first-born bond. He had taken care of her after the death of His earthly father, Joseph. They were close. He didn't want to leave her, but He knew she would be okay. Why? Because He had chosen John to take her in. I have to believe He chose John as a disciple for this purpose too.

You don't have to teach your children to love mom. They just do. But you do have to remind them to care for her. Dads, this is directed at you. "Taking care of Mom" doesn't start when you are no longer around. This starts when they are young. It begins with how they respect and treat their mom.

Your son must be taught that Mom is, first of all, your wife, whom you will protect. Your daughter must be taught that Mom is her friend, but not her "secret keeper"—as in keeping secrets from Dad. Jesus' example of how He cared for His mom should be taught to your children. Let them hear His words on this subject.

Was Jesus a mama's boy? Well, probably not. But it is obvious He loved His mother and wanted someone He trusted to take care of her. If your mom is still alive, call her today and thank her for all she has done for you. Perhaps you are estranged from her. Pray for guidance on how to make that right. Live life with no regrets, especially when it comes to family.

Father, thank You for godly mothers who try to follow You. I thank You for my mom. Thank you for her love for me when I probably didn't deserve it.

JUNE 21

LOOKING DOWN

Genesis 9

BEST VERSE: 16

When the bow is in the cloud, then I will look upon it, to remember the everlasting covenant between God and every living creature of all flesh that is on the earth.

Who doesn't like a rainbow? They are beautiful. Someone recently took a picture of our church with a double rainbow over it. The picture was awesome and inspiring.

But have you ever thought of this verse? God told Noah, right after he and his family had left the ark (after over a year inside a boat full of stinky animals) that this would be a sign. The rainbow was not just a pretty thing in the sky. God would look down and see it too. Then He would remember the covenant He had made with "every living creature of all flesh that is on the earth."

TEACHING MOMENT

Now, this is a story all children love to hear. What a fun story to tell. But don't leave out the context. Man had rebelled and had become exceedingly wicked. God had to "reboot" the earth. He had to reestablish His covenant with man and all creation. The flood came, and everything (except what was on the ark) died.

Can you imagine the questions Noah's family had the first time it rained again? But God set a reminder in the sky for them—a rainbow! And not only would they be looking up at it—He would be looking down on it. And at that moment, they would both be reminded of the covenant.

Have you stopped today to remember your covenant with God? Have you spent time today thanking Him for His faithfulness even in the storms of life? Have you thanked Him for the "rainbows" He sends to you every day to remind you of His covenant with you through His Son? If you haven't, why not stop right now and do that?

Look up! He's looking down! And you both can smile at the bow in the sky.

Lord, the rainbow is a beautiful sign of Your covenant with Noah's family. Your arc of colors was created by Your hand to remind us of the importance of a relationship with a covenant-keeping God. Thank You for loving me.

JUNE 22

BETTER THAN GERITOL

Joshua 14

BEST VERSES: 10–11

Now behold, the LORD has let me live, just as He spoke, these forty-five years, from the time that the LORD spoke this word to Moses, when Israel walked in the wilderness; and now behold, I am eighty-five years old today. I am still as strong today as I was in the day Moses sent me; as my strength was then, so my strength is now, for war and for going out and coming in.

Forty-five years have passed since Joshua and Caleb and the other ten spies had gone into the land of Canaan at Moses's command to bring back a report of the land. Of course, you know that only Joshua and Caleb said, "Let's go!" The other ten, whom I bet you can't name, were scared, and they discouraged the people.

Now, here we are in Joshua 14, at the same spot, ready to enter the land. Caleb steps up to Joshua and says, "I'm ready again! I am still strong and can fight. Let's go!" He's eighty-five! But God has sustained him all these years in the wilderness. Age is relative. God can give anyone the strength and power, if He chooses. And because Caleb has been obedient and faithful, God has empowered him.

TEACHING MOMENT

The next time your children come in from a long day of play and fall out on the couch or the floor, share this passage. Talk about how long Caleb was in the wilderness. Explain how discouraged he may have become knowing that he had done the right thing but still had to endure the forty years of wandering with those who were disobedient.

Sometimes fatigue is hard. Sometimes we feel we can't go on. Remind your children that God is our source of strength. It doesn't come in a Monster® drink or a dose of Geritol® (I'm telling my age now). Real strength to achieve great things only comes from the Father.

Are you tired? Are you weary? Do you feel you have been wandering in the wilderness? Turn to Him. He can refresh you and give you the strength you need to carry on. Remember, Caleb had seen the Promised Land. Those forty years may have seemed long and hard, but he had the image of what was to come. We have that same vision. We know what is coming.

Look ahead! Look to eternity! With that in mind, the things of this earth seem meaningless. God has prepared us a place. Prepare yourself for it.

Life Giver, give me the spiritual energy I need to carry Your message to a lost and dying world. I want to be invigorated by Your Truth and encouraged to go the distance.

COME AND EAT

John 21

BEST VERSE: 12

Jesus said to them, "Come and have breakfast." None of the disciples ventured to question Him, "Who are You?" knowing that it was the Lord.

I love the picture I get in my head of this scene. The disciples had been fishing all night. They were tired and probably very hungry. They see the Lord on the shore who tells them to cast their nets on the other side of the boat, which results in a huge catch of fish. Peter jumps out of the boat and swims/wades to shore ahead of the rest. But then they all arrive to a meal already prepared for them.

I can just smell the fire, the bread and the fish. But, as hungry as they were, their eyes were not on the food. Their eyes were on Jesus. After all, He had told them "I am the Bread of Life. He who eats of me will never hunger."

TEACHING MOMENT

How many times have you called your children to come eat? A thousand? And how many times have they come running to the table and without glancing at you start grabbing for the biscuits or chicken? The next time you call your children to a meal, why not read this passage? Remind them that our eyes should never be just on what is in front of us. We should have our eyes set on Christ.

If we are looking at Him, then all the things before us are more appreciated. Everything comes into focus when we look at Him first. He helps us prioritize life's "stuff." Our children can learn to rely on Him to show them the steps to take. Jesus can feed them with that eternal bread and living water. Then and only then will they be satisfied.

You are my provider. You set the table before me each day. Don't let me eat alone, God. Help me invite others to dine with You at Your table.

BAD NEWS

1 Samuel 28

BEST VERSE:17

The *Lord* has done accordingly as He spoke through me; for the *Lord* has torn the kingdom out of your hand and given it to your neighbor, to David.

In 1 Samuel 28, King Saul is in trouble, again. He is facing the Philistines and is scared. Seems a little like *déjà vu*. However, this time there is no Samuel to run to. Samuel had died, so what does Saul do? He goes to a "conjurer," someone who can talk to the dead (Samuel). Really? What part of wrong do you not understand, Saul?

But Saul is desperate. It's okay to do a wrong thing if it's for the right reason. Right? Wrong! And sure enough, Samuel tells Saul through the conjurer that all he had told him previously was coming true. Saul is not only going to lose the kingdom, but he and his sons will lose their lives that very day and be with him.

TEACHING MOMENT

It is so important that we teach our children to always choose the right thing. A wrong way is never right. What's wrong? Anything that goes against the Word of God. Your children will have lots of people tell them they can do something else. They will be told that there are other options. They will be told to not be so rigid and stiff with their morals. Wrong! Wrong! Wrong!

The Word of God is true for every generation. Its truths never change. Its commandments still guide. And if we choose to go another route, well, the Lord will bring us bad news. Discipline will follow. We will not like the consequences. But it is the result of disobedience.

Which route are you on right now? Are you following the Lord or some other guide? Some of you may be thinking, *Carl, times have changed. We have more choices today.* Nope, not true. Truth is still truth. You must choose to obey.

I want to encourage you today to make sure that every choice you make is based on His Word. Make sure every option you have before you is one that Jesus would choose. If there is ANY doubt, don't do it. Wait on the Lord.

Lord, give me wisdom today to make the right choice. Show me Your best path and I will follow!

MATCHMAKER

Ruth 3

BEST VERSE: 1
Then Naomi her mother-in-law said to her, "My daughter, shall I not seek security for you, that it may be well with you?"

Naomi loved Ruth as much as Ruth loved Naomi. She didn't want to see her live the rest of her life without a husband and children, so Naomi played matchmaker. She gave her some directions on how to let Boaz know she was "interested." Remember, Ruth was a stranger to the customs in her new homeland. Perhaps the directions Naomi gave were strange to her. But she followed her instructions completely.

Has anyone ever played matchmaker in your life? Well, be careful with that. Make sure your "matches" are approved by the Lord. He is the ultimate matchmaker. He always knows what is best for us. He knows who will make our best spouse, should we marry.

TEACHING MOMENT
Now this lesson is NOT about finding the right spouse for your children. I am sure we all have our preferences in that. No, this lesson is about teaching our children to follow instructions. Had Ruth not followed Naomi's instructions, she perhaps would never have married Boaz. Why is that important? Because Boaz is in the lineage of King David, who is in the direct lineage of . . . Jesus.

Ruth had no idea of that. How could she? But she was obedient, and God used her obedience to bring salvation to the world. I bet right now in heaven (and yes, I believe she is there) she is rejoicing to see the results of her obedience. We just never know how our decisions will affect others.

From what divine instruction are you pushing back? Relent! Follow Him! You may just be the key part of a successive reaction to change the course of history. You may be the key to someone's salvation a generation from now.

O God, You are the ultimate match maker. You are the only one with the fore-knowledge of my life. Help me trust You more so I can be used of You more.

JUNE 26

BABY WORDS
Matthew 21

BEST VERSES: 14-17

And *the* blind and *the* lame came to Him in the temple, and He healed them. But when the chief priests and the scribes saw the wonderful things that He had done, and the children who were shouting in the temple, "Hosanna to the Son of David," they became indignant and said to Him, "Do You hear what these *children* are saying?" And Jesus said to them, "Yes; have you never read, 'Out of the mouths of infants and nursing babes you have prepared praise for yourself'?" And He left them and went out of the city to Bethany, and spent the night there.

"Out of the mouth of babes." You have heard that saying, I'm sure. Well here we see that saying quoted by the Lord Jesus. He is quoting Psalm 8:2 which reads, "From the mouth of infants and nursing babes You have established strength because of Your adversaries, to make the enemy and the revengeful cease."

TEACHING MOMENT

Have you ever heard your child say something that surprised you? What parent hasn't, right? Sometimes it is the words they hear around the house. Sometimes it's words they hear from friends. But what a joy it would be if what they repeated were words of praise and adoration for our Lord. If we, as parents and grandparents, are mindful of those words coming from our mouths, I am sure our little ones would hear and repeat.

Teach your children to sing praises to the King of kings. Teach them His Word so that it will be with them later in life when they encounter difficult days. But most importantly, teach them to keep a lookout for Him so they too can join in and say, "Hosanna to the Son of David."

Lord God, I want my words to be echoed in the halls of my home by my children. I want them to sing and speak words of praise to You all day long.

JUST GOTTA TELL SOMEBODY
Mark 16

BEST VERSES: 8–11

They went out and fled from the tomb, for trembling and astonishment had gripped them; and they said nothing to anyone, for they were afraid. [Now after He had risen early on the first day of the week, He first appeared to Mary Magdalene, from whom He had cast out seven demons. She went and reported to those who had been with Him, while they were mourning and weeping. When they heard that He was alive and had been seen by her, they refused to believe it.

It is interesting that Mark is the only Gospel that implies that the women, who came to the tomb on Resurrection morning and saw the angel, did not immediately tell others what they saw. Verse 8 says, "and they said nothing to anyone." But you just can't keep that kind of story to yourselves.

Have you ever heard good news and decided to keep it to yourselves? Maybe you had been trying for months or even years to have a baby and you finally get the news that you are expecting. You may, for a little while, keep it to yourselves, but eventually you tell everyone you love. Heck, you may even tell a perfect stranger.

The news of Christ's resurrection is just as exciting today as it was when the women discovered the empty tomb. It is still empty. He is still risen. He is still seated at the right hand of the Father. The women, as recorded here in Mark, kept the news to themselves out of fear. But they had to tell someone.

So how do we teach this truth to our kids? By getting excited about it ourselves. We need to make a big deal about the Resurrection. We need to live as if we actually believe He rose from the grave rather than living as if He were still in it. We need to show them we believe that He is seated at the right hand of the Father, interceding for all who have accepted Him. We need to TELL SOMEONE! Have you done that? Your children will imitate you, you know. What better trait for them to imitate than your passion to share Christ with others.

Give me the boldness today, Lord, to tell someone about Jesus. Broaden my outreach to have contact with others who need to hear the good news of Christ.

JUNE 28

LIAR, LIAR

Judges 17

BEST VERSES: 3-4

He then returned the eleven hundred *pieces* of silver to his mother, and his mother said, "I wholly dedicate the silver from my hand to the Lord for my son to make a graven image and a molten image; now therefore, I will return them to you." So when he returned the silver to his mother, his mother took two hundred *pieces* of silver and gave them to the silversmith who made them into a graven image and a molten image, and they were in the house of Micah.

Did you ever notice in this story about Micah how his mother lied? Micah had taken 1,100 pieces of silver from her. When he returned the silver, she said she would dedicate it to the Lord. But she actually only used two hundred pieces for the image. What happened to the other nine hundred pieces?

We parents will often tell our children one thing but do another. We think because we are the adults, we can do what we want, even if that is not exactly what we expect from our children. Wrong! Wrong! Wrong! We have to be above reproach, especially when it comes to setting the example for our children.

The best way to teach this truth is by living it out for our kids. When we tell them not to lie, we shouldn't tell them to tell someone we are not home when we are, just to avoid a phone call. When we are at the store and we buy something that we know our spouse wouldn't approve of, we don't tell them to not tell Mommy. We can't do those things and then get on to them when they lie to us.

Micah's mother set a poor example for him. You should read the rest of the story about Micah to see how his life turned out. Not great. And his mama deserves part of the blame, I believe. Parents have to set the example for their children.

Are you doing that for your children? Are you hiding possessions or activities from them that you wouldn't want them to have or do? Moms and dads, don't ever ask your children to lie for you, even if that lie is an "innocent lie." There are no innocent lies, just lies.

Lord, I want to be the person in Christ You want me to be for my children. Let Christ live in and through me so they will allow Him to do the same in them.

JUNE 29

CHILDLIKE FAITH

Matthew 18

BEST VERSE: 2
And He called a child to Himself and set him before them.

Moms and dads, is there anything any better than having your child crawl up into your lap to get some hugs and kisses? I can't think of anything. Well, maybe grandkids doing the same.

Look at this verse again. Jesus called a child from the crowd to use as an example. Now it doesn't say specifically, but I have to believe that when it says, "set him before them" that He took that child in His lap, probably hugged him and kissed him. That is just the way Jesus was. He loved children. He was always referring to their faith as the faith we must have to follow Him. He used the child to teach.

What can you learn from your child? You know they can help us learn a lot about faith, if we just let them. They believe *simply*. They don't try to "figure things out." They just believe. They just trust. They just accept.

How about you? Are you so busy with your parenting that you have ceased to be a learner? Have you gotten too "mature" to believe all that nonsense? I certainly hope not. Having worked over thirty-eight years with children, I can tell you that I am still learning from them. They teach me every time I am with them.

Will you listen to your child's heartbeat for God and get in rhythm?

Lord God, open my eyes and ears to what You are trying to teach me through others, especially from my children. And when I learn from them

JUNE 30

BEST KNOWN

John 3

BEST VERSE: 16
For God so loved the world, that He gave His only begotten Son, that whoever believes in Him shall not perish, but have eternal life.

If you memorized Scripture as a youngster, this is probably the first verse you memorized, right? Many of us learned this verse in Sunday School or Vacation Bible School, and we learned it early. If you watch an NFL game, there is probably someone in the crowd (usually behind the goalposts) holding up a sign that reads "John 3:16." We all quote it and know it, but do we live it?

The real question is "Do we REALLY believe it?" Do you? If you do, how many people have you told lately about Christ? How many people have you gone out of your way to share the greatest news? I often wonder about Nicodemus, with whom Christ was talking in John 3:16. Once Nicodemus heard this, how diligent was he to share it?

TEACHING MOMENT

Teach your children this verse. Help them memorize it. But more importantly, help them really believe it. Help them see the importance of the "whoever" in this verse. God desires that all people be saved, and He wants to use us, your children included, in sharing the good news.

Talk with them about the contrast in the verse—perishing or eternal life. Which one do you desire for your children? What a dumb question. Well, God has the same desire for EVERYONE. We are ALL created in His image, so He desires for us ALL to come back to Him.

Will you share this verse with someone today? Will you tell them the story? Will you lead them to eternal life rather than allow them to perish? God wants to use you. Don't be like Nicodemus who came in the night to avoid being seen by others. He was fearful of the reprisal of others. Be bold and courageous.

Father, You loved me enough to send Your only Son to die for me. Help me today to love You enough to die to my pride and live boldly for You. Help me to share Your love with anyone I meet

FLATTERING LIPS

Psalms 11–12

BEST VERSES: 12:3–4

May the Lord cut off all flattering lips, the tongue that speaks great things; Who have said, "With our tongue we will prevail; our lips are our own; who is lord over us?"

Oh, brothers and sisters, beware of those who boast of themselves or others. People who are "good talkers" can win a crowd with their words. We see it all the time. Some politicians are great at it. Of course, they almost always boast of themselves. Lawyers are skilled at influencing jurors with their side of the argument. Even preachers can use their words (instead of God's) to sway a congregation.

We are warned about their motives. They say, "Our lips are our own; who is lord over us?" They truly believe no one is over them. What they say goes. Their tongues are their weapons of choice. Beware! If someone pays you unsolicited compliments, step back about ten feet and ask yourself what they really want.

TEACHING MOMENT

What is my point? We should only boast in the Lord! He is the only one worthy of praise, not ourselves, not others. Teach your children that. Boasting and bragging is not really flattering at all. It is conceited and obnoxious. It drives people away. Don't let your children get into this habit.

Teach your children to direct all praise about them upward. Give credit where credit is due. It is God who gives us the abilities to perform well. He gifts us with strong minds and bodies. When we see others excelling, praise God for their achievements, even if they don't.

Are you boasting about yourself? Are you bragging on your kids too much? Let the Lord do the exalting. He is quite capable of making these things known if they are worthy. Humbleness is rewarded in due time. Let the Lord boast on you.

Lord, the song says, "O Lord, it's hard to be humble, when you're perfect in every way." I know that is not true. Help me show the other side—humility—each and every day.

DEAL WITH IT NOW

2 Samuel 1

BEST VERSE: 21

Now when King David heard of all these matters, he was very angry.

I grew up with an older brother, an older sister, and a younger sister. We loved each other, but, boy, did we ever fight. My brother and I would wrestle all the time. I would get mad at my sisters from time to time. But one thing my parents did is they made sure we made things right.

The story here in 2 Samuel of David's children, Amnon, Tamar, and Absalom is a brutal one. Amnon rapes his half-sister Tamar, who is the sister of Absalom. David hears of this and does nothing, except get angry. As a result, Absalom kills Amnon and then flees, only to return and lead a rebellion against his father, David. What would have happened if David had dealt with Amnon when he first sinned against the Lord and his half-sister?

TEACHING MOMENT

This lesson is more for us parents than for our children. Siblings are going to fight. Can we all agree on that? They won't always get along. But we must ensure that they make things right afterwards, and we must discipline accordingly. I didn't always do that with my two children. To my own children, if you are reading this today, please forgive me.

Unforgiven sin and undealt-with disobedience will lead to more sin and disobedience. The Lord teaches us that. We must confess and make things right, or we will suffer the separation of fellowship from the Lord. He longs to bless us. He longs to hear us asking for forgiveness. He stands ready to forgive.

Do you have undealt-with sins in your life today? Do you, as a parent, ignore your children's harsh treatment of each other? Do the right thing now. Deal with your sin. Deal with your children. Make sure you are pleasing the Father in all aspects of your life. Unless you do this, you will become callous to the pain of sin. Before you know it, it just won't seem important to confess.

Oh Father, show me the sin in my life. Give me the determination to parent my children as You would. Help me teach them to honor You and treat others as your children.

THE WRONG QUESTION

1 Samuel 9

BEST VERSE: 11

As they went up the slope to the city, they found young women going out to draw water and said to them, "Is the seer here?"

Saul was looking for Samuel to find out where his father's donkeys were. He and his men had been looking for them without any luck and thought "the seer" could help. Why waste the time of a prophet of God looking for donkeys? They had no idea what lie ahead. Saul had NO idea he would be anointed as Israel's first king.

Sometimes when we go to God with a request, He has a completely different answer for us than we expected. Sometimes He probably thinks, "What a dumb request!" Now I am sure He doesn't really think that. But looking back at how He answers sometimes makes us realize we had really asked for the wrong thing.

TEACHING MOMENT

You have heard the expression, "There is no such thing as a stupid question, just a stupid answer." Well . . . sometimes questions are a little less than smart. But when our children ask questions, we should do our best to answer them with truthfulness. Sometimes their questions make us stop and think. Other times the answers are easy.

Hopefully our answers will teach them to keep asking questions. They won't learn how to do life without asking those probing questions. God wants them to ask Him questions as well. He wants to answer. That is the key. They need to keep asking God for direction and the answers to those challenging life questions.

What are you asking God right now? Has He EVER refused to answer? You may not like the answer, but I guarantee He hasn't refused to answer. Just listen. He will respond, sooner or later.

God, I know you are listening. I know You are ready to answer. Prepare my heart to hear what You say and not what I want You to say.

DOING IT RIGHT
2 Samuel 8

BEST VERSE: 15
So David reigned over all Israel; and David administered justice and righteousness for all his people.

Finally, David is able to rule and reign. Finally, he is able to concentrate on leading his people. Finally, he is able to be the king God had intended for His people. Why? Because David had honored God in each and every action.

In this chapter, after David defeats his enemies, God allows him to set up his kingdom to rule the people in justice and righteousness. What a legacy. In America, our Presidents want to leave a legacy when they leave office. They want to be remembered for some great accomplishment. David was known as the king who sought after God's own heart. Now that is a legacy worth leaving.

TEACHING MOMENT
We should leave a legacy for our children. I have a book on my bookshelf that is entitled *A Father's Legacy*. This book covers my entire life. It's one of those books you write in to complete. It gives your children and grandchildren something to read about you after you are gone. But that is NOT my legacy. I pray my legacy will be like David's. I want them to remember me as the man who sought after God's own heart.

And we need to all keep our legacies in mind as we make our everyday decisions. It is so easy to ruin a legacy by one quick indiscretion. We are teaching our children every day. We, too, should show forth justice and righteousness which will draw our children to Christ. Because it is only because of His justice and His righteousness that we can even begin to lead them.

Are you leading that way? Do your children see you leading well? If not, why not begin today? Even David made mistakes, some tragic (i.e., Bathsheba), but he went down as the greatest king of Israel. We do not have to be perfect to lead. We just have to rely on the Perfect One.

O Holy and Perfect Father, show me today how to lead in justice and righteousness. Show me how to model a broken heart for my family. Draw them to You through my life.

DON'T STOP

Genesis 2

BEST VERSE: 7
Isaac spoke to Abraham his father and said, "My father!" And he said, "Here I am, my son." And he said, "Behold, the fire and the wood, but where is the lamb for the burnt offering?"

Have you ever wondered what would have happened if Abraham had stopped short of the place where the Lord told him to go to offer Isaac? What if he had said, "Ah, this is far enough. No need to go all the way to the top of that hill. He's going to die anyway."

The provision of the ram was waiting for him at the very place God told him to go. How about you? Are you stopping short of the calling God has placed on you and thereby missing His provision? Don't stop! Even when the burden seems heavy and perhaps His calling makes no sense, proceed!

Abraham had to keep going, trusting and wrestling with what the Lord had asked of him. I have never been asked to kill my son, but I have been asked to do some things that really didn't make sense at the time. Most of these requests made more sense after the fact. Others . . . well, I am still waiting to see why.

Do your kids ever ask you why you read your Bible? If so, what a great opportunity you have to explain why! You are preparing for a journey, one fraught with detours and obstacles, some hidden. But you know the ultimate destination. You have to stay on the road (reading your Bible) so you will be prepared for whatever unexpected event that pops up. In fact, the next time the Lord gives you a challenge and you are able to use a biblical truth you have read, make sure your kids know that.

Trust Him! He will never lead you astray.

Thank You, God, for guiding me exactly where You want me. Help me recognize Your guiding principles and respond as I should. I really want to be where You want me.

JULY 6

EXHAUSTED AND SICK

Daniel 8

BEST VERSE: 27

Then I, Daniel, was exhausted and sick for days. Then I got up again and carried on the king's business; but I was astounded at the vision, and there was none to explain it.

When I read this verse, I said to myself, "I can relate to that." There have been times in my life when I felt just like that. I have wearied myself with ministry. I have been literally sick from seeing the world around me reject the truth and head straight toward hell. Daniel had been given a message, but it wasn't clear to him. He was burdened to know the truth of the message. Why? To show others how much he knew? To be seen as super smart? No! He wanted to make sure that if the message needed to be passed on, he could explain its meaning to others.

TEACHING MOMENT

Sometimes the Lord tells us things that are hard for us to understand, much less explain to others. But He tells us truth so we can share it, not hoard it. Children need to be discipled so that they can share the good news of the gospel to others. Sharing does NOT come naturally. But with the right guidance, anyone can do it.

There are a multitude of resources out there to choose from. Let me encourage you to find one to use with your children. Teach them to share truths that God gives them in His Word. Show them how exciting it is to share a truth and see it take root in someone's life. That means you have to model truth-sharing to them.

What truth has God revealed to you this week in His Word? With whom can you share that? Surely, there is someone in your sphere of influence that needs to be encouraged. Don't hold onto those nuggets God gives you. As you share them, the truths continue to come.

Holy Father, You are the giver of all good things. Help me share those truths with others. Let others cross my path today who need to hear from You.

JULY 7

WATER WARS

Genesis 26

BEST VERSE: 18
Then Isaac dug again the wells of water which had been dug in the days of his father Abraham, for the Philistines had stopped them up after the death of Abraham; and he gave them the same names which his father had given them.

The story told here in Genesis 26 shows the importance of water in the lives of Isaac and his people. We can't live long without water—about three days. Our bodies have to have it. Our animals have to have it. Our crops have to have it. If it is not there, we have to find it somewhere. You really need to read verse 16 to the end of the chapter to get the full story, but the short version is Isaac kept digging wells until he found one that they could use without being hassled by the locals.

TEACHING MOMENT
So, what truth can you share with your children about this passage? The next time you pour them a glass of water or open a bottle of water, tell them this story. People used to argue and fight over water. We still see that today in some drought-stricken areas of the world. They fight over physical water. How sad! But water is necessary to live.

Now here is the principle—we also can't live (eternally) without the Living Water, Jesus Christ. And the beauty of this water? We don't have to fight for it. We don't have to dig a well to find it. We don't have to search and search hoping to find it. All we have to do is bow before a Holy God and ask for it. He gives it away. And this water continues to flow in our lives and quenches our deepest thirsts.

Are you thirsty today? Have you drunk lately from that well of Living Water? He offers it fresh and clean each day. Will you take the cup from the Savior today? Ask Him to refresh you with His life-giving liquid.

Lord, will You fill my cup today? My soul is thirsting for Your liquid peace. Feed me with Your Word until I am full and complete.

JULY 8

IS ANGER UNGODLY?

Mark 3

BEST VERSE: 5

After looking around at them with anger, grieved at their hardness of heart, He said to the man, "Stretch out your hand." And he stretched it out, and his hand was restored.

Parents, do you tell your kids all the time to not get angry? We tend to do that a lot. We don't want our children to be mad at someone. We don't want them to lash out at another person to try to hurt them. That is good parenting. We want them to love others.

But you can see from this verse that there are times when anger is justified. In this story, Jesus is angry with those who opposed Him healing this man just because it happened to be the Sabbath day. The word "anger" in verse 5 really means anger. But it also has the definition of anger that God has toward sin. That's what *should* anger us—sin!

TEACHING MOMENT

We should teach our children that unrighteousness *should* anger us. Things done to harm others *should* anger us. Abortion *should* anger us. You get the picture. However, notice Jesus' reaction. He didn't lash out at the crowd. He simply healed the man.

We need to teach our children that we should go about doing good in the very presence of those who hate us and hate God. We should bless others despite their actions. We should follow the example of the Master. Be angry, but sin not. Now that's a lesson worth teaching!

Forgive my anger at things that just make me mad, Father. Let me be angry in agreement with Your righteousness. Let me forgive others as You forgive me.

ETERNAL RULE

Lamentations 5

BEST VERSE: 19
You, O Lord, rule forever; Your throne is from generation to generation.

Don't you just love these words of Jeremiah? Jeremiah acknowledges God's eternal rule. He sits on His throne forever. No one can ever depose our God. Why? Simple. Because He is God, and there is no other! No earthly king can overthrow Him. No heavenly creature can usurp Him. He is the eternal King of Glory.

Now, just think about that. Think about the thousands of kings who have ruled on this earth. They all thought they were supreme, but they weren't. They all died. They may have thought they could rule forever, but, sooner or later, death came calling. But not for our God. He has existed and will exist forever.

TEACHING MOMENT
This is somewhat of a heavy topic for kids, but they will understand about kings and thrones. Have them draw a picture of what they think God's throne looks like. Tell them to make it as beautiful and magnificent as possible. Ask them how long they think this throne will last. Then read them this verse and explain that His throne will never end.

When your children get older, they will begin to understand the concept of eternity. They won't ever fully understand it, but they will have a picture in their mind. Eternity is a long time. And all of us who are believers in

Christ will one day reign with Him in glory. We shall be in His eternal kingdom. We will worship the King of kings and Lord of lords forever.

Can you grasp this concept yourself? There are some things we just have to accept and not try to conceptualize. Some things are left better as a mystery, too big to define. That's eternity. That's God's eternal reign. We don't fully understand the longevity of eternity. But one day we will.

Eternal Father, You have promised me eternity only because You are eternal. You have made me an eternal home which I can't wait to see. But more importantly, I can't wait to just be with You.

JULY 10

A WISE WOMAN

2 Samuel 20

BEST VERSE: 16
Then a wise woman called from the city, "Hear, hear! Please tell Joab, 'Come here that I may speak with you.'"

Joab was on a mission for King David to find and kill Sheba, a man who was leading a rebellion against him. All this happened right after David's own son, Absalom, had unsuccessfully staged a coup. David was going to have none of this, so he ordered Joab to track down this Sheba and execute him. His search led him to the city of Abel.

Abel was known as a city where people went to seek wisdom. We can assume then that meant there were seers there who imparted advice and guidance. Thus, enters the "wise woman." Perhaps she was one of those seers. She doesn't want her city destroyed, so she cuts a deal with Joab to deliver Sheba over to them, or at least his head.

TEACHING MOMENT
Okay, this is another devotional when you may be thinking, *What in the world can I teach my child about this story?* For me, this is the point. God will sometimes place wise people in our path unexpectedly. He will speak through them to deliver guidance just when we need it. We, however, must be willing to receive it. Scripture doesn't give us this wise woman's name. All

we know is she was a woman and she was wise. But I bet everyone in that city knew her because of her wisdom.

Teach your children to listen to godly advice. Any advice they receive from anyone should be filtered through God's Word. If it conflicts with that, it is NOT godly advice. But if it agrees, listen closely. Teach them to be willing to change their course of action based on this wise counsel. Joab did, and he had the army to achieve his original plan.

Do you need wise counsel right now? First, go to the Lord. Ask Him to give it to you. Secondly, look out for those the Lord may place in your path today. He may just put someone right there who can guide you. Finally, when you receive the advice, follow it. Trust that the God of the ages is big enough to help solve your problems.

Father, I am good at asking for advice but not so good at receiving it. Show me what You would have me do today to please You. Open my eyes to those You send with Your message.

JULY 11

A FINAL GOODBYE

1 Samuel 26

BEST VERSE: 25

Then Saul said to David, "Blessed are you, my son David; you will both accomplish much and surely prevail." So David went on his way, and Saul returned to his place."

How many times have you heard of people speaking harshly to each other just before one of them dies? The survivor almost always has regrets of their last encounter. They wish they had a chance to correct their last words. But what's done is done.

David and Saul did not know that this encounter would be their last. Saul had been pursuing David for months trying to kill him. Here, at last, is the final conversation between the two. Saul finally relents to chasing David, after hearing David's voice and seeing how he spared his life again. They part with Saul's final words of blessing.

Children can get mad and say things they really don't mean at the time. Remember the movie *Home Alone*? Young Kevin gets in trouble and says he wishes he didn't have a family. Poof! The next morning, they are all gone, or so he thought.

This passage today is right before Saul and Jonathan die in battle. David did not know that was going to happen. Neither did Saul. But they left each other this final time with kind words, not angry ones. Our children need to see that their words can cause them to carry a lot of guilt, if spoken in haste and anger.

Who have you hurt lately with unkind or hurtful words? Do you need to make that right, before it's too late? Better yet, who has hurt you with unkind words? Forgive them, and then let them know it. Don't let your feelings keep you from the peace that comes from forgiveness.

Pray for those who have hurt you. It's really hard to be mad at someone you are praying for. The Lord will soften your spirit toward forgiveness very quickly.

I need to choose my words carefully, O Lord. I need to think before saying what is on the tip of my tongue. Help me to keep myself clean as I represent You.

JULY 12

HEAL MY CHILD PLEASE!

Matthew 15

BEST VERSE: 28
Then Jesus said to her, "O woman, your faith is great; it shall be done for you as you wish." And her daughter was healed at once.

Have you ever wondered why Jesus did not immediately respond to this mother's request to heal her daughter? Moms and dads, wouldn't you beg the Lord to heal your child if they were sick? No parent wants to see their child suffer. We would do anything we could to alleviate their pain and sickness.

This mom, like many of the ones I know, begged Jesus to heal her daughter. She even came close to arguing with Him. Why did Jesus test her so? I believe He wanted to make sure she was sincere in her faith in Him. Many came to Him for healing. Why was she coming to Him? What was her motive?

When she humbled herself, comparing herself to the dogs who eat crumbs from the table, he said those words to her, "Your faith is great." Moms, dads, don't you want the Lord to whisper those words in your ear? Don't you want to be told your faith is great? You can! Just trust Him. Just talk to Him. Daily implore the Lord on behalf of your children. After all, He loves them more than you ever could.

TEACHING MOMENT

Our children need to know that all healing is from the Lord. Sure, they may go to the doctor or nurse, but it is the Lord who gave these medical professionals their abilities. You may give your children medicine, but it is the Lord who allows the ingredients to be created to make that medicine. And finally, it is the Lord who made our bodies and understands exactly what kind of healing we need.

Father, You are the Great Physician. You made me in Your image—perfect and whole. Restore me to Your image today.

JULY 13

GOD'S FINGER

Exodus 31

BEST VERSE: 28

When He had finished speaking with him upon Mount Sinai, He gave Moses the two tablets of the testimony, tablets of stone, written by the finger of God.

God used His finger to write the ten commandments on the tablets. He didn't have to do that. He could have chiseled them with fire from heaven. He could have just spoke them into existence. But He touched them with His finger.

Can you imagine how Moses felt when he picked up the tablets? These two stone tablets had just been touched by God Himself. Moses knew the holiness of these commandments, not because of the words written, but because of who had written them. God Himself had truly touched these commandments.

TEACHING MOMENT

Your children have been touched by God also. The Word says we are knit together in our mother's womb. Who do you think does the knitting? God does. He creates new life Himself. He creates us in His image. That includes your children, no matter how they act.

Remind them that God touched them. Remind them that He has made them in His image. Remind them He has created them to be holy as He is holy. They have been fashioned and formed by God to be used by Him to draw others to Him. Their purpose is to glorify the Father.

Do you feel God's finger on you? Can you see His fingerprint in your life? As believers in Christ, we should see God's prints all over us. Others should see them too. The next time you are trying to get all those fingerprints off your windows or doors, remember God has His prints on you. Don't wipe those off.

Your prints, O Lord, are all over me. Forgive me for wiping them off. Forgive me for not showing those prints to others. Help me to teach my children this truth of Your touch on their lives.

JULY 14

QUICK TEMPERS

1 Samuel 11

BEST VERSES: 12-13
Then the people said to Samuel, "Who is he that said, 'Shall Saul reign over us?' Bring the men, that we may put them to death." But Saul said, "Not a man shall be put to death this day, for today the Lord has accomplished deliverance in Israel."

It is amazing how quick some people get all riled up. One minute they are fine, and the next they are ready to fight. Israel had just experienced a great victory, and the people wanted to punish anyone who had spoken against their new king. Fortunately, Saul was even-tempered (at this point in his life) and refused to allow them to carry out their plans.

Have you ever lost your temper? Maybe you overreacted to something. "Not me, Carl. I would never do that." Yeah, right! We have all "lost it" at least once. Our emotions can get the best of us. We get offended, or we take up someone else's offense. And before we know it, we are in a fight with someone. Take a breath, like Saul did here.

TEACHING MOMENT

Do I even need to say it? This is a crucial teaching for your children. When we learn to control our tempers at an early age, it helps us avoid a lot of chaos. It keeps us focused on Him and not us.

Try this little experiment. Get a pot and put some water in it. Then place it on the stove and bring it to a boil. Let it keep boiling until it starts to boil over. Your kids need to see this. Depending on what kind of stove top you have, you may have quite the scene. Our tempers are like that. Boiling water (our emotions) are good when kept under control. But when they are left to boil and boil, pretty soon we have a mess.

I pray you have control over your emotions. Don't let them control you. God gifted us with all kinds of emotions, which can be used for good or bad. You have to choose how you want to use them.

O Lord, You gave me my passions. You gave me my emotions. Help me control them and use them for Your glory!

OH, HOW SOON WE FORGET

Exodus 15

BEST VERSE: 24
So the people grumbled at Moses, saying, "What shall we drink?"

Here in Exodus we read about a very short-minded people. The children of Israel, just recently freed from slavery, had witnessed the parting of the Red Sea and the destruction of Pharaoh's army. They walked across the sea bottom on DRY GROUND. How cool was that?

And now, here they are three days later, and they are actually worried about not having water. Did they not think that the God who freed them could give them a drink? What ungrateful, unbelieving people.

TEACHING MOMENT
That reminds us of our children, doesn't it? At some point our children get brain-freeze and forget all that we have done for them. "Hey Junior, I just fed you a nine-course meal!" "Hey Penelope, didn't I just buy you a dress for homecoming." But past experiences can be so soon forgotten.

Before you get angry, take a moment to reflect on all the things the Lord has done for you which you have forgotten. Think back over the years at all the miracles God has performed in your life. Now—do your children seem so different than you? Probably not! Be grateful and celebratory!

Lord, You have blessed me beyond my expectations. Thank You for all You have done for me. I do not want to take any of that for granted. You are an awesome God!

WALKING WITH GOD

Genesis 5

BEST VERSE: 24
Enoch walked with God; and he was not, for God took him.

There were only two men in the Bible who never died a physical death, Enoch and Elijah. We have many stories about Elijah, but all we know about Enoch is he was the father of Methuselah. That's it! Oh yeah, ... Enoch lived on the earth for 365 years, the shortest lifespan of anyone mentioned at this point in the Bible, except for Abel whom Cain killed.

So, what is so special about Enoch? Scripture just says, "Enoch walked with God." What does that mean? Why did God decide to take him at such a young age (compared to others in chapter 5)? The Bible doesn't tell us, but we have to believe that Enoch was special to Him. So special that He wanted him closer to him than to earth.

TEACHING MOMENT

When was the last time you took a walk or hike with your child? There is something peaceful about walking in the woods down a trail. Your child is exploring every little stick and rock. You are admiring the beauty of creation. What a perfect time to share this verse with your son or daughter. Tell them how Enoch was just walking with God, and God decided He loved him so much He wanted him home.

Now, don't scare your child into thinking that if they walk with God, He is going to kill them. But they do need to know that when we walk with the Lord and focus on spending time with Him, we will much rather be with Him than here. We look forward to the day when we will see Him face to face. Don't you imagine Enoch was thrilled to come face to face with His God?

Are you walking with Him? A word of warning: Don't become so heavenly-minded that you are no earthly good! You may have heard that before. But most of us are never in danger of that. We probably could all afford to be a little more heavenly-minded.

Now, take that step today with Him!

I don't want to get ahead of You, Father, but I often do. Help me to walk with You and be restful in the walk. May I move when You move and wait when You want me to.

FOLLOWING DIRECTIONS

Exodus 39

BEST VERSES: 42–43

So the sons of Israel did all the work according to all that the Lord had commanded Moses. And Moses examined all the work and behold, they had done it; just as the Lord had commanded, this they had done. So Moses blessed them.

Have you ever attempted to put something together without looking at the instructions? What happens? Well, if you have never assembled this item before, you usually revert back to the instructions. Instructions are written for a reason. They make the assembly easier (at least most of the time). Following directions is easier than trying to wing it.

The craftsmen had followed all the Lord's commandments as given by Moses. They were diligent to get it right. They knew they were working on something holy and sacred. They knew everything they did was a reflection of their love for their God.

TEACHING MOMENT

How many times have you had to send your children back to their rooms to "reclean" it? This is exactly what I am talking about. We must teach our children that every task they do is a reflection of them and our Lord. We must do our very best at everything we do since we are known by others as believers in Christ.

I had a boss once that said, "Holy shoddy is still shoddy." So true. Excellence is expected. Pride in our work is expected. Show your son how to do it right the first time. Teach your daughter how excellence looks. Then praise them for their work. Moses blessed the workers when they had finished because they had followed directions and performed with excellence. We should too.

Are you guilty of halfway doing your job? Do you drag into work and drag along all day? Refocus your attention to pleasing the Lord in your work. By pleasing Him you will please your boss. Do your best at every task and see how He blesses.

Father, show me how to please You in every task. Show me how to honor You in my everyday tasks.

USED

Genesis 40

BEST VERSE: 23
Yet the chief cupbearer did not remember Joseph, but forgot him.

Have you ever been used by someone to get what they want? That feels bad enough, but what if they also completely forgot about you? That's what happened to Joseph. He had correctly interpreted the cupbearer's dream, but as soon as the cupbearer was free from prison and back in his lofty position with Pharaoh, he forgot all about Joseph. He had even witnessed the baker's dream come true, yet he still didn't mention Joseph.

I am sure, since Joseph was running the prison, he heard about all that was going on in Pharaoh's palace. Every big dinner would require the cupbearer to be there. I bet Joseph thought he would surely tell Pharaoh about him today. But days, weeks, months, and even years went by before his name was mentioned.

TEACHING MOMENT
What is the lesson in all of this? Simple— do what is right regardless of the outcome. Joseph did what was right. He had the gift, through God, to interpret dreams. He used it to help others. Our children need to learn to do the same. If someone has a need which they can meet, they should do it without any thought of payback.

Think of all the Lord has done for us. He doesn't expect any payback except our love. Children need to be directed in this by their parents. They need to see us doing the same. Our outward expressions of love to Christ and our efforts to come alongside a brother or sister in need speak volumes to them as they develop their own faith walk.

Won't you model service for your children today? Help them discover a way in which they can be of service to another. Teach them to give in a way

231

that expects no return. And then celebrate the joy that comes from being obedient to the Lord.

Lord, show me whom You would have me bless through an act of service today. Let me be the example for my children. Teach me to be unselfish and undemanding of others.

ACCEPTANCE

2 Samuel 15

BEST VERSES: 24–26
Now behold, Zadok also came, and all the Levites with him carrying the ark of the covenant of God. And they set down the ark of God, and Abiathar came up until all the people had finished passing from the city. The king said to Zadok, "Return the ark of God to the city. If I find favor in the sight of the Lord, then He will bring me back again and show me both it and His habitation. But if He should say thus, 'I have no delight in you,' behold, here I am, let Him do to me as seems good to Him.'"

Have you ever wondered why David didn't deal with Absalom more harshly? Surely David had heard what Absalom had been doing for the past couple of years. I am sure he was aware of Absalom's motives. But, as any father, he hoped for the best in his son. He was probably praying that the Lord would turn his heart.

But now here David is, fleeing the city. In the above verses, we see Zadok bringing the Ark of the Covenant out of the city to follow David. David, however, has too much respect and awe for God's will to see this done. He has seen how the Lord works and is willing to give up his throne if that is what the Lord wants. He knew the Ark belonged in Jerusalem, not following him who knows where.

TEACHING MOMENT
Children need to learn to make decisions as they get older, but they also need to learn to accept your decisions without arguing or whining. By teaching them this, we are preparing them to accept the Lord's decisions for their lives. They may never understand this side of eternity why some things

happen. But, just like David, they need to learn to trust the hand of God. He's got this!

Sometimes, your children will have to decide to just "be the wrong one" for the sake of peace and unity. That doesn't mean they are a doormat or a pushover. It is a sign of humility and grace in their lives. We can model that as parents when they see mom and dad disagreeing. We should seek to outdo each other in seeking peace. That's a lesson worth learning. Will you be like David and allow the Lord to redeem you when you've been wronged? He knows your heart and your motives.

O God, I have this problem. I always want to be the right one. Help me to be the wrong one, if needed, for the sake of peace. You are the Peacemaker, but You will use me.

JULY 20

TALKING BUSH

Exodus 3

BEST VERSE: 4

When the LORD saw that he turned aside to look, God called to him from the midst of the bush and said, "Moses, Moses!" And he said, "Here I am."

I don't know about you, but a burning bush that is not consumed is strange enough. Then it starts talking. I would have been running as fast as I could. Not Moses. He "turned aside to look" and then spoke back. What? Was he crazy? Of course not. He recognized the voice of God.

How did he do that? That's a question to ask Moses when we get to heaven. One day we will be ask him such questions about the burning bush, like *What did the voice sound like? Did it have a crackle, like the sound of a crackling fire? How did you know it was God and not the devil?* Regardless of how he knew, he knew.

TEACHING MOMENT

Hearing God's voice doesn't come naturally. You have to invest time with Him to recognize it. That's part of our job as parents. We need to bring our children to Him in prayer and teach them to listen. He speaks to all of us differently. He may sound totally different to one of your kids than He does to another. That's okay.

But more important than recognizing His voice is doing what He says. Explain it to your child this way. It's kind of like going to the doctor, getting his diagnosis, buying the medicine he prescribes and then going home and putting the medicine in the trashcan. Hearing what's wrong doesn't help you. Doing what the doctor says (taking the medication) is what will help.

Have you made one too many visits to the throne of grace and heard the Lord tell you what to do? Hearing and not doing is not faith at all. Faith does come through hearing, but faith is built through responding to what you have heard. Do what He says, and watch your life discover purpose.

Father, You are the only one who can give me the advice I need. No one else comes close. Only You can show me truth. Only You can give me the courage to do exactly what You said.

JULY 21

ENOUGH IS ENOUGH

Deuteronomy 3

BEST VERSES: 5-6
"Let me, I pray, cross over and see the fair land that is beyond the Jordan, that good hill country and Lebanon." But the Lord was angry with me on your account, and would not listen to me; and the Lord said to me, "Enough! Speak to Me no more of this matter."

How many times have you begged someone for something? I mean really *beg*. Moses had undoubtedly asked the Lord to allow him to go into the Promised Land more than once. But because he had disobeyed Him way back in the wilderness, God's decision was final. Do you remember that incident? God had told Moses to speak to the rock, and it would give water. Instead, Moses struck the rock with his staff. Water still came out, but Moses had not followed God's instructions. God said then that Moses would not enter the Promised Land. I guess Moses had held out hope that as they neared the Promised Land the Lord might reconsider.

How many times have your kids done this to you? You hand down a consequence for disobedience, and they start right in begging for mercy. How many times have you given in, just to get them quiet? Come on, be honest. You know you've done that.

Don't do it. It's okay to reconsider and lessen the consequence, but don't do it because of their whining. That teaches them the wrong thing. This will go with them into their adult life—whining, complaining, murmuring until they get their way. That won't work in the workplace or in their marriage. Be firm and hold them accountable.

You may be thinking, *Carl, it's too late. I have already created a monster.* No, it's not too late. Start today following the Lord's example. Moses got to see the Promised Land (that was a little compromise the Lord gave without changing the consequence), but he never stepped foot in it. God held firm in his judgment and decision making. You, too, hold firm.

Lord, I am so tempted to give in to pressure from others when they want me to change my mind on something that I know is right. Give me the courage and strength to stand firm. Help me teach my children the value of sticking to your word.

JULY 22

BIG MISTAKE

1 Samuel 5

BEST VERSE: 2
Then the Philistines took the ark of God and brought it to the house of Dagon and set it by Dagon.

The Philistines were under the impression that since they had defeated Israel, they had also defeated their God. They took the ark of God and presented it before their god, Dagon. But when they awoke the next day, Dagon was face down on the ground. The next day it happened again, and this time Dagon was even chopped up.

Then God turned His sights on the Philistines. He smote them with tumors. Obviously, they became worried. Now before you judge them too harshly, we do the same thing. We have to treat the things of God as holy, not flippantly or casually, as just another thing. What do I mean? How about His Word? It is HIS Word, not just some stories. How about the Church? It is HIS bride, not just some gathering.

TEACHING MOMENT

Children will watch how you handle God's stuff. They will learn from you how to handle His Word. They will learn from you how you treat His Church. They will learn from you how important you consider the day of worship.

Come on, Carl! Aren't you getting a little legalistic? I don't think so. I just think we don't teach our children to honor God anymore. He is the same God who smote the Philistines. He is the same God who punished those who rejected Him. Teach your children to have a holy reverence for Him.

Is there something of God's that you aren't honoring? Make that right? Ask God to forgive you for not standing in awe of Him. Ask God to forgive you for treating Him too casually. He deserves all your praise.

O Holy God, forgive me when I get too comfortable with You. I know You love me and call me Your child, but I also know You are worthy of my allegiance and obedience. I bow before You today.

JULY 23

DOWN AND DIRTY

Luke 5

BEST VERSE: 19

But not finding any way to bring him in because of the crowd, they went up on the roof and let him down through the tiles with his stretcher, into the middle of the crowd, in front of Jesus.

We always concentrate on the healing that takes place in this story. Of course, that is the point, right? But what about the poor homeowner? I mean, come on, there is a six feet by three feet hole in his roof now. It would have taken a hole about that big to let the man down on his pallet without dumping him out on top of the Savior.

How about the mess on the floor? All that roof top material had to go somewhere. People were crowded into the house to hear Jesus and all of a sudden stuff starts falling. What do you think they were thinking? And the poor house servant or wife! What a mess to clean up!

TEACHING MOMENT

Our children need to know that sometimes faith can be messy. It's not all about dressing up in our Sunday best (not that many people do that anymore—that's a whole other lesson) and going to church to show our faith. Sometimes when we exercise our faith, we can get dirty. Sometimes when we show Christ's love for others, we can get dirty. Sometimes when we reach out to lend that helping hand, we can get dirty.

In fact, let me encourage you to get dirty. Take your kids out and do a mission project somewhere in your neighborhood that requires you all to get dirty. Then tell them this story. Those men who lowered that pallet got their hands dirty digging through that roof. But their friend's healing meant more than clean hands. The servant or wife who saw the dirty floor didn't care when she saw that man get up and walk. So, get dirty for Jesus! Bet you haven't heard that before!

> Father, I know a little dirt isn't going to hurt me. And I am not afraid to work. My problem is with taking the time. Help me prioritize getting dirty for You.

JULY 24

STRONG OR STRONG-WILLED

Exodus 9

BEST VERSE: 35

Pharaoh's heart was hardened, and he did not let the sons of Israel go, just as the LORD had spoken through Moses.

Strong-willed! Parents, have you ever heard that term? You might have a child who is strong-willed. They look at you with those arms crossed and stomp their feet when you ask them to do something. Or perhaps they are teenagers now and consistently argue every point with you, demanding to make their own decisions regardless of your advice.

I truly believe Pharaoh was a strong-willed child. After all, he was raised to believe he was a god. Who wouldn't be strong-willed and arrogant and defiant if they had been told that since childhood? He believed he could do anything he wanted and that everyone else must bow to his decisions.

And then he ran smack into Jehovah God. Moses introduced Pharaoh to Him. "Let My people go!" Pharaoh resisted, mocked Him, defied Him until . . . he felt the full brunt of the wrath of God.

TEACHING MOMENT

What a lesson for our own children who may be strong willed and defiant! Now there is nothing wrong with being strong-willed as long as you understand that you are NOT God. Strong wills drive people to achieve great things. Don't discipline your child for that alone. However, allow them to learn that even the strongest of wills must bow to the Almighty Creator of the universe. When they learn that, they will truly be STRONG!

Thank You for giving us the drive to succeed. But Father, curb my stubborn streak. Make my will Your will. Only then will I be truly successful.

JULY 25

GOD DID IT

Exodus 8

BEST VERSE: 24A
Then the Lord did so.

It never ceases to amaze me how we pray for God's Will to be done, and then when God answers, according to His Will, we don't like the answer we got. God ALWAYS answers prayers. Sometimes it's *yes*, sometimes it's *no*, and sometimes it's *wait*. But He always answers.

God had instructed Moses and Aaron in the order of the plagues. I love this first part of Exodus 8:24. It just says, "Then the Lord did so." Period. End of discussion. Done! When God decides to do something, it's done. God warned Pharaoh time and time again. He had ample opportunity to yield, but pride and arrogance always gets in the way of hearing God.

It is so important that we teach our children to pray according to God's will. Now that is not the easiest task. How do you know God's will? How do you help your children understand God's will for their lives?

The easiest way I have found is to seek what will give Him the most glory. Pray that, and then see what He does. If we are willing to accept WHAT-EVER He does in answering our prayer, we have discovered God's will. Just teach your children that God will never do anything which goes against His Word or His character. Never!

What are you praying for right now? Like the Hebrews, do you need to be released from some sort of bondage? Seek the Lord. Ask Him what He is teaching you right now. Ask Him to show you the way out. Surrender to Him and allow Him to lead you to freedom.

Redeemer and Lord, You are the one who frees me from my everyday chains. Help me surrender my will to Yours. Help me lead my children to do the same.

JULY 26

SHOULD HAVE ASKED FIRST

Joshua 9

BEST VERSES: 14–15

So the men of Israel took some of their provisions, and did not ask for the counsel of the Lord. Joshua made peace with them and made a covenant with them, to let them live; and the leaders of the congregation swore an oath to them.

Even leaders make mistakes. This is obvious here in this passage. Joshua and the "men of Israel . . . did not ask for the counsel of the Lord." Now, before you start pointing fingers and judging them, how many times have you made a decision without consulting the Lord? If you are like me, plenty. Why don't we learn?

The Gibeonites come up again and again in the Old Testament. They were an issue with Saul and then later with David. All of this could have been avoided if Joshua had stopped and talked to the Lord before making promises. Hmmm, that sounds like very good advice, doesn't it?

Has your daughter ever invited a friend over to spend the night before asking you? Has your son promised his friend he could go with him to the movies before asking you? These are perfect times to talk about this story. You see, God knew that Canaan needed to be cleared of all the pagan people or else His children would be led astray. He knew what was best for them in the future, in the same way you can know what is best for your child.

Our children need to learn to trust us with their plans while they are small so they can learn to trust the Lord with their future. Once again, we are modeling for them what the Lord wants to do for them. But, in order for us to do that, we have to consult the Lord first. We have to make sure that we are directing them in the way the Lord wants us. Isn't that your desire? Don't you want to lead them wisely?

Are you on the wrong path right now? Is the Lord trying to steer you left but you want to go right? Is He pointing you in a whole new direction, but you are stubbornly refusing to budge? Don't be foolish! Allow the Lord to guide you.

If there is one promise I can give to you it is this: God will never lead you where He can't keep you. If He is leading, you are safe, no matter how dangerous it may appear. Trust Him!

O God, I do indeed need to come to You first before I make any decision. I should know better, but I follow my gut way too much. Help me pause and pray.

JULY 27

LIFE

Exodus 1

BEST VERSE: 17
But the midwives feared God, and did not do as the king of Egypt had commanded them, but let the boys live.

Every year at our church we celebrate Sanctity of Human Life day. It's usually the third Sunday of January. Having worked with ministries who assist mothers with unplanned pregnancies, this is near and dear to my heart. That's why this verse today stuck out to me.

Pharaoh had ordered the midwives to murder the male children upon birth. But they refused. They feared God more than Pharaoh. They knew they were held to a higher law. Understand something clearly. They knew they could have died for their decision, but they stood firm anyway.

TEACHING MOMENT

Parents must teach their children that when man's law clashes with God's law, God's law wins every time. We are fortunate here in America that we haven't been faced with that very often. But I fear the day is coming when we may. Your child may already be facing some decisions at school that come close to that. Be ready to support them and defend them.

But you know, your children are already facing those pressures to conform to a worldly standard by their peers. Hold them to the Word. Encourage them to stand strong. Read them this verse. Look at the result. Moses was saved and eventually was used by God to lead the people out of Egypt. Stand strong!

What are you compromising right now? When you attend that office party or company social event, are you tempted to let your standards down a little. Don't! Don't let the world dictate your standards. Only the Lord can do that. Hold true to the Word and let it guide you.

Lord, You are the Law Giver. I know that. But You are also the Grace Giver. When I fail You by compromising or giving in, please forgive me. Give me the courage to be bold in my witness and lead my children to stand tall and firm.

JULY 28

STRENGTH IN HUMILITY

Genesis 41

BEST VERSE: 16

Joseph then answered Pharaoh, saying, "It is not in me; God will give Pharaoh a favorable answer."

Everyone who has spent any time in Sunday School knows the story of Joseph. It is one of my favorite passages in Genesis. There are so many truths to be gleaned from the story. But what hit me today was the humility of Joseph, even in a very difficult situation.

God had given him a gift of interpreting dreams. In fact, that gift had gotten him where he was—a slave in jail in Egypt. His brothers had grown tired of his dreams and sold him off into slavery. Now, here he is again, interpreting dreams. This time for Pharaoh, who could reward him greatly or kill him. Joseph chooses humility and gives all the credit to God, not himself.

TEACHING MOMENT

How do we teach our children humility? How do we get them to understand that even if the Lord has blessed them with incredible talents, they must remain humble and not proud? It is not easy. But we must do all we can to model and teach humility.

First, we must model it for them. Have you ever had someone brag about you in front of your children? How you handle that praise will tell your children a lot. They will watch how you deal with that attention. Come on, who doesn't like attention? Right? Children sure do. But we have to point any praise to the Father.

Secondly, we have to hold our children accountable when we see them getting that proud, braggadocious spirit. Letting them get by with that will only lead to trouble in the future. There is nothing wrong with them being proud of their accomplishments. But when that pride is shown in order to put someone else down, well, that has to be addressed. Brag on your kids! You should! But also hold them accountable in how they treat others in the process.

So, how about you? What will it take for the Lord to teach you humility? Will it take a prison cell like Joseph? I hope not! Let love be your guide. It is hard to be proud and loving at the same time!

Lord, I don't like to be humbled. But I bow today in humility to You. Show me how to make myself less and You more.

CHOOSE LIFE

Deuteronomy 30

BEST VERSES: 19-20

"I call heaven and earth to witness against you today, that I have set before you life and death, the blessing and the curse. So, choose life in order that you may live, you and your descendants, by loving the LORD your God, by obeying His voice, and by holding fast to Him; for this is your life and the length of your days, that you may live in the land which the LORD swore to your fathers, to Abraham, Isaac, and Jacob, to give them."

Choose life. We hear that phrase a lot these days in regard to the Pro-Life and Pro-Abortion debate. We can even get tags for our vehicles in some states that read "Choose Life." I am solidly Pro-Life and believe that every life, from the moment of conception until the last breath is released, is precious in the eyes of God. But this verse isn't talking about that. Look at what it says.

In this passage Moses is telling the people of Israel just before they enter the Promised Land what life is all about: **1)** loving the Lord God **2)** obeying His voice and **3)** holding fast to Him. Those three things give life. What great principles to teach our children!

TEACHING MOMENT

First, Moses says to love the Lord. That one is easy to teach. Even the smallest child can understand love. We love a lot of stuff. But to love the Lord God means He is the only one deserving of our worship and praise. Teach them that!

Secondly, Moses says to obey His voice. Now this gets a little harder, doesn't it? Even for us adults, that is difficult. What better way to teach our kids to obey God than to teach them to obey the authorities in their lives? I see way too many children who are not taught to obey. Parents let little children pitch fist and then give them what they want. That is NOT teaching obedience. Teach them to obey!

Finally, Moses tells them to hold fast. Our children need to learn to hang on even when things get hard. Too many children (and adults for that matter) bail at the first difficult task or situation. Teach them to stay committed to what they have begun. They need to learn how to stick with something. After all, God will stick with them through eternity. Teach them to hold on!

Again parents, you have to model all three of these yourselves, because our little "angels" learn best by watching us. Love, obey, and hold fast! That is *life worth choosing*!

Father, show me the true meaning of life each day as I interact with those around me. Give me a renewed focus on life seen through Your eyes.

JULY 30

OUR PROTECTOR

Psalms 3–4

BEST VERSE: 3:3
But You, O Lord, are a shield about me, my glory, and the One who lifts my head.

When you read this verse, how do you picture the Lord as your shield? Do you picture Him as Captain America holding a shield in front of you to ward off any attacks? Or do you see Him as someone with a sword in one hand and the shield in the other?

I see Him ALL AROUND ME. The verse says, "a shield about me." I can envision Him above, below, beside, in front, and behind. NOTHING can touch me unless He allows it. That is so comforting. That allows me to relax and just follow Him, even if following Him means I walk headlong into a battle.

TEACHING MOMENT
When we teach our children the all-encompassing love and protection of the Lord, this is a great verse to use. You can even physically show this to them by wrapping them in bubble wrap. Wouldn't that be cool? I bet they wouldn't forget that.

Our children do need to understand that, as believers, God is our Protector. He is our Deliverer. He is the one who lifts our head, as the verse says.

He picks us up when we have fallen. He is ALWAYS there, even when we don't think He is.

How are you doing with this truth, Mom and Dad? Are you trusting Him as your shield? Do you believe He is there defending you? If so, then live like it. Allow the Lord to surround you with His protection. Stay inside that protective "bubble." Don't step out, unless He tells you to.

We struggle with wanting to defend ourselves. But we are no match for our spiritual enemies unless we allow Jesus to defend us. The puniest demon can whip us any day. But with Christ as our defender, we can take on the gates of hell with a water pistol and extinguish those fiery darts sent by Satan himself.

My Shield! My Defender! My Comforter! Lord, You are all of these. I thank You for being there for me at all times.

GOD'S UNSEEN PROTECTION

1 Samuel 29

BEST VERSE: 9
But Achish replied to David, "I know that you are pleasing in my sight, like an angel of God; nevertheless the commanders of the Philistines have said, 'He must not go up with us to the battle.'"

David had been hiding from Saul in the land of the Philistines for a while, and now the epic battle was about to go down, the battle where Saul and his sons, including Jonathan, would be killed. David was prepared, along with his men, to go along and fight. However, the Philistines did not trust David to fight with them. They were afraid he would switch sides in the middle of the battle and fight for Israel. We will never know what would have happened because Achish sent him home.

But think about this. If David and his men HAD fought against Israel in the battle where Saul and his sons were killed, he would have been seen by Israel as having taken part in that. That could have marred his reign as king to begin with. God knew that. Perhaps God was sparing David from that association. David didn't see it at the time, but God was actually fighting for him.

TEACHING MOMENT

Our children will have experiences that are disappointing. They may want a certain job or a certain boyfriend or girlfriend. For some unknown reason, things just don't go the way they wish. Could it be that God is sparing them some pain or hurt? When your child goes through that kind of situation, tell them this story of David's unseen protection from God. Hindsight is always 20/20, but isn't it nice when we can see God's protecting hands around us. Trust that He is always looking after your best interest, as long as you are seeking Him. David was seeking the Lord, even while in the land of the Philistines. God knew that and was working in ways David could not see.

Will you trust the Lord to work in your life? When you get that gentle nudge to do something that may seem ridiculous, but you know it will bring Him honor, just do it. Allow Him to work through you in amazing ways.

Thank you Lord, that I don't have to see You at work to know You are working. Today, help me to bow before Your sovereign hand.

THE YOKE IS ON YOU

Matthew 11

BEST VERSES: 28-30

"Come to Me, all who are weary and heavy-laden, and I will give you rest. Take My yoke upon you and learn from Me, for I am gentle and humble in heart, and YOU WILL FIND REST FOR YOUR SOULS. For My yoke is easy and My burden is light."

Don't you just love this verse? Christ offers to put a yoke on us and promises that it will be easy. Right! I've heard that before. I have heard that from previous bosses. Not me! No way!

Now wait a minute. Let's look at this. He said take "My yoke," not just any yoke. That yoke has a place for two. Jesus on one side and you on the other. He would be the one directing and leading. He would take the responsibility of the load, not you. He just wants you to come along and learn.

When someone back then yoked two animals together, they always had one that knew what they were doing. The other, perhaps younger, animal would sometimes pull against the older one in the yoke and cause chaffing or sores to develop. When the pain got too much, the younger animal would reluctantly go along with the older animal, thus reducing the strain on those sore spots.

TEACHING MOMENT

Don't you think our children pull against the yoke sometimes? You are leading them in one direction, but they are determined to go in another. Can I give you some advice? YOU are the lead oxen. YOU must lead them. YOU must show them how to plow or carry that burden. They do not know how to do this yet. Stop being so "child friendly" and be "yoke friendly." God has put you in that yoke for a reason—to lead them. But you can only lead them as you allow Jesus to lead you.

I don't know about you, but I don't like to hurt. Won't you allow Jesus to put His yoke on you? Won't you let Him lead? It is a lot less painful.

Lord, when you lead me, remind me to follow. I need to learn to lead, and only You can teach me. Help me lead others in the same way You lead me.

SEEING SPOTS

Genesis 30

BEST VERSES: 31B–32

And Jacob said, "You shall not give me anything. If you will do this one thing for me, I will again pasture and keep your flock: let me pass through your entire flock today, removing from there every speckled and spotted sheep and every black one among the lambs and the spotted and speckled among the goats; and such shall be my wages."

How shrewd! Jacob pulled a fast one on Laban. Do you know the story? He removed all the sheep and goats mentioned above. And then used what seemed like trickery to get the rest of the goats and sheep to have more spotted and speckled offspring, which Jacob claimed for his own.

This, of course, allowed Jacob to build his flocks at the expense of Laban, who had cheated Jacob all the previous years. I am not sure exactly what the purpose was, except the Lord wanted to bless Jacob and return him to his homeland a rich and prosperous man, just as He had promised him those many years ago.

TEACHING MOMENT

So, what can you teach your children with this story? Can you say, "Just trick your way to wealth!"? Or maybe "Use whatever you can to get ahead."? Of course not! The Lord does not want us to be deceptive or dishonest. He does, however, want us to work hard and be a blessing to others.

Jacob didn't steal a single lamb or goat. He made an honest deal with Laban and then went about doing all he could to build up his flock. Honest, hard work. There is nothing wrong with that. Our kids need to know that. And who did it bless? Jacob's children and even his brother Esau, whom he would see later.

Are you working justly? Are you working to please yourself or the Lord? He is the one who deserves our best efforts. When we please Him in our work, we will almost always please our employers (if we have one). It's all about pleasing the true Master.

O Lord, I want to please You. May You give me the strength to work as unto You. Let my work be a blessing for others.

JEALOUS

Deuteronomy 4

BEST VERSE: 24
For the Lord your God is a consuming fire, a jealous God.

Did you know your God is jealous? In fact, in Exodus 34:14 it reads, "for you shall not worship any other god, for the LORD, whose name is Jealous, is a jealous God" His NAME IS JEALOUS!!! Now that's serious.

But what does that mean? Does He stalk you like a jealous boyfriend? Does He call you incessantly if you break up with Him? Of course not. He is jealous in that He demands full allegiance. He wants your full attention. He does not allow you to "say" you love Him and then flirt with other "gods."

TEACHING MOMENT
Children need to learn that our Holy God will not allow them to make Him just another interest. He is not interested in sharing their attention. He is the ONLY God, and He requires us to recognize that. Our children will be bombarded by other religions and their false teachings. They will hear from others that there are many gods and many ways to heaven. There aren't!

I am sure your children will sooner or later have a jealous moment over a friend. That's a perfect time to share this verse. This verse will help them understand the emotions they feel in a jealous moment. You, as mom or dad, need to talk to them about how that type of jealousy is not of God. But also share with them how God is jealous for them. He will defend them. He will cherish them. They are HIS.

And you? Are you a jealous type? Do you get jealous over little things? Do you get jealous when you see your husband or your wife flirt with someone else? You should. You have sole rights as spouse. God has sole rights to you, too. Don't forget it. No other gods before Him.

I recommit myself to You today. Thank You for Your selfless love You have shown us by giving Your Son to die for us. I want to show You my love and devotion today.

THE TITHE

Genesis 14

BEST VERSE: 20C
He gave him a tenth of all.

Many believe this is the start of the ten percent tithe. Whether it is or not is really not important. The point is, Abram blessed Melchizedek king of Salem by giving him this gift. What a great example to follow!

I really love what Abram said when Melchizedek tried to give him part of the stuff he had brought back after defeating the king who had taken Lot. He said, "Nope, I won't take one thing. God is my provider." Well, that's not exactly what he said, but it was the general idea.

TEACHING MOMENT
Now this is something you have to model for your kids. But, if you aren't tithing yourself, it's hard to model it. And you have to show them what this means. They need to know how you give, not so much how much, but how. You need to teach them to give from their money, not yours.

"But Carl, they don't want to give their money." Well, they won't ever do it unless you help them. But the most important part is the joy that comes from being a blessing. The joy comes **after** you give. The joy comes from being obedient.

If you aren't "being obedient," start now. Giving is one aspect of life as believers we don't talk about much. Nor should we. What and how you give is between you and God. But you should give. Be a blessing. Be obedient. Be joyful!

Giver of all, I know I can depend on You to supply all my needs. Teach me to be a sacrificial giver. And Lord, help me teach others to give so they too will be blessed by You.

EXCUSES

1 Samuel 13

BEST VERSE: 8

Now he waited seven days, according to the appointed time set by Samuel, but Samuel did not come to Gilgal; and the people were scattering from him.

You really need to read chapters 13—15. In fact, from the moment Samuel anointed Saul as king of Israel, Saul started making excuses. It seems he was always justifying or rationalizing why he did what he did. This verse today is just another excuse. "Samuel, you are late. I had to do something."

We, of course, know what follows. God "rips" the kingdom from Saul and gives it to the boy David. Israel's first king may have been head and shoulders above all other men physically, but a young shepherd boy stood way above him in devotion to the Lord.

TEACHING MOMENT

Teaching our children to obey is hard, isn't it? A lot of the time they do not understand our rules or they try to change them. Sometimes they completely ignore them. Then there are consequences, and the excuses begin. We've all been there, right? Little Johnny can give you a hundred reasons why he did what he did, knowing he was going against your rules.

Listen Mom and Dad! You must hold true to your convictions. Don't give in to their excuses or tears. Samuel held the king accountable for disobeying the Lord. Saul offered the sacrifices, which wasn't his responsibility. He had no authority, even as king, to do that. So, he had to suffer the consequence of losing the kingdom.

Before you judge Saul too quickly, think about how many times YOU have rationalized your actions. "But Carl, I HAD to do something." Really? God is a "right on time" God. Sometimes He delays His actions just to see if we will be faithful and wait on Him. He is not tempting us toward evil. But He is testing our faithfulness.

Will you today allow the Father, through the Son, to remind you Who is in charge? It "ain't" you! We are to wait and wait and wait until God shows up. Then and only then will we see the hand of God working in our lives.

Almighty God of the universe, work as only You can work. I will wait on You, for You will NOT disappoint.

THERE ARE ALWAYS CONSEQUENCES

Deuteronomy 28

BEST VERSE: 15

"But it shall come about, if you do not obey the Lord your God, to observe to do all His commandments and His statutes with which I charge you today, that all these curses will come upon you and overtake you."

This is a tough chapter. While verses 1–14 tell about God's blessings for obedience, verses 15–68 describe the consequences for disobedience. I don't know about you, but I definitely prefer blessings over punishment.

I know what some of you are thinking. *Carl, this is Old Testament, so it doesn't apply to me as a Christian.* Really? Do you think a holy God is still going to allow you to thumb your nose at Him and live a life of disobedience? Not hardly. Now, if you truly are a believer, you should be very careful to obey Him. Why? Because you love Him. That's simple.

TEACHING MOMENT

I don't need to explain to you how to apply this verse, do I? As a parent it seems we are always dishing out either consequences or praises. I prefer to praise children. It is a lot more fun. I love catching kids doing the right thing. Let me encourage you to do the same. Look for the good stuff rather than the bad stuff.

I had a teenage boy in a children's home I served in once who was a very negative leader. But he definitely had leadership skills. After months of constantly disciplining him for his negative actions, I realized I needed to find ways to use his leadership skills in positive ways. So, I began to give him small tasks to do that would allow him to lead others. Slowly but surely, he started leading positively. "Blessings" rather than "curses" followed.

What are you focused on in life? Are you so distracted with your own pursuits that you don't even stop to make sure that you are living obediently?

Examine your choices and line them up with God's Word. You may be surprised with the outcome.

Thank You Father, for the blessings You send to me. I know the disciplines I receive from You are to shape me into a more useable vessel. Help me choose obedience every day.

REMEMBERING IS GOOD

Deuteronomy 24

BEST VERSE: 9
"Remember what the Lord your God did to Miriam on the way as you came out of Egypt."

Do you remember this story about Miriam? She and Aaron had complained about Moses' Cushite wife, so Miriam was stricken with leprosy (Numbers 12). God did heal her, but the ceremonial cleansing held up the entire nation from traveling any further. One woman's sin affected millions. Moses is reminding the people to not repeat such an offense.

Our sins do affect others. We may think it is only between us and God, but others may be forced to endure consequences brought about by our disobedience. How unfair is that? How dare we think we can live isolated and alone!

TEACHING MOMENT
You'll deal with this when one of your children does something to thwart a family outing. Such actions can affect the whole family. It is so important that you talk to all your children when or if this happens. They need to see that one person's actions affect everyone.

I can hear the kids screaming now, "That's not fair!" And it's not, but it's life. God does not want us living alone. We need each other, through the thick and thin of it. We need to hang together through the trials as well as the good times. And we need to be held accountable by others.

Will you be accountable today? Will you allow others' behavior to dictate how you react? Don't let it. No matter what they do, you do what you know is right according to God's Word. Maybe then you will be the source of progress and not holding up the group, like Miriam.

Lord, forgive my selfish attitude. Forgive me when I purposely choose to follow my desires rather than what is best for all.

WHO ARE YOU TALKING TO?

Matthew 7

BEST VERSE: 21

"Not everyone who says to Me, 'Lord, Lord,' will enter the kingdom of heaven, but he who does the will of My Father who is in heaven will enter.'"

Boy, I tell you what! There are many today for whom this holds true. I hear our nation scream out to God when a tragedy strikes, but then protest if a football coach prays with his players before a game. They cry out "Lord, Lord" and then slam the door in His face.

But the beauty of the Lord is He understands them. I may not, but He does. He knows their motives for prayer. He waits to hear that prayer of repentance, and then He can move in and do wonderful things for them. Now does that mean He will intercede for an unbeliever? He may, but it will be for one purpose—to draw that unbeliever to Him and to disclose Himself for the purpose of deliverance.

TEACHING MOMENT

When our children are just learning to walk and talk, we need to teach them to pray. It is so sweet to watch them fold their hands and pray for everyone under the sun, even the pets. But our teaching about prayer should always be pointing them to the most important prayer—the prayer of confession and repentance that leads to salvation. It is so important that our children learn to pray. God will draw them to Himself. When your children hear Him speaking to them, they will tell you. But in the meantime, keep teaching them about prayer.

Why are you crying out to God? What is your motive today? Will you bow first in confession to Him and ask for forgiveness and cleansing of your sins? Oh, how God wants to work in your life. Bow, surrender, confess, and then call Him Abba Father.

Father, I know You are listening. Give me the boldness to talk to You, even when I don't feel like it. Remind me today that You are just waiting to hear from me.

NOT FORGOTTEN
2 Samuel 9

BEST VERSE: 7
David said to him, "Do not fear, for I will surely show kindness to you for the sake of your father Jonathan, and will restore to you all the land of your grandfather Saul; and you shall eat at my table regularly."

This story of Mephibosheth has always blessed me. After David has solidified his kingdom he starts thinking about his old friend, Jonathan, Saul's son. They had been "covenant brothers." David had promised to protect Jonathan's family once he became king. So, David seeks out any of the family who may still be alive.

Can you imagine, though, Mephibosheth's fear when the king's soldiers arrive at his house to take him to David. He probably thought this was it. The day had finally arrived when David would kill him in order to rid the land of any of Saul's descendants. He probably had no idea of the covenant between his father and David. What a wonderful surprise and blessing when he was received by David with such love.

TEACHING MOMENT
Promises are something we need to teach our kids about. When we give our word, it means something. When we give our word, we need to keep it, not matter how long that means. Childhood promises made may not mean a lot when they are made, but the whole idea of making promises should not be taken lightly.

Probably the most visible "promise" your children see in you is the promise you made to your husband or wife (if you are married). They need to see you keeping your promises to love, honor, and cherish each other. You are teaching them, in the way you do that, how they will treat their spouse one day. Promises made should be promises kept.

What promise have you broken? What covenant relationship has become a forgotten one in your life? It's not too late to make that right. I doubt the other person has forgotten it either. Now, you can't make the other person keep their side of the covenant. But you can make sure they know you are sorry you failed to live up to your side.

Oh Father, this is a hard one. I have made mistakes. I have broken promises. Help me be more like David in this. Help me to be true to my relationships.

AUGUST 10

BRIGHT LIGHT

Psalms 35–36

BEST VERSE: 36:9B
In Your light we see light.

It's hard to see in the dark without a good light. We all know that. That's common sense. But this verse confused me. How do you see light in the light? That has to be a really bright light, right?

But if you look at the verse from a spiritual side, you can understand what David is saying. If we stay in God's light, we can see light. God gives us the ability to see the light around us. He allows us to recognize the light in others. He shines His light upon us so that we can see His light.

TEACHING MOMENT
Children love playing with flashlights in the dark. Get a good one and play along with them. Get in a really dark room and turn it on. Talk about the shadows it casts upon the walls. Talk about the things in the room you really can't see too well unless you shine the light directly on them.

Now turn on the room light, hopefully an overhead light. Now talk about how you can see everything more clearly. You don't need to shine your flashlight at stuff because you are in the light from the room. It makes things more visible. You can recognize all the things in the room easily. God will shine His light directly on us and, in so doing, He illuminates the world for us. He exposes the hidden things.

You see, God doesn't want us tripping. He doesn't want us stumbling. But if you are like me, sometimes I want to hide in the darkness. I have to remember that the light of Jesus dwells within me through the power of the Holy Spirit. I must stay in the light and shine my light, not for me, but for others. I need to point them to the Light.

Light of the world, You shine upon me. You are the brightest light. There is no other light that draws men like Yours.

AUGUST 11

IS IT OKAY TO LIE?

2 Samuel 17

BEST VERSE: 7

So Hushai said to Absalom, "This time the advice that Ahithophel has given is not good."

I bet you have struggled with that question before, right? If someone comes into your house at night to harm your family and demands to know where your children are, what are you going to do? You had better believe I am going to lie to protect my children. Evil is evil and won't honor you for telling the truth, no matter what.

Hushai knew Ahithophel's advice was the better advice. Absalom could have caught David quickly and killed the King, so Hushai lied to protect his King. He knew Absalom's rebellion was evil. What would you have done? I would have done the same.

TEACHING MOMENT

But now comes the hard part. How do you explain this to your child? How do you explain to your children that it is okay to lie sometimes? That's difficult. I can only see one reason to tell them to do that—to protect someone's life who is innocent. Other than that, there is no reason.

Your son might ask, "How about to protect my toys?" Nope, *things* don't matter. "How about to keep from getting into trouble?" Nope, truth will always come out, anyway. Only to protect the innocent life of someone.

Some of you may disagree with me on this, and that is okay. You can just be wrong. Seriously, we may disagree. You may believe that a lie is never acceptable. I truly believe that God will understand a lie to protect precious lives. He also protects the innocent.

Father, if I am wrong about this please tell me. I will lay down my life for others, but I can't see giving innocent lives to those who want to harm them. Give me the boldness to die for others.

AUGUST 12

DO YOU SEE THAT?

Mark 10

BEST VERSE: 51
And answering him, Jesus said, "What do you want Me to do for you?" And the blind man said to Him, "Rabboni, I want to regain my sight!"

You know, when I first read this verse I was like, "What a stupid question." I mean, Jesus, can't you tell what he wanted. He was blind, for crying out loud. Even a child could tell what he wanted.

But before we go there, think about it. This man was blind and was making a living begging. He didn't have to work. He sat around all day. People probably helped him get around when needed. Perhaps he put up with his blindness. After all, if he regained his sight, he might have to be "normal." It says he wanted to "regain," but we really don't know if he had been born blind or had lost his sight. Either way, the first thing he would see when healed would be Jesus.

Jesus wasn't one to assume anything. He didn't need to ask the question. Since He was God, He knew what Bartimaeus wanted. He knew his motive. How many times have you questioned your children when they asked for something even though you knew why they were asking? Did you refuse them? Did you give them what they wanted? Would you give them something that would harm them? Of course not. You would only give them things that blessed them or was good for them.

Our children need to know they can come to us for anything. But they also need to learn that we won't give them things that we know aren't good for them, no matter how much they want them. We want to open their eyes to see the difference between good and evil. We want them, like Bartimaeus, to see Jesus. What a sight to behold.

Open my eyes, Lord. I want to see Jesus. That's all I truly need to see. Help my blind eyes see the truth each and every day.

AUGUST 13

FAVORITES

Genesis 48

BEST VERSE: 19
But his father refused and said, "I know, my son, I know; he also will become a people and he also will be great. However, his younger brother shall be greater than he, and his descendants shall become a multitude of nations."

What was Israel (Jacob) thinking? Didn't he realize Manasseh deserved the blessing before Ephraim? Joseph tried to switch his father's hands, but Israel stopped hm. Why? Do you remember Israel's story? He had tricked his brother Esau into giving him his birthright, and then he and his mother Rachel had tricked his father into getting Esau's blessing.

But I don't think Israel did this as a repeat of his own deceitfulness. I believe he truly knew Ephraim would be greater than Manasseh. I am not sure why, but he knew. After his explanation, Joseph allowed his father to continue. To the best of our knowledge neither Ephraim nor Manasseh ever complained about it either.

TEACHING MOMENT

If you have more than one child, do you treat one differently than the other. Now, before you say "no" stop and think about it. It is natural to do so. They are different people who respond to you differently. Treating them differently is NOT necessarily tantamount to showing favoritism to one over the other.

Your children need to know that they are just as important as the other. Children get their self-image from what they believe their parents think about them. Did you know that? Although you may relate better to one over the other, they don't need to see that. Love them differently but love the same. Get it?

The Lord loves all believers the same—unconditionally. He does, however, love us differently according to how we respond to His guidance and direction. He is able to bless those who obey. So, are you allowing the Lord to love you as much as He wants to?

Remember, we all will receive the blessing!

God, I am thankful You see us all the same. You recognize our gifts and abilities and use us differently. But we are all equal in Your eyes. Help me to see others as You do.

AUGUST 14

TWO JUDGES

Psalms 49–50

BEST VERSES: 50:4–5
He summons the heavens above, and the earth, to judge His people: "Gather My godly ones to Me, those who have made a covenant with Me by sacrifice."

I will have to admit that I do not remember these verses. That happens a lot, though. I have read through the Bible many times, but each year I find verses that I just don't remember. These two today are in that group.

God is directing the heavens and the earth to gather His people. Look at how we are identified. God calls us "godly ones." We are the ones "who have made a covenant" with Him. We are protected by that covenant that was made through the blood of Jesus. I love that God has called us "godly ones."

TEACHING MOMENT
I know your children are precious to you. Whether they are three or thirty-three, our children are special. But are they godly? We know we are all born sinners. We are born in flesh. Only God's redeeming power can make us godly. There is not one thing in us that can do that.

So, one of your jobs is to make your children godly. You say, "Right Carl! I can't do that." That's correct. Your job is to direct them and lead them to the one who can. You provide the environment where they can discover the truth. You teach them God's Word, which will draw them to Him. You pray for them and with them to show them how to talk to God. He will do the rest.

Do you consider yourself to be a godly person? God does, if you are one of His. Start living like it, if you are not. Remember with whom you are in covenant. Let His attributes be lived out in your life each day.

Righteous Judge, You may send the heavens and the earth to gather me one day. I am excited about that. I am ready to see You. Help me share the good news with others while I am here.

WHERE IS YOUR TREASURE?

Luke 12

BEST VERSE: 34
"For where your treasure is, there your heart will be also."

I remember when I was a young boy, my father helped me open up a savings account at the Coats & Clark Credit Union. The plant he worked for in Pelham, Georgia, allowed children of employees to put money in a savings account. I had my own little savings book where I could record deposits and withdrawals (even though those were hard to get approved by my dad). I was so proud of that little book because it showed my "wealth."

It wasn't until I was older that I realized how little wealth I had. All those dollars and cents that seemed so big when I was little didn't really add up to a whole lot when I was older and really wanted to buy something expensive.

In the same way, all these "treasures" we build up on earth don't mean a lot when we think about their eternal value. You've probably heard the saying, "You've never seen a hearse pulling a U-Haul." It is true you can't take it with you. So, where is your treasure?

We need to point our children toward searching for spiritual treasure. This is the treasure we find in God's Word. His Word is so rich in life application truths. These are riches that defy words. These are riches which we can easily share with others without depleting the account. In fact, I have found that the more I give of these spiritual truths the more I get in return. Try that in the marketplace!

How rich do you want your kids to be? To what source of "treasures" are you directing them? Are you willing to "invest" in their future through God's Word? His blessings await.

Father, even though I may never be "rich" in the world's eyes, I am rich beyond measure. Your love and compassion enrich my life more than any earthly wealth. Thank You for blessing me.

AUGUST 16

WELL PLEASED

Matthew 3

BEST VERSE: 17
. . . and behold, a voice out of the heavens said, "This is My beloved Son, in whom I am well-pleased."

Jesus was always pleasing His Father. He knew no other way to live. Every thought He had was directed toward that. He had a mission to complete, which He knew would please the Father. Nothing else mattered . . . just please the Father by His works, by His words, by . . . everything He did.

Isn't that a worthy example to follow? Now, we weren't sent to earth to die for mankind. There is only one Savior. But we do have a mission. Our mission is to share the love of Christ with as many as possible. Our mission is to be Jesus to the lost around us. When we do that, we also please the Father. Then we can hear Him say, "This is My beloved in whom I am well pleased."

TEACHING MOMENT

Don't you love when your children are obedient? Of course, you love them regardless, but when they obey you willingly, doesn't it just warm your heart?

Tell them. They need to hear that. They say it takes ten praises to balance out one criticism. I don't know if that is true or not, but I do know it is much better to praise than critique.

The next time your son or daughter does something before you ask them to do it, praise them. Tell them you are well-pleased. Tell them how it makes you feel when you see them choosing right rather than wrong. And then tell them how their heavenly Father is also well-pleased with those choices. They really need to hear that.

Are you pleasing the Father today? Are you willing to accomplish the mission God has given you? If you are grateful for your salvation, share it. Tell someone today about Jesus. The Father will smile.

Father, I want to see You smile on me. I know You love me regardless, but I want to please You. Help me tell others just how great You are.

AUGUST 17

DO IT NOW!

Genesis 35

BEST VERSE: 1
Then God said to Jacob, "Arise, go up to Bethel and live there, and make an altar there to God, who appeared to you when you fled from your brother Esau."

I love the fact that God said, "Go," and Jacob went. He didn't ask any questions. He didn't make any excuses. He just went.

How about you? Has God clearly given you some directions in life, and you've just made excuse after excuse? *God, I can't do that. I'm too old. . . . God, that doesn't make sense. . . . God, are You crazy?* Well, maybe that last one is going too far. But you get the drift. We piddle around and ignore His direct instructions for our life. You may say, "But I haven't heard any direct instructions." If you read the Bible, you have seen the instructions.

TEACHING MOMENT
Don't you get frustrated with your children when you ask them to clean their room ten times and have to threaten them within an inch of their lives (just kidding) to get them to do it? Prompt obedience is so important. Teaching

your children to obey the first time prepares them for life in the classroom, the workplace, and with God. But it's not about control. It's about training.

They will obey as they see you obey. Will you be obedient the first time? Will you obey God no matter what He says? I promise He will not lead you astray. What He says may seem crazy, but it is not. It is the pure truth! Trust Him!

Father, help me to trust Your commands. Even when I don't understand them, help me to trust them. I want to obey. Give me that nudge I need today.

GOING ABOVE AND BEYOND

Joshua 4

BEST VERSE: 9
Then Joshua set up twelve stones in the middle of the Jordan at the place where the feet of the priests who carried the ark of the covenant were standing, and they are there to this day.

I've looked, and I can't find anywhere that God told Joshua to do this. He was supposed to take stones and set them up on the bank, cover them with lime and mark the commandments on them. But nowhere does God say, "Set up a monument in the Jordan." So, why does Joshua do this, and was it being disobedient?

Obviously, God didn't mind since Joshua wasn't chastised for it. We don't know how deep the Jordan was normally at the crossing site, but probably once the waters returned you couldn't see those rocks. But the people would know they were there. They could remember the wall of water that was backed up so they could cross. Maybe years later, when the river got low you could see them. Who knows?

TEACHING MOMENT
We need markers in our lives. Children need to be taught to mark milestones in their walk with Christ. When a prayer is answered, mark it down. When a healing occurs, mark it down. When a new direction is given, mark it down.

Why? Because we tend to forget the details of the pivotal moments. We need to teach our children to retail these stories to their children one day.

Every moment of our lives is watched over by God. He will direct us, if we will let Him. But He won't force us toward direction. Not forcing us, though, hardly means He is not keenly aware of what is going on. Children learn this by watching us in our own walk. Make them part of your journey.

Are you going through a "redirection" right now? Is God sending you down a new path? How about your children? Are they facing a big decision? Set up your stones. Mark the spot. One day you will look back and say, "That's where I crossed my Jordan."

O God, You are the One who tells me where to cross the Jordans in my life. Help me to trust that You know exactly the perfect spot. Teach me to lead my children in their own crossings.

AUGUST 19

I CAN'T STOP LOOKING

Daniel 7

BEST VERSES: 9–10

I kept looking until thrones were set up, and the Ancient of Days took His seat; His vesture was like white snow and the hair of His head like pure wool. His throne was ablaze with flames, its wheels were a burning fire. A river of fire was flowing and coming out from before Him; thousands upon thousands were attending Him, and myriads upon myriads were standing before Him; the court sat, and the books were opened.

Have you ever come across a scene that is both terrifying and incredible? I mean, you want to turn away, but you just can't. You have to try to take it all in. Every part of you screams, "Turn away! Stop looking." But you have to keep staring at the scene.

I imagine Daniel felt like that when he had this vision. Chapters 7–12 of Daniel are the prophecy section of the book. Fortunately for us, God did not leave him hanging. He not only gave him the vision of the end times, but he gave him (and us) the meaning. I just think it is fitting that these chapters begin with the vision of God on His throne. Terrifying but inviting! Astonishing and amazing!

On your next road trip or vacation, you may have the opportunity to see something amazing. Your kids will probably drop their jaws and scream, "Wow!" Take that opportunity to share this verse. Their imagination can fill in the picture. Explain to them that God sitting on His throne will be magnificent. And we, as believers, will see that one day. We will approach that throne with confidence, not in fear. We will see His glory! We will be bathed in His light.

Kids love to imagine stuff. Some of your children may have the artistic ability to draw or paint. Why not have them draw this scene? Let them put their imagination on paper! Why not? You may even get a glimpse of His glory through your child.

May I teach my child that You are always on Your throne. Thank You that You are an approachable, loving God. I love You, "O Ancient of Days."

AUGUST 20

HIDDEN GODS

Genesis 31

BEST VERSE: 34A

Now Rachel had taken the household idols and put them in the camel's saddle, and she sat on them.

Don't you bet Jacob had told Rachel about how he had deceived his brother, Esau? You know she knew the stories. So why wouldn't she deceive her father, Laban, by stealing his gods? She stole them and hid them. Those gods were NOT found when Laban searched for them, which means they traveled with Rachel all the way.

Now don't forget this—people don't steal gods just to keep them hidden. She obviously was worshiping them. She had even hidden them from Jacob. He had no idea they were there, at least not then. I wonder if he ever found out.

TEACHING MOMENT

Have you ever found something your child has hidden from you? Perhaps they stole it from a store or from someone else. Anyway, you don't recognize it and have no idea where it came from. What do you do? Do you just ignore it? Of course not. You confront your child about it. Why? Because these kinds of habits have to be dealt with quickly or they become hard to stop.

Are you teaching your little ones about truth and honesty? Do they know the importance of respecting others' property? Do you? Are you giving them a prime example to follow? Hidden things can become hidden "gods." They will drain all your energy trying to keep them concealed. They will rob you of your integrity. Put a halt to the hiding.

Father, I know that truth is always the best practice. Sometimes, though, it is so hard. Help me point my children to always be upfront and honest about ALL THINGS.

AUGUST 21

LISTEN UP

Deuteronomy 27

BEST VERSES: 9-10

Then Moses and the Levitical priests spoke to all Israel, saying, "Be silent and listen, O Israel! This day you have become a people for the Lord your God. You shall therefore obey the Lord your God, and do His commandments and His statutes which I command you today."

Two words stood out to me in these verses today. Can you spot them? Moses has just given the people the laws by which God will hold them accountable in the Promised Land. And then he says, "This day you have become a people for the Lord your God." THIS DAY! Wait just a minute! I thought they were already the Lord's people. Didn't He choose them, and didn't He lead them out of Egypt? Didn't He promise them this land they were about to enter?

Yes, but on this day, Moses was commissioning them through the power of God to be a brand new nation. All their past wanderings in the desert were over. All those who had rebelled against God forty years earlier were dead. They were indeed His people at last, and He was ready to usher them into the Promised Land.

The same is true for us and our children. We may grow up knowing all about God. We may teach our children about God. We may take them to church and Sunday School. They may make all the little crafts about Noah and the ark, Moses and the ten commandments or Jesus in the manger. But until we each surrender our lives to His will and become His child, we are not His people.

Read this passage to your children and tell them that they too must make a decision to follow Christ. They won't get into heaven with your faith. Just as the Israelites had to choose to follow the Lord into the Promised Land, they must choose to follow Christ. But once they do that, once they accept Him as their Lord and Savior, they are forever His.

Are you following Him today? Are you surrendered to His Will? Stop wandering in the desert. Listen up! Hear the Lord calling you today to be His child. Allow Him to point you in the direction He has for you today.

Lord, I trust You to guide me each day. I may not understand all the reasons I am going down this road, but as long as I end up with You in heaven, I am okay. I love You Lord.

AUGUST 22

GOOD HONEY OR BAD HONEY

1 Samuel 14

BEST VERSE: 27

But Jonathan had not heard when his father put the people under oath; therefore, he put out the end of the staff that was in his hand and dipped it in the honeycomb, and put his hand to his mouth, and his eyes brightened.

Without knowing it, Jonathan had disobeyed his father, Saul. He was busy fighting the Philistines and had not heard the command to fast until the battle was over. But he was faint from all the fighting and knew the honey would restore his energy to continue the fight.

It's interesting when he found out about the command that he remarked how foolish it was (verses 29–30). But when he came back to his father and it was revealed what he had done, he was willing to die for his disobedience (verse 43). He recognized his father's right as king to make any command.

So, what is this story about? How do we teach it to our children? One lesson we can get from this is Jonathan's submission to his father. Even though he disagreed with the command, he was willing to accept the consequence for his disobedience. He had disobeyed unknowingly, but he had still disobeyed.

Your children are going to question your authority. If not already, it will happen. Remember, questioning your authority does not weaken your authority. You are still the parent. Our children need to see that authority carries with it the requirement to lead them correctly and fairly. And when you blow it (and you will), you have the wherewithal to make it right.

What command of God are you questioning right now? Are you remorseful when confronted? Are you willing to accept the consequence? Be like Jonathan. Let God direct you. And when He does, follow. Period!

Lord, I may not understand or even agree with all your directives in my life, but I want to follow. Help me make my heart more submissive to Your Will.

AUGUST 23

HAND-ME-DOWNS

Deuteronomy 29

BEST VERSE: 5
I have led you forty years in the wilderness; your clothes have not worn out on you, and your sandal has not worn out on your foot.

How many of you have worn hand-me-downs? You know, the clothes your older siblings wore? When I was growing up, I would get some of my older brother's clothes. I couldn't wear his pants because my legs were so big, I wore husky-plus pants. Don't laugh! But I did wear a lot of his shirts and shoes.

The children of Israel had forty years of hand-me-downs. It says their clothes did not wear out, nor did their sandals. Now, how would you feel wearing your grandparents' hand-me-downs? The point of this is the Lord took care of them down to the very stitch of clothing and the soles of their feet.

The next time you pass down some clothing from one child to another, remind them of this story. Passing down clothing is a good way to fully utilize a resource God with which has blessed us. If you don't have other children, pass them down to another family or a thrift shop that can sell them.

Your child probably will not want to wear those hand-me-downs. And don't make them wear something inappropriate for them. But they need to know that we are to be thankful for everything we receive from the Lord, even hand-me-downs.

How about you? What has the Lord "passed down" to you? Are you avoiding "wearing" it? Perhaps, your church has appointed you, due to your giftedness, to handle a responsibility there. Are you rejecting that? If you know that "fits," you must pick it up and serve.

We tend to reject hand-me-downs. We prefer the newest fashions. God, however, has been passing down hand-me-downs for generations. We should gladly receive any and all hand-me-downs He gives us. That seemingly worn out "gift" may be just what we need to fulfill our walk with Him.

Father, You know exactly what will fit us. I trust You to "fit" me. You know my size.

AUGUST 24

GENEALOGIES

Ruth 4

BEST VERSES: 16–17

Then Naomi took the child and laid him in her lap, and became his nurse. The neighbor women gave him a name, saying, "A son has been born to Naomi!" So they named him Obed. He is the father of Jesse, the father of David.

Don't you just love the story of Ruth? Here is a young woman who is widowed at a young age. She travels back with her mother-in-law to a land she has never been. She humbles herself to serve her mother-in-law, to the point of even following her instructions to get married to a relative she didn't really know. Do you think that would happen today? Not hardly.

But God used Ruth in the line of Judah to accomplish His plan for mankind. She gave birth to Obed, the grandfather of King David. I bet Ruth had no idea the impact her son would have on the nation of Israel—and eventually mankind itself.

TEACHING MOMENT

Is there someone in your family tree whom you can point out to your child who made an impact on your family? Perhaps there is some interesting, little known fact about them that they should know. In the same way, your child may have an impact on your family or the world. We never know how one life can affect thousands or even millions.

Read them the story of Ruth, if possible, in one sitting. It won't take long. This would be a great bedtime story. Explain how we should be willing to serve the Lord in the same way Ruth served Naomi—unselfishly. Laying down our rights for the benefit of another is a humbling thing. The Lord will bless us for it.

Can you relate to Ruth? Are you willing to lay down your pride for the sake of others? You never know how God may take that action on your part and bless it to benefit the following generations. Being God's vessel in the life of another is a privilege and an honor.

Lord, use me today in the life of someone who needs change. Allow me to be part of your master plan for their life.

AUGUST 25

LISTEN THE FIRST TIME

Daniel 4

BEST VERSE: 37

"Now I, Nebuchadnezzar, praise, exalt and honor the King of heaven, for all His works are true and His ways just, and He is able to humble those who walk in pride."

Chapter 4 of Daniel is the story of Nebuchadnezzar's humiliation. He had a dream. It was interpreted by Daniel. Daniel warned him. He didn't listen. The dream came true. AND then he realized God was right all along.

Boy, he could have sure used those seven years differently, couldn't he? Instead of living wild and eating grass, he could have been serving the Lord. Instead of being out of his mind, he could have had the mind of God. Instead of his hair and his nails growing out, he could have been growing in his knowledge of the Lord.

TEACHING MOMENT

Unfortunately, there are some things our children have to learn on their own. Trusting the Lord's Word to be true is one of them. Sure, we can tell them and show through our own lives, but they still have to experience it themselves. They have to come to a point where they make that decision to believe Him.

Our prayer must be that they learn this quickly instead of making a mess of things. Our prayer must be that they decide at an early age to follow Jesus rather than the world. Our prayer must be that they bow their knees in worship rather than beg for mercy and restoration.

Nebuchadnezzar learned the hard way. How about you? Are you hardheaded and proud like he was? We have the benefit of God's Word to show us how to live. Turn to it today and ask the Lord to show you what HE wants you to do. He will.

O Lord, I prefer not to live with the beast and eat grass. I prefer to sit at Your banquet table and feast on Your Word. Forgive me of my haughtiness and pride. Let me live today totally submissive to You and Your Will.

AUGUST 26

PROPHECY

Psalms 21–22

BEST VERSE: 22:1

My God, my God, why have You forsaken me? Far from my deliverance are the words of my groaning.

These words of David, spoken way before Christ, are the same words Christ spoke on the cross. Did David know his words would be used by the Messiah, the Son of God? No! David was just a man like the rest of us, but he did have a heart to please the Lord. He, in penning these words, was being guided by the Holy Spirit, just like every other author of the Bible.

Don't you think God can use us in the same way? Now I don't mean in writing prophecy. I mean don't you think if we are yielded, He can use us to speak into the lives of others the truths of His Word? Of course He can. But we have to be willing to be used. We have the advantage of knowing His complete Word, something David didn't have. We have the blessing of the permanent indwelling of the Holy Spirit, something David didn't have.

TEACHING MOMENT

We can teach our children to speak into the lives of others using God's Word. Our part is training them in the Word. We must be deliberate in teaching them to get the Word inside their hearts, not just their minds. By "ingesting" the Word, they will always have it at their disposal to share with others.

Just last night I was at a funeral visitation and had the opportunity to share a short word with one of the family members. He was saying how he was about to crash after "being strong" all week for everyone else. God gave me the opportunity to speak truth into his life (without preaching) in just a few short words using His Word.

Our children need to see us doing that. And as we do it, they see how God can use us, if we are willing. Will you allow the Lord to speak His Word through you today? Will you "ingest" the Word today and then share that with someone?

I will be watchful! God, send those people who need me. I am willing to be used as You see appropriate.

AUGUST 27

BELIEF STARTS WHEN?

John 2

BEST VERSE: 12

After this He went down to Capernaum, He and His mother and His brothers and His disciples; and they stayed there a few days.

As I read this passage about Jesus' first miracle, turning the water into wine, I was struck by verse 12. Why did His mother and brothers follow Him to Capernaum? Of course, Mary knew all about Jesus and the message she received from the angel about His purpose on earth. Why else would she have asked Him to help with the wine issue. But His brothers? Maybe they thought He could help them out. You know how brothers are. Did they start believing in Him here or were they just along with Mom?

TEACHING MOMENT

I get asked all the time by parents how old should a child be before they place their trust in Jesus. Well, do they understand the simple truths of the gospel? Do they believe He died for them, was buried, and rose again? Do they admit they are a sinner and need cleansing? If so, there you have it.

Your children can't ride your coat tails into heaven. There is no "family plan" for salvation. Being born into a Christian family no more makes them Christian than being born in a garage makes them a car. They must come to a point where they recognize their own sin and need for a Savior. Are you listening to your children when they talk about Jesus?

We don't know when Jesus' brothers recognized Him as the Messiah. But being born into the same family as Jesus did not give them any more heaven points than anyone else. For that matter, and this is going to make some people mad, even Mary wasn't guaranteed salvation unless she too bowed her knee to her Son, her Savior.

Don't rest on the fact that your children have always attended church and sang all the songs and memorized all the verses. Lead them to the miracle worker, Jesus Christ, their Savior and Lord.

Father, let me be pointed and direct concerning the necessity of salvation for everyone. Help me be loving, but clear of the need of each one to repent on their own. Thank You for my own salvation.

AUGUST 28

FAMILY TIME

Genesis 36

BEST VERSE: 6

Then Esau took his wives and his sons and his daughters and all his household, and his livestock and all his cattle and all his goods which he had acquired in the land of Canaan, and went to another land away from his brother Jacob.

Why? Why did Esau leave? I know what it says. It says because between his and Jacob's flocks and herds, the land wasn't big enough. But he had been there all this time. He had stayed when Jacob left all those years ago. Now, Jacob is back, and packs up and leaves.

Maybe he figured it was his time to travel. We don't really know what he was thinking. But don't you wonder what Jacob thought? He had "survived" his homecoming with Esau, and now his brother leaves. I bet Jacob had hoped he would have more time with Esau.

TEACHING MOMENT

We need family. Sometimes though, time and space separate us. We move away from each other. Your children need to realize how important family is. How can you instill this in your children? Only by continually making family time important. Brother and sisters should always have that connection with each other.

How do you handle those sibling rivalries? Do you ignore them and hope they will go away? Don't think this will just fix itself. Just look at what happened with Jacob and Esau. Over twenty years went by and still they parted.

Do you have a family member with whom you are at odds? Restore it now. But understand this: you can't do it alone. Only Christ can give you the love and mercy and grace to deal with these people. Through Him you can do it. Let Him be the source.

Lord, keep me close to those I love. Help me to show them the love of Christ. Help me keep my children close.

AUGUST 29

MISPLACED GRIEF

2 Samuel 19

BEST VERSES: 5-6

Then Joab came into the house to the king and said, "Today you have covered with shame the faces of all your servants, who today have saved your life and the lives of your sons and daughters, the lives of your wives, and the lives of your concubines, by loving those who hate you, and by hating those who love you. For you have shown today that princes and servants are nothing to you; for I know this day that if Absalom were alive and all of us were dead today, then you would be pleased."

This is a sad story. Absalom, David's son, had rebelled against his father. During battle Absalom is killed. That was done against David's orders, but Absalom was trying to overthrow his father's kingdom and probably would have killed David if given the chance. But as any father would do, David was mourning for his son, even though Absalom meant him harm.

The problem with this was it was the wrong time to mourn. David's army had defended his reign and were left to feel like they had failed. David's mourning for his son was seen as a slap in the face to those who had fought for David. David's mourning wasn't wrong. It was just misplaced, at the wrong time.

TEACHING MOMENT

I pray your children never have to mourn. There is nothing sadder to me than to see a child crying over the death of a loved one. But we as parents must teach our children that mourning is a natural, healthy thing. We are flesh and blood. We feel true loss when someone we love dies. That could be a relative, friend or even a pet. But mourning is meant to last for a season, not a lifetime.

Our mourning should never cause others to feel uncomfortable. Our mourning should be directed towards the Lord. He is the only one who can truly comfort us. As believers, we know that death is only a temporary separation from our saved loved ones. So, do all you can to lead those you love to Christ.

Are you mourning appropriately? I know it may sound trite or callous, but ask the Lord to guide you in your grief. Let Him be your comforter and solace. He knows your deepest emotion and can fill you with peace.

O Lord, send your comfort on the grieving hearts today. Fill them with your everlasting peace.

WANDERINGS

Deuteronomy 2

BEST VERSE: 7

"For the Lord your God has blessed you in all that you have done; He has known your wanderings through this great wilderness. These forty years the Lord your God has been with you; you have not lacked a thing."

Deuteronomy begins with a recap of how the Lord has led the Israelites since they left Egypt. Moses reminds the people in verse 7 how God sustained them as they wandered in the wilderness. Now, don't forget that the wandering was punishment for not going into Canaan. But still God, even in the midst of their punishment, sustained them.

God's love for them and His purpose for them had not changed. He took care of them all through those years. This was no small feat. They were a great number. Some estimate anywhere from two hundred thousand to over two million. Can you imagine the amount of water that was needed for that crowd? But God provided it.

TEACHING MOMENT

The next time your child "rebels" against you and has to be disciplined, remind them of this story. You are not going to stop feeding them just because they are in trouble. You don't withhold clothing from them because they are grounded. No! You still love them and protect them, even though you have to carry out the discipline.

Do you enjoy disciplining your child? Neither does God. He has to because He loves us, but He had much rather see us walk in fellowship with Him. He had rather have us obey. He had much rather bless than correct.

Let me ask you this question. What are you doing right now to obey God? Is He pleased with your walk right now? It is so important for us to walk worthy of our Lord. Others are watching. They are watching to see how we handle life. Will you let the Lord guide you?

O God, I am so guilty of wanting to do things my way. I am just like the Israelites in my rebellion against You. Forgive me and set me back on the right path.

WATCH THIS, BUBBA!

Exodus 14

BEST VERSES: 13-14

But Moses said to the people, "Do not fear! Stand by and see the salvation of the Lord which He will accomplish for you today; for the Egyptians whom you have seen today, you will never see them again forever. The Lord will fight for you while you keep silent."

Sometimes it is fun to just watch. We can watch something good and worthwhile or something silly and a waste of time. Whichever it is, we just watch. Somebody else is doing all the action. Similar to watching a football game. The guys on the field are doing all the running and tackling. We just watch.

God is telling Moses to tell all the people to just watch Him work. He was going to take care of the Egyptians once and for all. He was done warning them. He was done with their threats towards His people. All Moses and the people had to do was watch Him do His thing.

TEACHING MOMENT

Do your kids ever watch you work? There is nothing they can do but watch. You don't expect them to help. It is beyond their ability and skills. You even tell them, "Don't touch anything. Just sit there."

The next time this happens, remind them of this verse. The people got to see God do an amazing thing. They had to just watch and believe. Just like your children watch you, they need to be taught to trust the powerful hand of our Savior who will do amazing things if we will just trust.

Are you too busy doing to watch? Is God wanting to work in your life, but you want to do it yourself? Let Him work. Let Him fight for you. He will always be victorious. He will always fight for you.

Lord, I am thankful You want to work in my life. I am thankful You want to show me how You are on my side. Help me to trust You and allow You to overwhelm with Your grace.

DECEPTION

1 Samuel 19

BEST VERSE: 13

Michal took the household idol and laid it on the bed, and put a quilt of goats' hair at its head, and covered it with clothes.

This story of how David escaped Saul's attempt to kill him in his own home has always intrigued me. Why did David and Michal have an "household idol" in their house? Why did David, the man who was after God's own heart, allow this? It seems this was a large idol, probably something like a bust of a person. It was big enough to put into the bed and cover up in the attempt to fool Saul's men.

It was common for Israelite women to have these idols. So, here is Michal, the king's daughter, deceiving her father who was trying to kill her husband. I wonder where she learned such deception? Hmmm? She must have seen him doing similar deceptive things. She was worshiping this idol in her home, which is the ultimate form of deception, the deception of ourselves.

TEACHING MOMENT

Children will follow our lead most of the time. I can still remember my son mimicking me when he was little. That was cute then, but it made me think very hard about the things I said and the things I did. Did I want him mimicking everything I did?

What are you modeling for your kids today? Are there deceptive idols in your home that are influencing your children? What has become the center point of your family? If it is anything except the Lord Jesus, it is an idol. I am not going to name things. You can figure that out all by yourself.

Are you sold out to the one true God? Obviously, Michal wasn't. That idol had no place in the home. God only has room for one God in your life—HIM! All other gods must go! They are false anyway, with no power and no authority.

Will you ask the Lord today to reveal all those things that are placed like idols in your life? As He reveals them, deal with them. Don't let ANYTHING divert your full attention towards God. Remember, your little ones are watching.

Father, thank you for being my All. Thank you for being my Everything. Show me those things that distract me, and give me the courage to get rid of them today.

SIBLING RIVALRY

Genesis 4

BEST VERSE: 9

Then the Lord said to Cain, "Where is Abel your brother?" And he said, "I do not know. Am I my brother's keeper?"

I grew up with an older brother. Boy, did we have some fights! I guess most of that is normal. After all, it's been going on since creation, right? But do you know why? Because of the fall of man. If sin had not entered the world, Cain and Abel would have been fine.

It all came down to greed and jealousy. Cain's offering "of" his fruits was not received by the Lord, while Abel's offering from the "firstlings of his flock" was. Cain obviously did not give God the *first* fruits. Man, that sounds like my fights with my brother. Most of them were over greed or jealously. Nothing much has changed.

TEACHING MOMENT

If your kids don't fight, count your blessings. But it's pretty safe to say that at some point, they'll have disagreements. This passage about Cain and Abel is the perfect story to read to them. Now make sure you point out that the way Cain dealt with the problem was NOT the correct way.

Explain to your children that their fighting is part of the old sin nature. As believers, that old nature has been defeated by the blood of Christ. They need to know that it has no more power over them—if they have given their life to Christ. There is no need to yield to the temptation.

But how about your greed or jealousy or strife? Do you still battle those hot-headed emotions? We all do, unless we are surrendered to His will and His way. Show your children how to die to self and allow the love of Christ to be your guide.

Lord of Peace, let peace reign through me. Give me the peace that passes all understanding. Let me be at peace with my brothers and sisters today.

IT'S A HEART MATTER

1 Samuel 16

BEST VERSE: 7

But the Lord said to Samuel, "Do not look at his appearance or at the height of his stature, because I have rejected him; for God sees not as man sees, for man looks at the outward appearance, but the Lord looks at the heart."

Man, I love this verse. How many times have you looked at some smart, good looking young person who has a great personality and charisma and thought, "Boy, if God got a hold of him, He could really use him"? That is such wrong thinking. That is exactly the kind of man Saul was according to 1 Samuel 9:2 (read it).

So, it seems God, in choosing the second king of Israel, deliberately chose a young man, David, who was not even thought enough of by his father to have him come in from the fields to line up for Samuel. Why would God choose the youngest of the eight brothers?

TEACHING MOMENT

This is a perfect verse to show your children how God determines the usefulness of people. They may think they don't "have what it takes" to be used, but God can take the most unlikely boys and girls and make them into kings and queens. God even knew all the mkistakes David would make in the future, but He still chose him to be the king.

What strengths does your child have? Help him or her develop them. But also look at their weaknesses, and do all you can to strengthen them. All the while, remember that is not up to you to determine the outcome. That's God's business. God will use anyone who is surrendered to Him. It may take time for His perfect will to be seen by your child (or you), but when it is revealed it will make perfect sense.

Some children know at an early age what God is leading them to do. Others may take, well, . . . longer. Encourage, direct, teach and train! But don't push. Let God draw them into the path He has for them. That will make their journey with God so much sweeter.

Father, I rejoice to see my own children following Your Will for their lives. I pray today for all the children who have yet to discover that. May they wait on You to reveal it.

SEPTEMBER 4

BE JUST

Deuteronomy 16

BEST VERSE: 20
Justice, and only justice, you shall pursue, that you may live and possess the land which the Lord your God is giving you.

Have you ever wondered what it meant to be just? Well, it simply means to show justice. Do what is right, according to God, not man. Man can pervert justice. Man can change the rules to fit what they want it to say. But man cannot change what God calls justice. He is justice. He demands justice.

And by living that way we are given a promise. I believe this promise to the Hebrew children, as they were preparing to enter the Promised Land, applies to us well. We may not be going in to possess a land, but we are promised to live and possess what the Lord is giving us (whatever that is) if we pursue justice.

TEACHING MOMENT
Children don't learn justice naturally. Their sinful flesh will always pursue what it wants. It doesn't care about others. But as God comes to live in and through them in the Holy Spirit, justice will win out. The Holy Spirit will demand it.

Sometimes showing justice (being just) is not comfortable. Sometimes it will cost us something or even a lot. But God has promised that if we do what is just, He will bless us.

Justice is fair. Justice is right. Justice is good. Whether we believe it or not, justice will make us stronger. Justice will bring us to look more like Him. So, why wouldn't you want to be just and live justly?

I shall submit to You for You are just. Guide my every decision. As a believer, You will guide me in living a just and holy life.

SNOWBALL EFFECT

2 Samuel 12

BEST VERSE: 13A

Then David said to Nathan, "I have sinned against the Lord."

Here we are at probably one of the two most told stories about David. The other is when he kills Goliath. That's a great story. But here . . . well . . . this is another side of David we haven't seen. This is a story of his failure.

It starts out innocent enough. He accidentally sees a lady bathing on a rooftop. But that look turns to lust, which leads to sin, which leads to another sin, and another sin. You get the picture. Once David decided to go against God's commandments, he started down a slippery slope.

TEACHING MOMENT

Have you ever caught your child in a lie? They are caught red-handed, but they begin to fabricate a story to try to get out of it. One lie leads to another lie. That's exactly what David did. This would be a great story to share with your child at such a time. Now, depending on their age, you may want to "adapt" what you tell them started all of this. But they need to see how lies can build until someone gets hurt.

How can we teach our children the importance of always telling the truth and doing what's right? Simple. Teach them God's Word. Teach them to follow His commands. If they do that, they are safe. But the moment they decide to do things their way . . . well, . . . they are subject to failure.

How are you doing with this? Are you making your decisions based on what you think is best or what you want to do? Or are you seeking the Lord before you make that decision? We are just as tempted as our children to do what we think is best. We are just as tempted to follow the example of David, if we think we won't get caught.

Decide today not to take that first step. Don't put one foot on that slippery slope. If you do and you fall, it's tough to recover. The only way out is confession. If that's where you are, then confess it now. Stop what you are doing and let Him cleanse you.

Father, I have sinned against You and You only! Forgive my sin! Cleanse my heart!

FABRIC HOUSE

Exodus 26

BEST VERSES: 1–2

"Moreover you shall make the tabernacle with ten curtains of fine twisted linen and blue and purple and scarlet material; you shall make them with cherubim, the work of a skillful workman. The length of each curtain shall be twenty-eight cubits, and the width of each curtain four cubits; all the curtains shall have the same measurements."

Do you know how long twenty-eight cubits is? It's forty-two feet. So, each curtain was forty-two feet long and six feet wide. That's a lot of fabric. Where did all this fabric come from? Remember, they are in the wilderness, right? There wasn't a neighborhood Walmart to run to. There wasn't a Hancock's Fabrics to order from. All this material came from the people who had brought it with them from their Egyptian masters. Remember they had "plundered" Egypt when they left.

My point is this—God had a plan for the tabernacle long before the people left Egypt. The people had no idea why they were carrying all the material with them except maybe to have clothes along the way. God had a bigger plan. He was going to have them build His temporary "home" among them with these items.

TEACHING MOMENT

A lot of the time your children do not understand why they have to do the things you ask them to do. They don't see the big picture. They only see the "now." Teaching them manners now will benefit them later. Teaching them how to dress properly will be good to know when they get older. Teaching your sons to respect their sisters will show them how to treat other women in their lives. The list goes on and on.

Details matter. Read a portion of this chapter and ask them what they think about all these numbers and measurements. They will probably say, "I don't know. I hate math." But once you explain the whole story to them, they may just begin to understand that God had a plan long before the Israelites started building this tabernacle in the desert. He has a similar plan for their lives as well.

What is God trying to build in your life? Are you confused by the "materials" He is using? Maybe He is using hard times. Maybe He is using a new boss. Perhaps He is using your past experiences. God only uses what is absolutely necessary to "build" us into the shape He wants us. Enjoy the process.

You are the Master Builder, God. I know that. I know You have the blueprint of my life written. Help me trust You in the process.

SEPTEMBER 7

ANGEL JOY

Luke 15

BEST VERSE: 10
"In the same way, I tell you, there is joy in the presence of the angels of God over one sinner who repents."

ONE REPENTING

Don't you just love that? The angels are rejoicing when ONE sinner repents. He didn't say hundreds or thousands. Just ONE! Remember, Jesus had witnessed this. He had been in heaven and watched the angels rejoice. He was speaking not only with all the wisdom of God, but from eyewitness experience.

I wonder what the angels think when they see a sinner repenting. They don't understand repentance like we do. They are heavenly beings and have lived with God since their creation. They have never had to repent. But I am sure when they see the Father smile at the repentance of His children, they smile too.

TEACHING MOMENT

I am sure it won't be long until your daughter comes to you and says she is sorry for something she has done. When you forgive her and smile, as I know you will, bring up this verse. Tell her right now in heaven the angels are smiling too. That's a thought she won't soon forget.

Helping our children learn the value of repentance is key to their growth as believers and followers of Christ. Every believer must be a repenter. They go hand in hand. And the repenting never stops. I wish it could, but until we reach heaven and are free from the presence of sin, we will need to stay "confessed up."

Are you "confessed up"? Are you a consistent repenter? Maybe this verse will help today. Just think each time you repent you make the angels smile. That should quicken your repentance time.

Father, I thank You for forgiving me each and every time I come to you and repent. I am sorry for how frequently I do that, but I know You want me to. Smile angels!

SEPTEMBER 8

WHAT BAIT DID YOU USE?
Matthew 17

BEST VERSE: 27
"However, so that we do not offend them, go to the sea and throw in a hook, and take the first fish that comes up; and when you open its mouth, you will find a shekel. Take that and give it to them for you and Me."

I love to fish, but sometimes it is hard to figure out what the fish are biting. You have to use the right bait. Now that could be live bait or an artificial bait. Either way, if the fish don't want it, they are not going to bite it.

The first thought I had about this verse was, *What kind of bait was Peter using to catch that fish with money in its mouth? I think I want to find that bait and use it here. I could always use a little extra money.* Seriously though, I bet Peter (who was a fisherman) never caught a fish before or after with money in its mouth.

TEACHING MOMENT
So how can we teach our children this verse? I mean, come on, what lesson does this teach us? What did Christ do? He obeyed the law. He payed his taxes. He just got very creative in doing it. Our children can learn from this verse that Jesus was obedient to those in power, even if they were scandalous.

It seems a lot of young people today do not respect authority unless they agree with the authority. Our children must learn to obey the authorities in their lives, unless they are asked to do something illegal or immoral. They may not "like" the person in charge, but they have been placed over them for a reason.

How about you, Mom and Dad? Do you have a boss you don't like? Tough! Submit! The Lord has placed them in your life for a purpose. You must allow the Lord to teach you through them. Perhaps the Lord has placed you there for them. Will you be obedient to Him? Submit and allow Jesus to show you how He will use that in your life.

You see, this verse isn't about fishing after all!

Help me to submit to all my authorities today. Give me the desire to serve them willingly, knowing You have placed them over me.

SEPTEMBER 9

BRING THE BABIES

Luke 18

BEST VERSES: 15-17
And they were bringing even their babies to Him so that He would touch them, but when the disciples saw it, they began rebuking them. But Jesus called for them, saying, "Permit the children to come to Me, and do not hinder them, for the kingdom of God belongs to such as these. Truly I say to you, whoever does not receive the kingdom of God like a child will not enter it at all."

One of the joys of my ministry as a children's pastor is seeing babies as soon as possible after they are born. I like to take them in my arms and pray for them and the family. I've said it many times, but I am amazed each time at the beauty of childbirth and the miracle of a new life. Jesus was too, I am sure of it.

The word for "babies" in verse 15 can be translated as newborn, infant or even a baby in the womb. Perhaps some of the moms came for Jesus to lay hands on their enlarged bellies. I have to imagine the love and power of Christ had compassion on these women too.

Our children need to see us blessing others, especially other children. Do they have friends you can pray for? When they have a friend over for the night, do you pray with them just like you do with your own child? If you do, don't stop this as they get older. Pray over their teenage friends. Pray over the boy or girl they are dating (especially them).

Encourage your children to pray for their friends and other children. Encourage your children to do all they can to bring other children to Jesus. Christ says it clearly in this passage. He desires they all come to Him to "receive the kingdom."

Be a bridge, not a moat!

Jesus, how good and loving You are to love children. You want all of Your children to come to You so that they can be touched and blessed. Teach me to show my child how to bless others.

SEPTEMBER 10

MY SON

Psalms 1–2

BEST VERSE: 2:7

I will surely tell of the decree of the Lord: He said to Me, "You are My Son, today I have begotten You."

I have a son. His name is Christopher. I couldn't be prouder of him. He is a good husband and father. He works hard for his family. He is the kind of son who makes his father proud. I am quick to claim him. If anyone knows me, they know that.

I so desire the same from my heavenly Father. I want Him to say to me, "You are My son, today I have begotten You." I long to hear those words of affirmation. I want to make Him proud. I want to live in such a way that He will point me out and say to those around His throne, "Look, there's My Son."

TEACHING MOMENT

We want our children to make us proud. But we should be proud of them, regardless. They are, after all, ours. We begat them (to use some Bible lingo).

We have raised them. We are proud. They make some bonehead decisions, but we will always love them.

But just like myself, I long for children to be seen not so much as my children, but as the son and daughter of God. I want them to be known as someone who seeks God first. I want them to be known as someone who longs after Jesus. That makes me proud.

What do you base your pride on? Are you boasting on their achievements or their following your rules? Stop that. Boast on how they follow the Lord. Boast on what they do to lead others to Him. That lasts. That is eternal.

Father, I want You to claim me as Your Son. I know I am Your child because of the blood of Christ. But I want to always make You proud of my obedience to You.

SEPTEMBER 11

THIS MAKES NO SENSE

Luke 17

BEST VERSE: 33
"Whoever seeks to keep his life will lose it, and whoever loses his life will preserve it."

This passage in Luke 17 is in the middle of the teaching of Christ about His return. We, as believers, all long for His return, don't we? But this verse is not one we want to dwell on.

What He says here goes directly against our instinct to survive. He says if you spend all your time trying to preserve your life, you will lose it. But if you lose your life you will preserve it. Huh? That just doesn't make sense. How can we preserve our life by losing it?

One of the greatest lessons we can learn is how to die to self. We have to lay down our own desires and wishes and way of life and embrace the life the Savior has for us. By doing that, what seems to be a sacrificial thing ends up being a fulfilling one. We are filled when we empty ourselves. We are lifted up when we fall down on our knees before Him.

TEACHING MOMENT
How can you, as mom and dad, model this behavior? When you mess up (and we all do) are you able to admit that to your child? When you let your

flesh get the best of you, can you go to whomever you have offended and apologize? Your children are watching you. They learn from your behavior.

I am anxiously looking forward to Christ's return. But I know between now and then I must lay down my life for Him daily. It is no secret why He put that statement in the midst of this passage about His return. He wants us to be living empty of ourselves and full of Him when He returns. Why do you think it will happen "in the twinkling of an eye"? If we are surrendered to Him daily, that transformation to glory will just be another day of surrender to Him. If we are full of Him here, being with Him there will just seem . . . natural.

How I long for the day, O Lord, of Your return. But help me be ready for that any time or any day. I want You to find me ready and waiting.

SECRET PLACE

Deuteronomy 34

BEST VERSES: 5–6
So Moses the servant of the Lord died there in the land of Moab, according to the word of the Lord. And He buried him in the valley in the land of Moab, opposite Beth-peor; but no man knows his burial place to this day.

Isn't it amazing that the only person whom God buried was buried in a private, "for family-only" service? Why was that? I think there were a couple of reasons. First, if the people had known Moses' gravesite it would have become a shrine. God did not want that. Secondly, God needed to be alone with Moses when He died. He did not want a crowd of millions wailing and crying over Moses's death.

God had a personal, intimate relationship with Moses. Perhaps, other than Adam and Eve in the Garden, Moses was the closest to Jehovah. God loved him and chose him for a very specific purpose. Now that was done, God wanted Moses to come home, his real home—Glory!

TEACHING MOMENT
Death is reality. We parents do not need to shield our children from this. They need to know that when someone dies, we will NOT see them again

this side of eternity. Depending on their salvation status (saved or lost) we may or may not see them there. Telling our children anything else is deceptive and not helpful. You need to decide at what age it is appropriate for them to know this, but don't hide this truth from them.

I have heard parents tell their children that grandma or grandpa had to "go away" and one day they would see them again in heaven. Two things are wrong with this. They didn't "go away." They died. And secondly, they will only see them again if they both end up in the same place, heaven or hell.

This may be the heaviest devotion I have written. Speaking of where someone will spend eternity is sobering, but it is so important. Are you sure where you are going one day? Do you know for sure that you will spend eternity with our loving Savior?

How about your children? Have they asked the Lord Jesus in their hearts to secure their name in the Lamb's Book of Life? There is no other decision on earth that is more important.

Thank You, Lord, for confirming my eternity. I am thankful my name is written down with permanent ink. There is nothing that can remove my name.

SEPTEMBER 13

GESUNDHEIT

Genesis 49

BEST VERSE: 28
All these are the twelve tribes of Israel, and this is what their father said to them when he blessed them. He blessed them, every one with the blessing appropriate to him.

Have you ever heard the expression "gesundheit" after someone sneezes? Maybe you have even said it without realizing what it means. You know that can be dangerous. (That's a whole other story.) Well, "gesundheit" actually is German for "healthy (*gesund*) hood (*heit*)." So, when you hear that, you are actually hearing "healthy hood" or "I wish you good health."

We commonly say in America "bless you." That is exactly what Jacob did here in chapter 49 of Genesis. He brought in all his sons, plus Ephraim and Manasseh, whom he had claimed as his, and blessed them. This was important in their culture. The father's blessing on his child was highly desired. It should be today also.

TEACHING MOMENT

Now this verse today is more about our actions as a parent than teaching our child. Of course, everything we DO teaches, right? Fathers, I want to encourage you to bless your child every day. Find some way to praise them and bless them. Pray over them, not just for them. Let them hear you praying God's blessings on them. And don't just do it for your sons. Your daughters need to hear words of blessing, too.

And moms, you can do the same. If you are a single mom, find a godly man who can pray over your children with you. Children need that blessing of a father figure. This is not to diminish your role. There is just something a child craves from a father that can only be filled by a godly man.

So, let me ask you today to be that person, men. Bless your child. Bless a child. Step in to help a single mom when you can. Now you can only do this with the blessing of your wife and with her full knowledge. Your integrity and reputation are important in this process. But be that blessing to a child who needs it.

Heavenly Father, You have blessed me beyond my highest expectations. You have delivered me. Give me the vision to bless those around me, especially my children.

SEPTEMBER 14

JUST REST

Psalms 45–46

BEST VERSE: 46:10A
"Cease striving and know that I am God."

Have you ever felt like living the Christian life is too much work? Most of us, at one time or another, have probably felt that way and maybe even said it. But this verse speaks to that perfectly. When we realize it is NOT up to us, we can rest and "cease striving."

We will never walk perfectly with God. We are going to have ups and downs. We are going to fall flat on our faces. We are going to do or say things that aren't godly. Not on purpose, mind you, but accidentally (sin for a believer should always be an accident and not planned). God tells us to let Him work through us. He can do all things.

TEACHING MOMENT

This is one of the best lessons we can teach our children. When our children realize that they cannot live the Christian life on their own, they will have learned the secret to holy living. It's Christ IN us, the hope of glory. He is the one who will live through them.

When they mess up, point them back to Him. When they feel like failures, point them back to Him. When they make real stupid mistakes and are afraid to tell you, point them back to Him. He is their source of faith, not you.

Have you ceased striving? Or are you still trying to get it all done through your strength or intellect? Stop it NOW! Let Jesus live in and through you by the power of the Holy Spirit. He can do it.

Lord of glory, teach me to rest in You. Help me to let go of my striving. Take my hand and lead me into the green pastures.

SEPTEMBER 15

BUT I SAID "LORD"

Luke 13

BEST VERSE: 27

". . . and He will say, 'I tell you, I do not know where you are from; depart from me, all you evildoers.'"

Jesus was asked who would be saved, and as usual, He launched into a story. In this story He told His disciples that there would be many who would "think" they are saved but aren't. How can that happen? How can someone think they are going to heaven and not get in? Unfortunately, it happens far too often.

So, what is the secret to getting into heaven? There's no secret. It's simple. You simply have to admit you are a sinner, believe Jesus is God's Son and died for you, and finally confess with your lips He is Lord. Too many people think just going to church or doing good things will get them there. Nope. Those won't do it.

TEACHING MOMENT

There is nothing more important than making sure your children understand this. Going to church since they were born does not get them into heaven. Singing in the children's choir or having all the badges on their AWANA vest will not save them. Only the drawing of the Holy Spirit and accepting Christ as their Savior does that.

Heaven truly is the icing on the cake. But let me rush to say this: being saved isn't all about going to heaven. Living for Him here is totally worth it. Living a joy-filled life here on earth is worth it. Living in peace is worth it. Heaven is our reward for trusting Him. I can't wait to go, but I enjoy living heavenly here.

Mom and Dad, are you settled about your eternal destiny? Have you confirmed your entry to heaven? If you haven't, do that now. Make sure **you** are going! And do all you can to make sure your children are "signed up" too.

Father, I am looking forward to spending eternity with You. Heaven is my true home, and I can't wait to "come home." But while I am here, help me live heavenly.

SEPTEMBER 16

GOD'S EXACT TIMING

Exodus 12

BEST VERSES: 40-41

Now the time that the sons of Israel lived in Egypt was four hundred and thirty years. And at the end of four hundred and thirty years, to the very day, all the hosts of the Lord went out from the land of Egypt.

God doesn't guess! He knows exactly what He is doing every second. These verses struck me that way today. They stayed in Egypt 430 years "to the very day." It wasn't 430 years and one day or one week or one month. It was 430 years exactly.

All of God's word is exact. Everything He does in our lives is exact. He has every hair of our heads counted exactly. He knows exactly the moment a sparrow falls to the ground. Do you get the picture? There is no "supposing" with God.

TEACHING MOMENT

The next time you are on a road trip with your little ones, and they ask for the fiftieth time, "Are we there yet?", use this verse. Tell them, "No, but God knows exactly when we will arrive." You can springboard into telling them God knows exactly what is going to happen in their lives. He knows who and when they will marry. He knows the names of their children and whether they will have boys, girls, or both. He knows when they will go to live with Him in heaven, if they are believers.

Children desire security. What more secure place can they be than under the watchful eye of God? He is always watching and protecting. He offers them EXACTLY what they need EXACTLY when they need it. They just have to trust Him and let Him have His perfect will done in their lives.

Let me ask you a question. Are you trusting the exacting God today? Do you let Him have His way? Do you really believe He knows exactly what you need today? Let Him show you that He is EXACT in all His ways.

O God, You are always on time. You are exactly right all the time. Let me live in that truth today.

SEPTEMBER 17

ARE WE THERE YET?

John 6

BEST VERSE: 21
So they were willing to receive Him into the boat, and immediately the boat was at the land to which they were going.

This miracle of Christ walking on the water is told in three of the four Gospels (Matthew, Mark, and John). But only here does the story mention this detail. Matthew includes Peter walking on the water. Mark says they were in the middle of the lake, and Jesus saw them struggling from land.

But John is the only one that says "Bam! They teleported to land." Well, he doesn't say that, but he does say, ". . . immediately the boat was at the land to which they were going."

I know road trips can be fun, but there comes a point when you just want to get there, right? Imagine a scenario where you are on a road trip, and the kids have asked you for the one hundredth time, "Are we there yet?" Your son and daughter are fighting in the back seat. The dog has thrown up in the floorboard. You are just so ready to get to your destination, so you push the teleport button on the dash, and instantly you arrive at your location. Wouldn't that be awesome?

TEACHING MOMENT

But, like the disciples who had just witnessed Jesus feeding the five thousand with a little boy's lunch, we too forget the little "miracles" along the way. We forget watching the kids giggle and laugh over silly songs. We forget them sharing the last fruit rollup. We forget the road games they played together peacefully.

Don't be in such a rush. Why not enjoy the boat trip across the lake? I mean the road trip in the car! You won't have that many more road trips with them, I promise. Before you know it, they will be too cool to go on vacations with Mom and Dad. They grow up and move out (you hope), and all you have left are memories.

I bet the disciples sat around after Christ's departure and told stories about those three years. "Hey Peter, remember the time. . . ." "I remember when James and John. . . ." Mark your memories and "miracles."

My Father, You have filled my life with events that are memorable. Give me the ability to mark those events. Help me make the same kind of memories with my children.

WASH, WASH, WASH YOUR HANDS!

Mark 7

BEST VERSES: 1–2

The Pharisees and some of the scribes gathered around Him when they had come from Jerusalem, and had seen that some of His disciples were eating their bread with impure hands, that is, unwashed.

I used to teach Red Cross Child Care courses to teen moms. One of the courses was "Preventing Infectious Diseases." In this course, the video had a Health Fairy (I know, kind of lame) that taught a song (sung to the tune of "Row, Row, Row Your Boat") that had the lyrics "Wash, wash, wash your hands; play the handy game, rub and scrub, scrub and rub, germs go down the drain." Cute, huh? Feel free to use that with your kids.

It would have been nice if the Pharisees were just concerned about germs, but their hand washing was more ceremonial than hygienic. It was all about appearances. Did they look clean? Did they act clean? Did they follow all the laws about staying clean?

TEACHING MOMENT

Well, while we may not wash our hands before meals to keep the law, we do other things that we think keeps us "clean" before the Lord. And the sad thing is we force those ideas on our kids. Do I need to remind you that we are under Grace, not Law? We are free because of the law of liberty, as James says.

So, the next time your kids run in from playing outdoors and their hands are dirty and before you say, "Go wash your hands," think why you are saying that. After all, a little dirt never hurt anyone, right Mom?

I want to be clean internally, not just externally. I want to wash myself and free myself from the stains of this world. I need You, O God, to use Your cleansing power in me today.

MIND YOUR OWN BUSINESS

Mark 5

BEST VERSE: 17
And they began to implore Him to leave their region.

This chapter begins with the story of the demon possessed man in the region of Gerasene. Can you imagine having a man living in the local cemetery who screamed all night and ran around with chains hanging from him and cutting himself with rocks? Wouldn't that be a little scary? Wouldn't you be a little happy if he left the area or stopped behaving that way?

Well, Jesus shows up and casts all those demons out of the man. He became calm, and everything looked great. So, why did they ask Jesus to leave in verse 17? Because he had cast the demons in the pigs, and they had run off the cliff and died in the sea. He was costing them money. Two thousand pigs just died, and the locals were basically saying, "Why don't you mind your own business? We were just fine before you got here. Why don't you just leave?"

TEACHING MOMENT
We need to teach our children that we WANT Jesus "messing around" in our daily lives. We WANT Him in our homes. We WANT Him in our playtime with our friends. No matter what He does, it is ALWAYS for our good. We just have to trust Him.

So, the next time you hear your kids say, "Won't you mind your own business?" make sure they aren't talking to Jesus. Our business IS His business.

Lord God, please get in my business. I want You to "meddle." I need You to help direct my everyday decisions so they always honor You.

WHAT ARE YOU BUILDING?

Genesis 12

BEST VERSE: 8

Then he proceeded from there to the mountain on the east of Bethel, and pitched his tent, with Bethel on the west and Ai on the east; and there he built an altar to the Lord and called upon the name of the Lord.

Abram stops his journey long enough to build an altar in order to worship the Lord. The Lord had told him to leave his homeland and go where he told him. Here he is, on his way, but he stops and builds an altar. He builds another one in Genesis 13. Abram was an altar builder. He wanted to hear from God.

What are you "building" in order to hear from God? Are you too busy "doing life" to stop and listen for God's direction? Have you been too busy throwing stones rather than gathering them to build your own altar of self-sacrifice? I heard Charles Stanley say once, "When people throw stones at you, pick them up and build an altar." I have never forgotten that. But I still want to throw those stones back. My flesh does not want to crawl on the altar.

TEACHING MOMENT

Our children will learn self-sacrifice one way—by observing us. Yep, sorry! We have to model sacrificial living for them to truly understand it. The day will come when they will face situations that demand sacrifice. Then they will reflect back on your example. Whether they yield to temptation or to the Lord is their decision. But we must be sure we set the right example.

What can a child sacrifice? A lot. When their friend wants to cheat off their paper in school, they may have to sacrifice friendship for honesty. It may happen when they are asked to compromise their purity for "love." Our children today are faced with so many challenges to their faith. We have to be constantly modeling self-sacrifice.

So today, when you are faced with that choice of building an altar and hearing from God or throwing rocks at someone who has challenged your faith, what are you going to do? Lay it down, crawl up on that altar of self-sacrifice, and die to self. Only then will you truly live!

Thank You, Lord, for reminding me that I need to be building and not throwing stones at others. Help me to stop my busyness to worship You and listen for Your direction.

OOPS! DID I DO THAT?

Joshua 10

BEST VERSE: 14

There was no day like that before it or after it, when the LORD listened to the voice of a man; for the LORD fought for Israel.

In order to get a clear picture of what I am going to say, you should go back and read Joshua 9 and the first 13 verses of chapter 10. Israel, specifically Joshua, made a big mistake right off the bat after they had entered the Promised Land. They mistakenly signed a treaty with a city they should have destroyed because they didn't take the time to seek the Lord about it. Gibeon became an ally when they were in fact living inside the land that the Lord told Israel to wipe clean of foreign occupants.

But then we see how the Lord used this to incite the other cities and people of the land to attack Gibeon and eventually come after Israel. Perhaps the Lord knew that the people of Israel would need a little incentive to attack and wipe out the pagans and unbelievers in the future who threatened their existence in this land God had promised. I don't believe God planned for Gibeon to trick them into a treaty, but He allowed it to happen and then used the circumstances to escalate Joshua into action.

TEACHING MOMENT

Have your children (or you) ever made a mistake? Have they ever made a decision that they knew the Lord would not approve of? Of course! Haven't we all? But once we come back to God and surrender to His will, He can take that mishap, that circumstance, and use it to teach us and direct us. Now God is not asking us today to go in and possess a physical land. But He is asking us to stake a claim in the name of Christ in a dark and foreboding world.

Your children can learn to stand up for righteousness. Just as Joshua and the people of Israel stood with Gibeon because of the treaty (they had given their word to them to protect them) your children can learn to stand for the cause of Christ. Even when they may have first missed it, they can allow the Lord to redirect them into a holy stand for Him.

Mom and Dad, will you do that? Will you take that stand? Will you surrender your mishaps to His divine will and allow Him to make lemonade out of lemons? He will!

You are a God of corrections. You can take my big faults and turn them into strengths. You are the One who lifts me up and gives me the second chance.

HOW QUICKLY WE FORGET

Judges 2

BEST VERSE: 10
All that generation also were gathered to their fathers; and there arose another generation after them who did not know the Lord, nor yet the work which He had done for Israel.

Isn't it sad? One generation! After all the struggles of the Israelites in Egypt and then the wilderness, one generation after entering the Promised Land, they forget God. The verse actually says, "did not know the Lord."

This is why I am always harping on the fact that we, as parents, have to be so diligent to teach our children and lead them to the saving knowledge of Christ. If we don't, it takes just one generation for the church to decline. Our calling as parents also involves advancing the kingdom of Christ here on earth.

TEACHING MOMENT
Share this verse with your children today. Explain to them that they have the same mandate from God as you. They must teach their children about the Lord. They must make sure their children don't just know about God, but

that they *know* God. Knowledge without personal experience does not cut it. They must truly know Jesus as Lord and Savior.

Your children, once they believe in the Lord and are saved, become missionaries to the next generation. They have the responsibility to share the gospel with their family and friends. Nothing is more exciting than to see your own children follow the Lord. A parent can rest in the joy of kingdom growth through their own children. Rejoice!

Have you done that? Does your life draw your children to Christ or repel them? Everything we do as parents must model Jesus so our children will want to model, not us, but Christ in us. Be His reflection and image today.

You are the generation builder, O Lord. I know if I rely on You for my strength, You will give me the ability to reach my children and grandchildren for Christ. Thank You, Lord.

SEPTEMBER 23

MAKING PREPARATIONS
Exodus 28

BEST VERSE: 1
"Then bring near to yourself Aaron your brother, and his sons with him, from among the sons of Israel, to minister as priest to Me—Aaron, Nadab and Abihu, Eleazar and Ithamar, Aaron's sons."

You are probably wondering, *What in the world can we apply to our lives as parents from this verse?* Well, let me tell you. First of all, every word of God's Word is inspired and has a purpose. Yes, even those verses in Leviticus.

We see in this verse God choosing Aaron and his sons as His priests. He gave Moses special instructions in anointing them, clothing them and making sacrifices for them. He was specific in His instructions to make sure these men were set apart for a special purpose.

TEACHING MOMENT
For what purpose are our children set apart? What does the Lord have planned for them? Well, let me ask you this. Are you following the Lord's

instructions in preparing your children for service? Are you anointing them? Are you preparing the proper clothing for them? Are you presenting them to the Lord as a sacrifice, just as Abraham presented Isaac?

How our children serve the Lord depends a lot on how we prepare them. Will you make the preparations?

Help me, Lord, prepare my children to serve You. Give me the tools and wisdom I need to direct them towards You. I know that serving You is a lifelong process that requires constant learning.

SEPTEMBER 24

JACOB'S LADDER

Genesis 28

BEST VERSE: 17
He was afraid and said, "How awesome is this place! This is none other than the house of God, and this is the gate of heaven."

You've probably heard of the phrase "Jacob's ladder." I even remember as a child playing with string and making a "Jacob's ladder" without realizing where this expression originated. Well, it's right here in Genesis 28. Jacob had a dream and saw angels ascending and descending on it. This caused me to think, *If angels all have wings, why didn't they just fly down?*

Anyway, back to the story. Jacob wakes and proclaims this place has to be the entry to the house of God, so he names it "Bethel," which means just that. Was it really the doorway to heaven? Probably not, but Jacob knew he had been in the presence of God and that He had given him a message.

TEACHING MOMENT
How many times have your children recalled their night's dream to you? Some of them can be quite entertaining, can't they? The next time they tell you their dream, listen intently. Maybe the Lord is trying to speak to them through the night. I know He has done that in my life. God may want you to "interpret" the meaning for them.

But also, tell them this story. Explain how the Lord does speak to us in all kinds of ways. Most importantly, He speaks through His word. He speaks through answered prayers. He speaks through godly counsel. He speaks through their pastor. But He speaks. We need to teach children how to listen.

Are you listening for God's words? Maybe He has been speaking to you in the still of the night. Is your mind so preoccupied with worldly events and activities that you can't hear Him? Spend some time before bed in prayer or in the Word so your mind is clear to hear Him if He speaks.

Open my ears, Lord. Open my mind, Lord. I want to hear You as You speak to me, whether it is through my dreams or during my waking moments. I want to hear Your words.

SEPTEMBER 25

AN EYE FOR AN EYE

Deuteronomy 19

BEST VERSE: 21
"Thus you shall not show pity: life for life, eye for eye, tooth for tooth, hand for hand, foot for foot."

So, this is where that saying "an eye for an eye" comes from. Have you ever wondered that? I have read this before, but never really stopped to realize just how harsh this was. God was insistent on keeping evil and disobedience out of His people. He was not going to tolerate outright evil.

But isn't it amazing how different grace is? When Christ came, He told us to turn the other cheek, to go the second mile. What? Isn't He the same God who spoke these words in Deuteronomy? Yep! But He knew from the beginning that law would not save us. We needed grace. We needed a Savior.

TEACHING MOMENT
Children have a natural tendency to want to "get them back" if they have been hurt by someone. Has your child ever said that? Maybe your child came home from school fuming and spouting off about so and so from class who had embarrassed them. Then they start making plans for payback. Nip that in the bud.

Take them to this passage and then explain how Christ came to fulfill all the laws of the Old Testament. Explain how He died for that boy or girl who just hurt their feelings. Explain how we, as believers, are to do everything in our power (through the Holy Spirit) to win them to Christ, not pay them back. That's the world's way.

I bet you have never gotten revenge on someone, have you? Right! We are all probably guilty of that to some degree. We may not have taken "an eye for an eye," but we get back at others. Repent. Confess that as sin. Remember, Christ died for each and every one we encounter in our life's journey—even the mean ones.

Giver of Grace, remind me daily of the forgiveness I have received from You. Help me forgive others in the same way. Help me love them as You love them.

SEPTEMBER 26

JEALOUSY

1 Samuel 18

BEST VERSES: 8-9
Then Saul became very angry, for this saying displeased him; and he said, "They have ascribed to David ten thousands, but to me they have ascribed thousands. Now what more can he have but the kingdom?" Saul looked at David with suspicion from that day on.

Saul liked all the attention. After all, he was the anointed King of Israel, the first king. He should be the one getting all the praise. So, when David began getting all the attention, Saul couldn't stand it. Jealousy began to build up.

The young boy who had been chosen to play the harp to calm Saul became the object of suspicion. The young man who had killed Goliath became a challenger to the throne. David was getting what Saul wanted—the love of the people. Verse 9 says, "Saul looked at David with suspicion from that day on." The word "suspicion" means Saul tried to find some iniquity or fault in David. But he couldn't.

As parents, we need to watch out for that evil monster of jealousy in our kids. Siblings can show it against each other. Children can show it against their friends. They want what the other person has. And it begins. Jealousy leads to evil actions. It is never good when it is directed against others.

If we are not careful our children can allow this jealousy to control their every action. They will even, like Saul, try to find some "dirt" on the other person to expose. Then they will appear better than that person. Johnny doesn't get picked to be on a ball team, so he decides to trash someone who did. Susie likes a boy who likes someone else, so she decides to spread rumors about the other girl.

Don't allow this. Stop it quickly. And don't show signs of jealousy in your life. You know what I mean. Even we adults get jealous when we see someone else getting something we want. Confess that now! Give that to the Lord.

Lord, I confess to You now any spirit of jealousy that comes on me. Lord, I want to be content with whatever You choose to bless me with. You know exactly what I need and can handle. Thank You, Father.

SEPTEMBER 27

LOSING YOUR HEAD

2 Samuel 4

BEST VERSE: 7
Now when they came into the house, as he was lying on his bed in his bedroom, they struck him and killed him and beheaded him. And they took his head and traveled by way of the Arabah all night.

I am sure you have heard that expression "lost their head." Most of the time when we hear that, it means someone just went crazy for a bit. They got angry and spouted off. But in this story, Ish-bosheth literally lost his head, but it wasn't for anything he had done. He was murdered. And to make the matter worse, the two who murdered him thought they were doing David, the new king, a favor.

In fact, those two men are the ones who "lost their heads" as the expression goes. They took matters into their own hands and acted on behalf of someone for whom they had no business representing. And it cost them their lives. David would have no part of an innocent man's murder.

TEACHING MOMENT

Children can get upset and "lose their heads" sometimes too. As parents, one of our jobs is to teach them to maintain their cool. Emotional stability is important. No one wants to be around someone who is constantly blowing up and railing at others. Your children need to learn to stop, breathe, and ask the Lord for peace.

Now, this all sounds easy. It is not. But remember, peace comes from within. The Spirit of God gives our children, if they are believers, the peace they need to handle any situation. The only real peace is that which comes from the Father. He is the ultimate peacemaker and peace sustainer.

Are you a model of peace in your home, or are you the one who is always "losing your head"? What will your children learn from you? Does the peace that transcends all understanding control you? Let His peace transform your mind today.

God, I know Your peace can fill me. I have felt it before. Help me stop and rest in Your peace. Help me model that for others.

A FATHER'S BLESSING

Genesis 47

BEST VERSE: 7
Then Joseph brought his father Jacob and presented him to Pharaoh; and Jacob blessed Pharaoh.

Joseph had undoubtedly told his father Jacob all about how Pharaoh had treated him. I am sure he heard the whole story about the dreams he interpreted. I am sure Jacob couldn't wait to see this man whom the people of Egypt considered a god. But what does Jacob do? Does he bow down and worship him? No, Jacob blesses him.

Now, just what does that mean? Jacob only knew one way to bless him. He blessed him in the name of Jehovah, the one true God. Jacob blessed the man whom others thought was a god by the name of the ONE who was and is God. What boldness! What a testimony.

TEACHING MOMENT

We should bless our children. They learn by hearing us do that. We bless them in the name of the only true God, Jesus Christ. But we also should bless those who bless our children. And when we do that, make sure your children hear you.

Bless their teachers. Bless their coaches. Bless their employers. Bless all those who impact the life of your child. Jacob blessed the one who had blessed his son. We should do the same. And our children will see and hear us and learn.

Whom are you blessing today? Are you mindful of all the people who bless your child? If you aren't, you should be. As we bless them and let them know they are being prayed for, hopefully they will see their impact on our children as a holy calling. Wouldn't that just be perfect?

O Holy Father, You are worthy of all my praise. I bless others in Your name because I know it is worthy. Help me recognize and bless all those who impact my life along with the lives of my loved ones.

SEPTEMBER 29

WHO'S AFRAID OF THE BIG, BAD WOLF?

Deuteronomy 31

BEST VERSE: 8

"Be strong and courageous, do not be afraid or tremble at them, for the LORD your God is the one who goes with you. He will not fail you or forsake you."

Dreams! Nightmares! The Boogie Man! The big, bad wolf! Do you remember your childhood fears? How about your children? Do they have bad dreams at night? Are they scared to go to sleep at night without the light on? We have all had those fears as a child, or our child has had or is having them. So, what do we do with that fear? How can we not be scared?

These words in Deuteronomy were spoken by Moses to the people of Israel right before they were to enter the Promised Land. He is telling them, "Don't worry about anything! God's got this! He will always be with you. You just have to trust Him." Moses knew that the people were scared, and not just because they were going to face obstacles in the land promised to them. They were going to cross the Jordan without him. Moses, their faithful and fearless leader of the past forty years, was not going with them. God had told him he couldn't enter because of his disobedience at the waters of Meribah. The people were panicked. "What do we do? How can we go in without Moses?"

TEACHING MOMENT

Our children are going to face obstacles as they grow up. Mom and Dad aren't always going to be there. When they face "an enemy" in the lunchroom, you won't be there to hold their hand. When they are taking a test, and are tempted to cheat, you won't be there to tell them "no." When they face those tough decisions between right and wrong, you may not be around or available to give them the answer. But "God is the one who goes with you. He will not fail you or forsake you."

What a perfect lesson for our kids to learn from this verse. As a believer, we have nothing to fear. John tells us perfect love casts out all fear. There is no obstacle too big for us to face if we trust the Lord to guide us. And if He is guiding us, He is also protecting us. Nothing can touch us unless He allows it. So, who's afraid of the big, bad wolf? Not I!

Lord, I have nothing to fear. I know that, but sometimes things get scary, and I panic. Calm my fears and let me see You defending me.

SEPTEMBER 30

ONE!

Deuteronomy 31

BEST VERSE: 4
Hear, O Israel! The Lord is our God. The Lord is One!

Every Jewish person knows this verse. It's part of their daily prayers. Our God is One! There is no other. It's kind of like us chanting at a ballgame, "We're Number One! We're Number One!" But this shout is directed at the world to acknowledge that Jehovah is the One and Only God.

Shouldn't we be shouting the same thing? Our God is Number One! He is the Only One! He is our Everything! There is no other god! Instead, we try to apologize for our God when the world "blames" Him for evil. We try to make our God politically correct. Pardon me, but God does not care about being politically correct. He IS correct, all the time and in every situation. He is THE Truth!

TEACHING MOMENT

We must teach our children this basic principle. The following verses in Deuteronomy 6 say that. Why not have verses written and hanging all over the house? Put them on the fridge. Put them on the bathroom mirrors. Challenge your child to memorize one verse a week. Write it out for them or have them do it if they are able. Then post it in their room, in their bathroom, and even put it in their lunchbox.

The great thing about knowing and believing that God is One is there is no confusion about who to worship. Our children need to know that. There are no worries about offending another "god." Unlike other people in the world, we focus all our adoration on our One God who exists in Three! Our God died for us. He doesn't ask us to die for Him. Our God lives in us. He is not in some far off place that is unreachable or unachievable.

Are you living today as if you truly believe that God is ONE! Do you want to have the ONE guiding you? Why don't you right now just stop whatever you are doing and thank Him for being ONE? Thank Him for taking you into His family. Thank Him for rescuing you from the domain of darkness.

Thank You Father for seeing me Number One, too! You gave Your Son just for me! I choose to live like it!

FOCUSED

Proverbs 3–4

BEST VERSES: 4:25–26
Let your eyes look directly ahead and let your gaze be fixed straight in front of you. Watch the path of your feet and all your ways will be established.

Have you ever been hiking in the woods? My wife and I love to do that. In fact, we need to do that more. Just being outside enjoying the creation of God is refreshing. But part of hiking is keeping your eyes on the trail, right? I mean, you can get off the trail quickly if you are not careful, and then you're lost.

Trails look different according to how much light you have, too. Walking in the woods at night requires a well-defined path. You need to be extra mindful of each step you take, or you can step in a hole or trip over something.

TEACHING MOMENT

Most children love to go into the woods to explore. But we must teach them how to navigate the trails. In the same way, we must teach them to navigate the trails of life. The next time you are in the woods with your kids, use this verse. Expound on the fact that we have to keep our eyes on the trail. If you want to look around, stop and take it all in, but don't walk and do that.

The Lord tells us here in this passage to look, let our gaze be fixed and to watch. Three times in two verses he talks about how we should see. He wants us to teach others the same skill. We must stay focused on the path, or we are prone to wander off.

How are you walking today? Are you hopelessly lost in the woods with the trail nowhere in sight? Have you forgotten how you got there? Stop where you are! Ask the Lord to direct you back to His path. He has blazed it! He will guide you! You just have to trust that His path is the best one for you. Break out your compass and let Him lead you to "true North," back to Him.

O Lord, keep my eyes focused on You. Keep my path straight. I need to be more aware of those things in my path that could trip me up.

NO POWER!

Matthew 4

BEST VERSE: 1

Then Jesus was led up by the Spirit into the wilderness to be tempted by the devil.

It is always curious to me that the third person of the Trinity led Jesus, the second person of the Trinity, into the wilderness TO BE TEMPTED BY THE DEVIL. Why would he do that? For what purpose? Did Jesus need testing? I don't think so.

God needed to show the devil that he had NO POWER over Jesus. Jesus was God and had always been God. No evil temptation was going to lure Him to sin against His heavenly Father.

That same Spirit lives in us today as believers. When you face temptation, remember that the devil has NO POWER over you, either. That Spirit is in your spirit to empower you to have victory over the devil. Isn't that amazing? Isn't that glorious?

TEACHING MOMENT

The next time your family are in the middle of a power outage, use this verse to teach your children. Just like the house has no power unless the electricity is on, the devil has no power unless the Lord gives it to him. He is powerless to influence them. And he can only tempt them with the limited power and presence God gives him. How frustrating for him, but how great for us!

Father, You are the source of all my power. I know that, but remind me today of the unlimited power that is available to me through Your Son, Jesus Christ.

WHAT A JOURNEY!

Deuteronomy 1

BEST VERSE: 2

It is eleven days' journey from Horeb by the way of Mount Seir to Kadesh-barnea.

Don't you love GPS? I mean, come on, don't you love that voice that pops up whenever you miss your turn shouting, "Rerouting! Rerouting!" Then the map resets and gives you a new route. Sometimes, that new route can take you on quite a journey. If you had just trusted the directions the first time, you may have avoided a rather lengthy reroute.

Think how the Israelite children felt. A journey that could have taken as little as elven days got "rerouted" into a FORTY-YEAR JOURNEY. Why? Because they missed their turn? Well, kind of. They missed their opportunity to trust the Lord who had told them to trust Him. They missed the opportunity to go into the Promised Land and enjoy the blessings of the Lord. They, instead, wandered in the desert for forty years until that generation was all dead. They missed it! So sad!

TEACHING MOMENT

Our children can learn a lot from this lesson. No, I don't mean if they don't obey, they are going to wander in the desert and die. But they may miss a blessing because of disobedience or lack of trust. They need to learn to trust the Lord's direction given through His Word. They need to learn to obey Mom and Dad when you are giving godly counsel. They need to learn to rest in the fact that God ALWAYS knows best.

Will you model that trust for them? Will you let them see you resting in the Lord's commands? If you lead, they are much more likely to follow.

Lord, I will follow. Give me the faith to trust that You always know the best route for my life. But I am thankful You are there when I get off course. I can hear You shouting, "Rerouting."

TEARS

Lamentations 2

BEST VERSE: 11

My eyes fail because of tears, my spirit is greatly troubled; my heart is poured out on the earth because of the destruction of the daughter of my people, when little ones and infants faint in the streets of the city.

Jeremiah was heartbroken for his people. He knew the judgment which had fallen on the nation was because of the sins of the people. They had turned away from the Lord God and sought after other gods. Because of their rebellion God had to correct them.

But look at this verse, especially the last phrase: "when little ones and infants faint in the streets of the city." These were innocent victims of their parents' sin. Jeremiah was weeping for these babies and children who were only guilty of being the children of those who had turned their backs on God.

TEACHING MOMENT

Now, understand me. We are ALL guilty until forgiven. We are born with a sinful nature. But sometimes the innocent suffer because of others. Having worked for almost forty years with children, I can tell you that children suffer due to their parents' sin. Divorce wrecks homes, and children suffer. Alcohol and drugs destroy the children as well as the parents who have the addiction.

As a parent, keep in mind that your sins will have an effect on your children. The way you choose to live your life will likely determine the life your children will face. Most of us only want what is best for our children. We want them to have it better than we did. We want them to succeed. If that is you, then choose righteousness. Let that be their inheritance.

Are you causing your children to "faint in the streets"? Are your sins forcing your children to struggle? Repent! Go before the Father right now and beg His forgiveness. Ask Him to cleanse you of your desire for sin. He will! Do it for your children. Don't let your rebellion put your children in the very center of wickedness.

O Lord God, I repent of my sins which have been the cause of my children's struggles. Forgive me of choosing my desires over yours. Let me see the effect my sin has had on my family and cleanse me of all of that.

HEAVYWEIGHT

Joshua 23

BEST VERSE: 3
And you have seen all that the Lord your God has done to all these nations because of you, for the Lord your God is He who has been fighting for you.

I don't know why, but I have this picture in my head of a heavyweight boxer when I read this verse. I know, dumb, right? I can just see our Father punching out the devil and all his minions who attack us. This verse reminds me that God is the one fighting my battles, not me.

Sure, I try to fight back. I get all mad and puffed up and think I have the moral superiority to fight. But, in my own power, I won't last one round with the puniest demon. Thanks be to God that I don't have to go fifteen rounds with my attackers. I just have to tag out and let my loving Father take over. He is always there to defend me. He is always there to fight for me, just like He did for the children of Israel.

TEACHING MOMENT

Has your son or daughter gotten into a fight with someone yet? Chances are it will happen. Sometimes those fights are more than just a misunderstanding. Sometimes they are true life lessons. How your child responds to adversity is so important. Read this verse, better yet the entire 23rd chapter of Joshua, to them. Let them see and understand that the God who led the children of Israel is the same God who will lead them.

Now, I am not saying that your children should stand there and "take it" when someone physically attacks them. We should always teach our children to defend themselves and the defenseless. But I am saying that many "battles" we take on are better left to the Father. He knows how to respond. He can calm our spirit. He can direct us how to respond to others, even those who are against us.

With whom are you having trouble today? Who is "pushing your buttons" right now? Lay it down. Talk to the Lord. You may have to examine yourself. In fact, you should examine yourself first to make sure you are not the problem. When you are "confessed up" and are sure that you are not the problem, how about this? Pray for your enemy. Yep, I said that. Give them over to God. He can handle them.

Today, put down your fleshly attitude and allow the Lord to take over. He can handle anything you give to Him.

My Defender, You are the One who comes to my rescue. You are the One who defeats my enemies. I thank You for being there when I am at my weakest.

OCTOBER 6

NOT MY HAIR!

Judges 16

BEST VERSE: 17
So he told her all that was in his heart and said to her, "A razor has never come on my head, for I have been a Nazirite to God from my mother's womb. If I am shaved, then my strength will leave me and I will become weak and be like any other man."

My wife almost always hates it when I get my hair cut. I like it short, and she likes it a little longer. I especially like it short when it's hot out. It just makes it easier to wipe off and go!

But unlike Samson, I know my strength is NOT in my hair. Samson, mistakenly built his confidence in his outside appearance (his hair) and thought because he didn't cut his hair due to the Nazirite vow, he was okay with God. But, if you read the whole story about Samson, you realize his life was nothing close to the life of a Nazirite.

TEACHING MOMENT
What a great story to use to teach our children about obedience to God. Obedience has nothing to do with how we look on the outside. God is only interested in the heart. Now, should we keep up our appearance and look respectable? Sure! I truly believe the Lord wants us to present ourselves so as to not offend anyone. But our holiness is not tied to our appearance.

Your children are going to push the limits with their desires for dress or appearance. You may face that challenge of piercings, tattoos, and shaven heads. Remind your children that they, as believers, are representing the Lord in how they look. If they have a peace about their decision after truly searching the Scriptures and praying, then we must trust their decision. Of course, I am talking about an older child who has that ability.

But, before you judge your child, how about you? Are you keeping your body physically fit to honor the Lord? Sometimes we are so quick to judge others, including our own children, while we aren't doing our best to represent the Lord.

Lord, take ALL of me. Let my life honor you in all I do and all I am.

OCTOBER 7

BUT YOU DON'T KNOW WHAT THEY DID

Genesis 50

BEST VERSES: 19–20
And Joseph said unto them, "Do not be afraid: for am I in God's place? As for you, you meant evil against me, but God meant it for good, in order to bring about this present result, to preserve many people alive."

Wow! That's the first word that comes to mind. Joseph saw through the pain of rejection and deception from his brothers to the ultimate purpose of God in his life. He saw, perhaps second-hand, that God put him where he was to save his family, even those brothers who had done him so wrong.

Can you do that? Can I do that? Can we accept wrongs done to us as God's purpose for our lives? Can we see through the pain and perhaps tears? Can we allow God to have His perfect will in our lives, even if it means pain and suffering?

TEACHING MOMENT
Today's devotional entry focuses on family hurts. Your children are going to have those throughout life. They need to learn now how to manage those feelings when someone close hurts them. What a perfect story. Just like

Joseph, they can forgive their sister or brother, mother or father, husband or wife, when they intentionally or unintentionally hurt them. But there is a secret to it.

Without Christ we can't. There is NO WAY!!! We will get bitter and vengeful. We will seek to "repay" those who have hurt us or our loved ones. Our flesh is just that way. Outside of Christ, we are evil.

But . . . in Christ we can do all things. We can love the most hateful person. That doesn't mean we have to love their behaviors. Heavens no! But we must love them. Remember—Christ washed the feet of Judas just before he betrayed Him. Whose feet can you wash today?

Give me the power, Lord, to love others. Let me love them through You. I can love, but only as I allow You to love.

OCTOBER 8

DOING WHAT'S RIGHT

1 Samuel 31

BEST VERSES: 11-12
Now when the inhabitants of Jabesh-gilead heard what the Philistines had done to Saul, all the valiant men rose and walked all night, and took the body of Saul and the bodies of his sons from the wall of Beth-shan.

This is, I must admit, a pretty somber story. Saul and his three sons were killed in battle by the Philistines. The Philistines, trying to humiliate the Israelites, fastened their bodies to a wall. How awful! How denigrating! So, the men of Jabesh-gilead came and took them down. The Philistines could have killed them for this, but they came anyway.

Now, why would they risk that? Because Saul had rescued them from Nahash, king of the Amorites, years ago when Saul had just begun his reign as king. They had not forgotten Saul's courage and what he had done for them. This was payback for the kindness shown them. They had to do this.

TEACHING MOMENT
Kindness is something that is hard to teach our children. They learn this best by observing it. So, Mom and Dad, be kind! We are told in the Word to put

on kindness. I believe the Lord knows that it just does not come naturally to our flesh. But it is expected.

Find some ways for your children to show kindness to others. Take some cookies to the local fire station and thank the firemen for their service. When you see a police officer in a restaurant while you are out eating, buy his or her meal. Walk up to a soldier and thank him or her for their service to our country. Take a meal to a shut-in at your church. These are all ways to show kindness and gratitude to others.

Who has done something for you in the past for which you have not thanked them properly? Do that today. Pick up the phone and call them. Send them a gift card. Whatever you choose to do, just do it. You might just make their day.

Father, thank you for sending people in my life who bless me. Show me today how to bless them.

OCTOBER 9

IN HIS HANDS

Psalms 31–32

BEST VERSE: 31:5
Into Your hand I commit my spirit; You have ransomed me, O Lord, God of truth.

Do you recognize the first half of the verse? Jesus said those words on the cross when He gave up His last breath. He voluntarily gave it up. No one took it. In the same way, we have to voluntarily give up our lives to the Father. He won't just take it.

And why do we do that? Look at the second part of the verse. He has ransomed us. Because Jesus gave up His life for us, He paid the ransom so we can give up our lives for Him. How cool is that? Are you committed to Him today?

TEACHING MOMENT
Do your children have commitment problems? Some kids have a real problem sticking to something. They start playing a sport and drop it when it gets

hard. They may begin a new hobby but get bored quickly. They may even drop friends.

Learning to be committed is something that we parents must teach them. We need to hold them accountable to their commitments, especially when it affects others. But the main commitment we need to teach them is being committed to the Lord. And that is best modeled by us. As they see us living up to our commitment, they will learn.

Are you living up to your commitment? Are you following Jesus each day? If you aren't, that lack of commitment could cause someone else to turn away. They may see you saying you are a believer but not living like it. Don't do that. Live for Him today and draw others into His presence.

Lord, I am committed today to follow You. I know I have said that a lot and fallen flat on my face. But today, Lord, I recommit myself to You, knowing others are watching.

OCTOBER 10

DEVILED HAM

Matthew 8

BEST VERSE: 32
And He said to them, "Go!" And they came out and went into the swine, and the whole herd rushed down the steep bank into the sea and perished in the waters.

I have always loved this story. My uncle was a hog farmer, so I saw pigs a lot. They are nasty animals. They smell. They stay dirty. They are just nasty. But to see them full of demons—now that would be a sight. And then to see them all run in the water and drown—that would have been crazy and perhaps sad to see.

But that is exactly what happened. Jesus commanded the demons inside the two men to leave. But notice He just said one word: "GO!" The demons had chosen the pigs. I guess pigs are better than nothing. With one word He sent them. They didn't leave until He said, "Go!" But then they obeyed Him.

TEACHING MOMENT

There are a couple of lessons here for our children. One, Jesus loves everyone, even those who may appear a little crazy. He had compassion on these two deranged, tormented souls. He set them free. We don't know what happened to them afterwards, but I have to believe their lives were changed and they couldn't help but tell the story to everyone.

Secondly, children need to understand that Jesus is the ultimate authority. Even the demons have to obey Him. And if demons, who hate Jesus, have to obey Him when He speaks, why wouldn't we, who love Him, want to obey Him? Hearing the Lord's voice is one thing, but obeying it is so much more important. And they obeyed immediately. They didn't ask for more time or a better breed of pigs. They obeyed.

Are you obeying the Lord's commands? Or are you picking and choosing which commands fit your schedule or your lifestyle? Obedience is not optional. If you are a follower of Christ, you must obey His commands. Followers follow. Ask Him right now what His orders are for today. He may just surprise you.

Father God, thank You for sending Your Son to rescue me. I, too, was tormented and deranged before He came into my life. Help me obey each day and do it with joy.

OCTOBER 11

WHERE DO YOU KEEP THE WORD?

Deuteronomy 11

BEST VERSES: 18-21

"You shall therefore impress these words of mine on your heart and on your soul; and you shall bind them as a sign on your hand, and they shall be as frontals on your forehead. You shall teach them to your sons, talking of them when you sit in your house and when you walk along the road and when you lie down and when you rise up. You shall write them on the doorposts of your house and on your gates, so that your days and the days of your sons may be multiplied on the land which the LORD swore to your fathers to give them, as long as the heavens remain above the earth."

Can I ask you a question? Where is your Bible? Do you even know where it is? Is it on a shelf somewhere covered in dust? When you come home from church on Sundays, does it stay right where you put it until next Sunday?

For many that is the sad truth. But according to this passage we should have it with us at all times. We should "bind it" to our palms and forehead. Now we can't literally walk around all the time with the Bible in our hand or tied to our forehead. I mean, we could, but we would have a hard time getting anything done. So, how can we teach our children this truth?

TEACHING MOMENT

We must be quick to pick up our Bible (bind it to our palms) when we need an answer. The Bible truly has the answer to all of life's questions. But in order to find the answer, we have to read the book. We must be able to lay our hands on it at any time. With today's smartphones and Bible apps, that is so easy.

We also must have the Word of God memorized (bind it to our foreheads). Scripture memorization is difficult for some. I know the older I get the harder it becomes. But when all else fails— hard copies, apps, computer software—we can always have the Word in our memory. Help your children memorize Scripture, maybe just one verse a week!

I will admit that I wasn't consistent about teaching my kids the Word when they were young. Sure, we read the Bible, and they were in church, but I don't believe I did all I could have done to impress on them the importance of God's Word in their life. Christopher and Casey, forgive me for not being more diligent about that. Don't be like me, parents. Use God's Word daily in your kids' lives. After all, verse 21 promises a blessing to those who do!

Give me a renewed desire to memorize Your Word, O God. Help me retain the words in my mind and in my heart so that I will always have them with me.

WHAT ABOUT ME?

Genesis 43

BEST VERSE: 23B
Then he brought Simeon out to them.

How would you like to have been Simeon? He was left behind in jail after the first trip to get grain. Instead of a quick return, the brothers weren't allowed to return with Benjamin, as requested by Joseph. When all the grain they had brought back was gone, only then did Jacob allow them to return.

How long were they gone? We don't know. We do know that each trip took at least 10 days or more. That means if they had returned immediately it would have taken 20 days. But since they stayed until the grain was gone, it may have been months before they returned. All that time, Simeon was in jail. And then when they do come back, all it says is, "Then he brought Simeon out to them." There is no mention of hugs and tears and, "We missed you brother."

TEACHING MOMENT
There will come a time when your children will feel they are invisible to their friends or someone they really like. They may feel abandoned by someone. What a perfect verse to share with them. Even though Simeon may have felt abandoned, God was working out His plan. In the end, he was restored to his family. Likewise, if your son or daughter will trust the Lord, they will see God's plan.

That doesn't necessarily ease the pain and hurt at the time. I know that. But we have to show our children that God always has a plan. He is never caught off guard. He is always prepared. He is never surprised. But our children must allow Him to do His will in their lives. When they learn to accept that, life is so much easier.

How about you? Are you struggling with some "injustices" in your life? Do you feel you have been mistreated? Ask the Lord to show you His purpose in all of this. He will, in His time. He will reveal why He has allowed you to go through the things you are facing. Trust Him.

God, I don't like some of the things I am having to go through right now. I don't care for the discomfort, but I am going to trust You. I believe You know exactly what is happening and why. Show me in Your time.

OCTOBER 13

ONE WAY

John 14

BEST VERSE: 6

Jesus said to him, "I am the way, and the truth, and the life; no one comes to the Father but through Me."

I read about a Christian minister who actually said that Christianity was NOT the only way to heaven. Well, I don't know about you, but what do they do with this verse today? I mean, it's pretty clear to me. Jesus said it. I didn't.

The world, including some "ministers," want to diminish the importance of Jesus. They say, "Surely a loving God would not send anyone to hell." Jesus matters. He IS the only way. He is the ONE way. There is NO OTHER WAY! Don't let anyone tell you anything different.

TEACHING MOMENT

Listen to me, moms and dads, your children are going to be bombarded with these "don't believe Jesus" statements. They are going to hear from all sides how God either doesn't matter or is unimportant. They are going to be told that Jesus is cool and all, but. . . .

Read them this verse. Better yet, have them memorize it for their defense. Jesus is the only way, the only truth, and the only life. Your children need to believe this. Nothing is more important than this.

Okay, so I seem to be on my soapbox. But I get a little passionate when I hear my Savior's relevance questioned. I want everyone to know what a great and mighty Lord He is. I want others to experience the joy of knowing Him before it's too late. I don't want them to wait until the end. I want them to live with Him and for Him.

O Father of life, You are the only reason I live. You give me focus. You give me purpose. Give me the opportunities today to show someone this truth.

A LIGHTWEIGHT
Daniel 5

BEST VERSE: 27

"'TEKEL'—you have been weighed on the scales and found deficient."

Belshazzar had a problem. He had received a handwritten message on the wall of the palace but couldn't read it. He and his drunken partiers had seen a hand write the message and were terrified. Only Daniel was able to interpret it. While part of that message does not apply to us (i.e, we won't be overthrown by the Medes or Persians), I believe this phrase does.

I don't know about you, but I have always struggled with my weight. I have probably lost and gained 5 tons in my lifetime. I have never had someone tell me, "You have been weighed on the scales and found deficient." But that is NOT what the Lord is referring to here. The king's character and humility were deficient. How about yours?

TEACHING MOMENT

Our children will definitely glean from us how we live our lives. They will model our humility or pride. They will remember our integrity or dishonesty. They will repeat many of our selfish or selfless acts. So, what are you teaching them? There is no guarantee they will follow our godly examples. Belshazzar didn't follow his father's repentant behavior. Instead he partied hard. He thumbed his nose at the very God who had punished and delivered his father.

But we parents must do all we can to set the godly example for our children to follow. We do not want them to be "weighed on the scales and found deficient" anymore than we want to be told that. Will you vow this year to weigh every action you take in light of how your children will repeat it? Will you ask yourself, "Do I want my son/daughter to do what I am doing?"

I know I will never be perfect, but I sure want to be. Why? Because my Father in heaven is. I want to be just like Him. I want to be remembered as a replica of Jesus. How about you?

Oh, how I long to be a heavyweight for Jesus. After all, He did and does for me, I desire for my character to be one that reflects my Lord. Help me to be aware and remember my children may model and repeat my actions and behavior. This is a very humbling thought and responsibility.

SHOULDA, COULDA, WOULDA
Joshua 15

BEST VERSE: 63
Now as for the Jebusites, the inhabitants of Jerusalem, the sons of Judah could not drive them out; so the Jebusites live with the sons of Judah at Jerusalem until this day.

What did God tell them to do? Destroy the people. Don't leave one alive? Why? He didn't want His people to get pulled into idolatry and heathen living. If the inhabitants of Canaan were to be left to live among them, there would be confusion and moral failures.

But here we see that the Jebusites lived among them. Stupid! And what happened later? Intermarriage, rebellion, strife. The same is true for us. When we allow our past "pagans" to live among us, our walk with Christ is hampered. We can't focus on righteous living as long as we allow our past to influence us.

TEACHING MOMENT
Does your child have that special item which it seems will never leave their side? Do they have habits that belong to their life before Christ? We need to show them the blessings that await to a totally surrendered life. They need to see how those unhealthy paths lead to destruction.

What do I mean? I am referring to anything in their lives that does not point them to Jesus. Idolatry can be seen in a lot of seemingly innocent things. Our children need to be reminded of that covenant they made with God at salvation. This covenant demands total surrender.

What are you dragging along in your walk with Christ? Whatever it is, lay it down. Let the love of Christ fill you to overflowing, so there is no room for any "wrong" thing.

Lord, I know You are holy and demand whole-hearted devotion. Thank You for the reminder that I, too, am holy in Your eyes. Help me to live that way each day.

BETTER THAN A DURACELL

John 8

BEST VERSE: 12

Then Jesus again spoke to them, saying, "I am the Light of the world; he who follows Me will not walk in the darkness, but will have the Light of life."

Don't you hate it when you grab a flashlight to go into a dark room or out into the night, and the batteries are weak or dead? It is so hard to keep fresh batteries in those things. I think there is some kind of little gremlin that sneaks around and sucks all the energy out of batteries.

I just love this verse today. We are promised by the very mouth of Jesus that, if we have His light, we will not walk in darkness. We will have the Light of life. Wow! Never ending light. We never have to walk in darkness. Now of course this is talking about a spiritual light, not a physical one. But isn't it even scarier to walk in spiritual darkness, not knowing what's out there? Not with Jesus. He lights the way.

TEACHING MOMENT

The next time your children ask to use the flashlight (and you know they are going to leave it on and drain the battery) read them this verse. Explain to them that just like the flashlight you are giving to them can light the room or the path, Jesus can light their spiritual dwelling and walkways. Go into a dark room with them and turn on the flashlight. Kids understand concrete things. Show them the effect of the light in a dark place. Then explain the effect of Jesus' light in a dark world.

And as we possess the light of Jesus through salvation, we let His light shine through us. We illuminate the dark things around us by our godly living and testimony. We become the flashlight, which is only powered by the batteries (Jesus). The only difference is the Jesus batteries never run out because He is Light, not just a source of light.

So today, moms and dads, won't you shine for Jesus? Won't you let your kids see you being that human flashlight, yielded to the touch of the Light?

You are the Light of the world. Illuminate me so I can shine You on others. I don't want to walk in darkness anymore.

OCTOBER 17

A GOOD REPUTATION
1 Samuel 22

BEST VERSE: 14
Then Ahimelech answered the king and said, "And who among all your servants is as faithful as David, even the king's son-in-law, who is captain over your guard, and is honored in your house?"

Ahimelech is in a tough spot. He has been summoned before King Saul and accused of treason with David, who had fled from the king's presence because he was trying to kill him. Ahimelech was an innocent bystander in this saga. All he knew was that David was highly respected, a commander in Saul's army, and the king's son-in-law. Why was Saul accusing him?

David had built his reputation as a respected man. People all over the nation knew his name. When David's name was mentioned they only thought good things. No one would have ever suspected David of treason. The lesson here is your name means something.

TEACHING MOMENT
What a great story to share with your children. The next time they do something that could possibly bring them public shame (stealing, lying) share this story. Our children need to know how important having a good name is. It could actually save their lives one day.

If we are known for good, rather than evil, we can have a stronger influence on others also. Who wants to listen to a known liar? No one. Who wants to trust someone who they know steals? No one. Teach your children the importance of a good reputation, not for themselves, but for the Lord. We represent Him as believers.

Are you representing the Lord with your reputation? Do people hear your name and think only good things? Does your name bring a smile or a frown on the face of others? Do your children hide the fact they are your children or wear your name proudly?

What are you doing today to build up the name of Jesus? If you are a believer, do nothing to bring shame on His name. Let all who know you as a Christian know that you stand for truth and honesty. Let them see pure joy and love in your countenance.

I want to allow You Lord to shine through me today. Be my mouth, eyes and ears today so that all I do brings You honor.

BUT . . .

Genesis 6

BEST VERSE: 8
"But Noah found favor in the eyes of the LORD."

That is not such a small word, you know. Take for instance, "I might die, BUT I might live" or "I could have won that race, BUT I fell right before I crossed the finish line." "But" changes things. "But" can often change the whole direction. Just do a word study through the Bible on the word "but." You will be amazed.

Here God has determined to destroy all of mankind. BUT Noah found favor in the eyes of the Lord. Noah turned God's head. Noah's life caught God's eye. Because of the way Noah lived, his family was spared. Do you think Noah knew God's plan when he was living that righteous life? No, BUT he lived it anyway.

TEACHING MOMENT
I bet your children have used that word "but" a lot, haven't they? "But Mom!" "But Dad!" Right? The next time they throw that out to you, pull out this small verse. Tell them how important that word is. It shouldn't be used as an excuse maker. It should be used a direction changer.

When they think they can't do something, show they how they can. "You think you can't do this, BUT I know you can." "You think no one likes you, BUT I love you." What a huge three letter word.

The next time you pick up the Word, watch for those "buts." See how God uses them in Scripture to change things. And then apply them to your life. I bet they change your life too.

But God, I know You are my everything. But God, I love you. But God, I trust You completely.

OCTOBER 19

STAYING PURE

Daniel 1

BEST VERSE: 8

But Daniel made up his mind that he would not defile himself with the king's choice food or with the wine which he drank; so he sought permission from the commander of the officials that he might not defile himself.

It is so easy to just go along with the crowd, isn't it? When everyone around you is choosing the wrong things, it is easy to get caught up in the moment. Making the right choice can be frowned upon by society. Taking a stand for purity is scoffed and made fun of.

Tim Tebow, a famous college and professional athlete, has been mocked because of his decision to remain pure until marriage. His choice of virginity is virtually unheard of today, especially among men. But, like Daniel, he has chosen the ways of the Lord over the ways of the world.

TEACHING MOMENT

Teaching purity to our children begins early. You can't start talking about purity when they reach the teen years. Oh no! It starts back when they are old enough to start having conversations. We have to be mindful of what they allow their eyes to see. We have to be careful of outside influences.

And the best way to do this is to ground them in the Word. That's what saved Daniel. It wasn't his own self-righteousness that kept him pure. It wasn't his own self-will that made him choose the right thing. No, he knew God's Word demanded purity, and he chose that.

What choice have you made? When all the guys at work are joking and laughing at coarse jokes, what do you do? When the ladies in your club continually invite you to events where you know your desire to please God will be challenged, how do you respond? Taking a stand is hard sometimes. But God promises to be with us through it all.

Father, thank You for giving me the courage to make a stand on Your principles. Thank You for allowing me to represent You to the world. Help me point others to You!

ANOTHER KING

1 Samuel 8

BEST VERSE: 7
The Lord said to Samuel, "Listen to the voice of the people in regard to all that they say to you, for they have not rejected you, but they have rejected Me from being king over them."

We don't have a king in America, so it's hard to comprehend that type of rule. But the people of Israel wanted one. They wanted someone to lead them, since Samuel's sons were not following in their father's footsteps. The people wanted a leader like everyone else.

You probably are thinking, *I would never do that Carl. I love the Lord. I would never replace Him.* Are you sure about that? They say you can determine your god by examining where you spend your time and money. Where is yours spent?

TEACHING MOMENT
This lesson is all about loyalty. Our children must learn from us what that is. This is another one of those traits that is better caught than taught. We must show them what loyalty looks like by being loyal ourselves. How do we do that?

Loyalty can be seen in a number of ways, but for the purposes of this lesson, it is seen in how we talk about our God. Everything we say and do should honor Him. Our decisions should be weighed in relation to what He would have us do. Our children need to see us doing that, and when they do, we need to explain our loyalty to God.

To whom are you loyal? Are you loyal to your spouse? Are you loyal to your employer? Are you loyal to your friends? Most importantly, are you loyal to God? Do others know you are "sold out" to Him? Can others see your loyalty?

Before you judge the Israelites for wanting a king, check out your own loyalty. And remember that as you follow Him, others will reject you. They, like the Israelites, are shunning you as much as they are the Lord. That's okay. You just be loyal.

Father, help me to be loyal to the point that all who know me will know with whom I stand and who stands beside me. You are faithful. Help me to be more faithful.

OCTOBER 21

BEGGING GOD

1 Samuel 1

BEST VERSE: 11
She made a vow and said, "O Lord of hosts, if You will indeed look on the affliction of Your maidservant and remember me, and not forget Your maidservant, but will give Your maidservant a son, then I will give him to the Lord all the days of his life, and a razor shall never come on his head."

Have you ever begged God for something? I mean, really beg? Perhaps your son or daughter fell ill, and the doctors couldn't figure out why, so you made a vow to God. You promised Him you would do whatever He asked, if only He would heal your child. We get desperate in times of trials, don't we?

Hannah was desperate for a child. She promised to dedicate her son to the Lord. She followed through on that promise, and thus, we have Samuel. Samuel grew to be a great man of God who helped lead the nation of Israel for years. But it all started with a mother's vow.

CRUSTLESS BREAD

Deuteronomy 8

BEST VERSE: 3

"He humbled you and let you be hungry, and fed you with manna which you did not know, nor did your fathers know, that He might make you understand that man does not live by bread alone, but man lives by everything that proceeds out of the mouth of the LORD."

Hey moms, have you ever wondered if the Israelite moms cut the crust off their children's manna? Call me strange, but I have. My grandma would do that for me. She would make the best peanut butter and jelly sandwiches on whole wheat bread. Her sandwiches were so good because she would mix the peanut butter and jelly together and then spread it on the bread. I still make mine that way. But then she would cut the crust off, so the sandwich was soft from edge to edge. Wow! I think I may have to go to the kitchen.

TEACHING MOMENT

This passage today would be a great story to share with your kids while you are making them a sandwich. Ask them if they think the manna bread had crust. But then talk about what the passage is really saying – that life is not about bread or pizza or ice cream or anything we eat. It is about eating God's Word. Now that is sure to raise some eyebrows, so you can then talk about how we need to read, study, meditate and really "digest" God's Word so that it, just like food, can nourish us and make us stronger. Explain how some foods can make us stronger while others really don't have any nourishment at all. But God's Word is the best nourishment for our soul.

Okay, I'm off to the kitchen. I sure hope I have some whole wheat bread and some peanut butter. Yum!

Lord, You are the bread of life. Give me a hunger for Your Word above all else. Let me feast on Your truth today.

COMPLETION

Lamentations 4

BEST VERSE: 22A

The punishment of your iniquity has been completed, O daughter of Zion; He will exile you no longer.

Have you ever been through a grueling, physical challenge? I remember some extreme practices when I played high school football. I remember my first running class in college. I remember going through my stem cell transplant in 2010. Physical challenges can be extreme. But they all come to an end (in one way or the other) at some point. And the relief when they are over is sweet.

Jeremiah is telling the people that their punishment will end. The siege against Jerusalem by Nebuchadnezzar had been extreme. People were starving. Physical pain from hunger and thirst was real. But the Lord was bringing an end to it. Their punishment had been fulfilled. He would exile them "no longer."

TEACHING MOMENT

I pray your child never has to go through an extreme physical challenge. Nothing is more trying for parents than to watch their children suffer. But, if this occurs, rest assured there is always an end to it. Our job as parents is to encourage our children during these times and continue to point them to Jesus. After all, He is the only true source of relief.

What am I talking about? Your child could face an illness or an injury requiring months of physical therapy. They could simply be pushed physically as they compete in some sport. Whatever it is, point them to Jesus. Let Jesus coach them through it. And stay strong yourself so you can lift them when they are down spiritually.

This may seem like a "Debbie Downer" devotional today. Sorry. Life can get us down sometimes. Life isn't always easy. But no matter what we or our children face, we have a God who has "exiled" us no longer. He has provided a way out—His precious Son.

Lord, sometimes I get low. I don't think I can take another step. Remind me on those days that I don't have to take that step. You are there to carry me, if I will just trust and call on You.

THIRSTY FOR GOD

Psalms 41–42

BEST VERSE: 42:1
As the deer pants for the water brooks, so my soul pants for You, O God.

I recently began working out again in the gym after a month and a half break due to neck and back injuries from a car wreck. At my age, that's like starting all over again. One thing I noticed (besides the sore muscles) is the need to drink water during my workouts. My panting and, yes, groaning make me very thirsty. I just need a small sip of water to quench my thirst for that moment.

We should have the same desire for that soul-quenching water from the Lord. As we go through our daily walk with Him, He is always ready to give us exactly what we need to continue the journey. We must have our soul's thirst quenched to keep moving in the direction He is pointing us.

TEACHING MOMENT
How do we get our children to have that same thirst for God? How do we instill in them the knowledge that He is always there when they are feeling faint and in need of a drink from the Spirit? Well, this is something we can't teach. We can't teach them to get thirsty. We can teach them to recognize the thirst, but they have to be willing to ask for what they need from the Savior.

Our job is to point them towards Jesus. Our job is to show them to come to Him for comfort and relief in those times when everything seems to be falling apart. When they don't have the answer, we point them to Jesus. We can give them advice, but we should always use God's wisdom from His Word, not our own wisdom.

The next time your child runs in the house after playing outside and asks for something to drink, use this verse. Explain how just as their physical body craves liquid to satisfy its thirst, their soul cries out for the quenching water of the Lord.

O God, I am thirsty today! My soul is parched for Your precious liquid. I want to drink deeply and often. Your well never runs dry.

UNUSUAL CHOICE

Judges 11

BEST VERSE: 29A
Now the Spirit of the Lord came upon Jephthah. . . .

Jephthah was a judge of Israel. What is so interesting about this judge, though, is he was born of a harlot out of wedlock. He wasn't the image of the one to be chosen to be a judge of Israel. But God used him to deliver the children of Israel from the Ammonites who threatened to take back part of the land which the Lord had given to them.

But notice what happens BEFORE he goes to battle. This verse says, "the Spirit of the Lord came upon Jephthah." The Spirit of the Lord does not come upon someone unless He has blessed them and given them His power to carry out a divine task. My point is this: God even used the illegitimate son of a harlot. God can use anyone He desires to accomplish His will. We just have to be willing.

TEACHING MOMENT
I think the object lesson for today is pretty clear. We need to teach our children that God can use anything or anyone He wants. God can choose them to accomplish great things for Him, if they will just surrender to His will. He can empower them through His Holy Spirit to do what they never thought was possible.

And they will have one advantage over Jephthah. In the Old Testament, the Holy Spirit did not live in the hearts of the people He indwelt. He would come and go, only empowering them at certain times. As Christians, your children ALWAYS have the Holy Spirit living in them, thus they always have His power.

Do you believe that? Do you understand that, as a believer in Christ, you have access to the Holy Spirit at all times? He lives in you. He empowers you. He comforts you. He emboldens you. So why aren't you living in His power? Why aren't you walking confidently before your enemies?

We all have bad days. We all face challenges. But, as believers, we have NO EXCUSE for not walking right into the battles before us knowing that God is with us. He indwells us. And He will fight our enemies for us. Just like Jephthah, who was chosen by God for a specific purpose, we have been chosen by Him before the foundation of the world. We have a purpose.

Show me my purpose, O God. I know You have chosen me. Your Holy Spirit is living in me.

WAS THAT GOD TALKING?

Deuteronomy 18

BEST VERSE: 21
"You may say in your heart, 'How will we know the word which the Lord has not spoken?'"

One of the most difficult spiritual concepts to teach children is how to know when it is the Lord speaking to them or just indigestion. Seriously, how do we teach them to listen to the Lord's voice and not be swayed by friends, culture, or even a misinformed teacher?

Moses answered his own question he proposed to the people by saying they would wait and see if what the prophet said became true. So, the answer is "Are your children hearing the truth as compared to THE Truth?" Our children need a measuring rod for what is true and what is false. We know as believers that the only real truth is God's Word. We have to use that to compare anything. If what we are hearing does not match up to what God says in His Word, then we are not to be swayed by it.

TEACHING MOMENT
That is why, parents, you must use God's Word, not your knowledge or wisdom, as the reason behind disciplining your children. We should always

point them to scripture when we correct. Not as a battering ram or a baseball bat, but as the gentle guide it is in our own lives. We need rules and guidelines, and God gives us those so clearly in His Word.

Your children are going to have many questions as they get older that will need clarity. Whom do they date? What will be their majors in college? Whom do they marry? Whom do they cast a vote for in an election? All these questions can be answered by clinging to His Word. Point them there. After all, if God says it, that simply settles it.

Father, I know the devil wants to confuse me. Help me distinguish Your voice from all others who would attempt to lure me away. I want to respond only to You.

OCTOBER 30

WHAT ARE YOU GIVING GOD?

Deuteronomy 26

BEST VERSES: 1–2

"Then it shall be, when you enter the land which the Lord your God gives you as an inheritance, and you possess it and live in it, that you shall take some of the first of all the produce of the ground which you bring in from your land that the Lord your God gives you, and you shall put it in a basket and go to the place where the Lord your God chooses to establish His name.

Everything we have belongs to God. He is the one who blesses us each day with food, drink, clothing, housing, and so many other things. He is the Great Benefactor. But He is not just that. He also expects us to honor Him by giving back in worship.

The people were commanded to give the Lord the first fruits of the land after they entered it. They would remember Him by giving to Him. Did God need these offerings? Of course not. He is THE ALL IN ALL. He can make something out of nothing. He doesn't NEED our offerings. But He smiles when we give back to Him in recognition of all He has given us.

TEACHING MOMENT

One of my regrets is that I don't think I taught my children to give to the Lord. I mean, we talked about it, and I encouraged them to give, but I didn't really sit down and explain the giving process to them fully. They are both adults now, and they have to decide that on their own.

Talk to your children about giving. Set up a jar in which they can deposit their offering money for the Lord. They can tithe of their allowance or from any chores they do for pay. They can tithe of any gifts they receive from friends or family. But don't just show them *how* to give. Tell them *why* we give. That will stay with them forever.

What are your first fruits? Where are they? Does God just get your crumbs? He wants to bless you more than you know. Giving to Him expresses to Him that we KNOW from whom our blessings come.

God, remind me of the joy of giving. Let me give with an attitude that honors You. Thank You for allowing me the privilege.

WHAT'S FOR LUNCH?

Mark 8

BEST VERSES: 14–21

And they had forgotten to take bread, and did not have more than one loaf in the boat with them. And He was giving orders to them, saying, "Watch out! Beware of the leaven of the Pharisees and the leaven of Herod." They began to discuss with one another the fact that they had no bread. And Jesus, aware of this, said to them, "Why do you discuss the fact that you have no bread? Do you not yet see or understand? Do you have a hardened heart? 'HAVING EYES, DO YOU NOT SEE? AND HAVING EARS, DO YOU NOT HEAR?' And do you not remember, when I broke the five loaves for the five thousand, how many baskets full of broken pieces you picked up?" They said to Him, "Twelve." "When I broke the seven for the four thousand, how many large baskets full of broken pieces did you pick up?" And they said to Him, "Seven." And He was saying to them, "Do you not yet understand?"

How many times have your kids asked, "Mom (Dad), what's for lunch?" They just assume, because you fed them breakfast, that there is more food coming. Right? They don't even question the fact that you would let them go hungry.

Then tell me why the disciples got all worked up about not having enough bread on the boat. They had just seen him feed over five thousand and then over four thousand. But now they were worried about lunch.

But before you get all spiritual and judge them, how many times have you questioned God's provision in your life? We wring our hands when the checking account balance gets low or when we don't see how we are going to pay that bill. We are just like the disciples. We question God's ability to meet our needs.

TEACHING MOMENT

The next time you are faced with that kind of situation, bring your kids in the room and share with them about the need. Then lead them in praying for that need. When the need is met, and it will be in His time, make sure they know how it was met. It may just surprise you how this will encourage them in their walk with Christ.

Father, give me this day my daily bread. I pray that believing You are going to meet all my needs. Thank You for allowing me to even ask.

HUNGER PAINS
John 4

BEST VERSE: 32

But He said to them, "I have food to eat that you do not know about."

I don't know about you, but I enjoy a good meal. Sitting down to a home-cooked meal is one the true enjoyments of life. Now that meal may vary from country to country, but knowing it is home-cooked makes it so much better.

The disciples had gone to town to fetch food, and now upon their return they had obviously prepared the meal and were encouraging Jesus to come eat. He, however, had no appetite for worldly provisions. His heart had been touched, and His words had gone forth to a Samaritan woman, a despised Samaritan. He had offered her living water, and she ran off to tell her neighbors. Was Jesus so eager for their return to hear about the living water that He had no appetite to eat?

Jesus was always kingdom-focused. He came with a purpose to seek and to save that which was lost. Surely, this Samaritan village was lost and in need of a Savior.

TEACHING MOMENT

How about you? Are you so kingdom-focused that you are always looking for opportunities to share the gospel, to offer that cool drink of living water? Your children are watching and observing how you take those moments to minister. You are teaching them to seize every chance they have to share the good news with someone.

You might just be preparing the next Billy Graham to be bold in their witness. They may be filing away those lessons on witnessing until they are old enough and have the opportunities themselves to be a witness. I promise you they will have plenty of chances in this lost world in which we live. But you, Mom and Dad, are the ones who will role model that behavior. Will you?

Are you willing today to "take a chance" and pray to the Lord that He will give you an opportunity to share with someone? You never know how the Lord will open the door for you to speak truth in the life of another.

O God, I have the best story in my possession through my life in You. Give me the opportunities today to share that story with someone else. I want to tell the story.

BOUNDARY LINES

Exodus 19

BEST VERSES: 10-12A

The Lord also said to Moses, "Go to the people and consecrate them today and tomorrow, and let them wash their garments; and let them be ready for the third day, for on the third day the Lord will come down on Mount Sinai in the sight of all the people. You shall set bounds for the people all around, saying, 'Beware that you do not go up on the mountain or touch the border of it. . . .'"

Borders! Boundaries! Limits! It seems as parents we are always stating those to our children. "Don't leave the yard!" "Don't get out of my sight!" Why do we set these limits? Because we want to keep our children safe, duh!

The Lord God set limits for His people. He told Moses in this passage as they approached Mt. Sinai to set boundaries around the mountain so the people would not sneak up and try to get a glimpse of Him. He wanted to **1)** keep them safe and **2)** see if they would obey.

It is interesting that these instructions were given not once but twice (just like we have to do for our own children). After giving these instructions to Moses, He told him to go back down and tell them again. Moses said, "God, I've already told them. We're good." But God sent him back to tell them again, to just make sure.

TEACHING MOMENT

As you set those limits for your children, make sure they are limits for their safety and not just to make you feel better. And make sure they understand the boundaries. Keep them clear and concise. Kids think concretely. Draw them a picture if necessary. God has drawn us all a picture of our boundaries. They are all found in His Word. Use it!

Thank You for boundaries, Lord. Keep me inside Your fence so I can remain safe and secure in You. You are my stronghold.

NOVEMBER 3

THERE HAVE ALWAYS BEEN "WICKED"

Judges 19

BEST VERSE: 23

Then the man, the owner of the house, went out to them and said to them, "No, my fellows, please do not act so wickedly; since this man has come into my house, do not commit this act of folly."

Chapters 19—21 of Judges contain probably one of the most confusing stories in Scripture. It involves concubines, homosexuality, rape, war, death, and forgiveness. It is apparent that wickedness has always been among us. People, left to their own decisions, will wallow in wickedness. Let's face it, sin feels good for a season. But there are always consequences for our sins.

Israel and the tribe of Benjamin are at war WITH EACH OTHER. It's brother against brother. This is NOT what God intended. They were doing what was good in their own eyes and not relying on the direction of the Lord. This story is a perfect example of how NOT to live.

TEACHING MOMENT

When your children hit their teen years and are determined to live how they want to live, read them this story. Show them how totally chaotic and wrong things can go when we are not following the Lord. Your children, even though they know the right way to live, can choose another path, resulting in wickedness. It's important they understand that wickedness always brings consequences.

The Lord won't let believers wallow in wickedness. He will discipline them at some point. God will not allow His holy name to be besmirched by us. His name means something. He won't be partnered with evil. So, just beware.

Is your life reflecting good choices or wickedness? Can the world even tell you are a believer by the way you live? Do your children feel drawn to Christ by the way you act around the house? Turn to Him today and ask Him to guide your every step.

> O Lord, I am prone to live just like the Benjamites in this story. My flesh's desires are strong. Give me the strength to always choose right, not wickedness.

GREATER IS HE THAT IS IN ME

Luke 4

BEST VERSE: 13
When the devil had finished every temptation, he left Him until an opportune time.

Don't you just love the audacity of Satan? Jesus, the Son of God, was led by the Holy Spirit (another part of the Trinity) into the wilderness. He hadn't eaten in forty days. He was hungry and probably a little tired. And when everything was JUST RIGHT Satan pounced. He pounced even though he knew he was taking on the Son of God. Jesus was not a stranger to him. But that did not deter Satan from trying to thwart God's plan for mankind.

TEACHING MOMENT
This is a great truth for our children to learn. If Satan would take on the very Son of God, surely he will try to lead us astray. He will try to tempt us in the same ways he tempted Jesus—physically, emotionally, and spiritually. Our children need to know that Satan is a real threat. But just like Jesus, with the power of God, not our own power, we can defeat him and resist the wiles of the devil. Greater is He that is in me!

The song "Greater Is He That Is in Me" has a verse that talks about Satan being a lion who is trying to kill us and eat us. Before we are in the gentle, protective hands of Christ, we are nothing but devil's food. But once we are in Christ, allowing Him to rule and reign in our hearts, Satan literally has no power over us. We are free! And Satan goes on a diet.

But he won't stop coming after us. Just look at the verse for today. He left Jesus after the temptations until another time presented itself. Boy is he stubborn! He wants us to be useless for the kingdom of Christ if he can't have us for himself. The secret for our children (and us) to remember is that Jesus is the key. He is the one who will make Satan flee. Let Jesus be the one you run to when Satan comes after you physically, emotionally, or spiritually. He truly is greater, and He lives in every believer through the Holy Spirit. Hallelujah!

God, You are the lion tamer. You are the one who shuts the devil's mouth when he comes to devour me. I know You are there to defend me.

NOVEMBER 5

GIVING TO OTHERS

Deuteronomy 14

BEST VERSES: 28-29
"At the end of every third year you shall bring out all the tithe of your produce in that year, and shall deposit it in your town. The Levite, because he has no portion or inheritance among you, and the alien, the orphan and the widow who are in your town, shall come and eat and be satisfied, in order that the Lord your God may bless you in all the work of your hand which you do."

I love the fact that the Lord had a plan from the beginning for us to meet the needs of those who lead us spiritually, as well as the less fortunate (aliens, orphans, and widows). It is just sad that we don't do a better job of it in the church or individually.

I serve on the board of a ministry called AMG International. AMG stands for Advancing the Ministries of the Gospel. It was founded in the 40s and then was led for several decades (beginning in 1947) by Dr. Spiros Zodhiates. One of the most recent ministry opportunities that has been given to

AMG is the refugee ministry in Greece, where thousands of refugees have come trying to get into Europe. What an opportunity to live out these verses!

TEACHING MOMENT

Our children, for the most part, love to give to others. How many times has your child asked to give something to the person beside the road with the sign in their hands? We adults are the ones who get hard-hearted and look the other way. Kids look AT the person and want to help.

In this case, they are teaching us. We need to listen to them. They are living out these verses. Whether it is assisting an Iraqi refugee in Greece or a homeless vet in Chattanooga, we need to do as the Lord leads and not fear. Give of your blessings. I promise you will be blessed so much more.

Lord, all I have is Yours. Direct me to give in the way You want me to give. Help me to hold all I have with an open hand.

NOVEMBER 6

INNOCENT BUT GUILTY

Luke 23

BEST VERSE: 25

And he released the man they were asking for who had been thrown into prison for insurrection and murder, but he delivered Jesus to their will.

I have often wondered what Barabbas thought of his release. He knew he was guilty of insurrection and murder, but Pilate released him anyway. Did Barabbas ever realize just who took his place that day? Did Barabbas ever acknowledge Christ as his Messiah? The Scriptures are silent on this, so we assume he never did. It would seem that if he had, that would have been big news and would have been recorded somewhere in one of the Gospels or another book.

We are just as guilty as Barabbas. We are known sinners. There is nothing we could have done to ever demand our release from the grips of sin. We were doomed for eternal punishment. But the one who is able secured our release from death. We have acknowledged Him as our Messiah. We have accepted Him as our Savior and Lord.

Your children are guilty too! They may not appear as a "Barabbas," but they are sinners from birth. Now, you may think your children are just too precious to be sinners. Just wait! Their true flesh will reveal itself. But there is hope for the vilest of sinners. Our job is to point them to the one who can free them from the power of sin.

Wow! This is a little heavy, isn't it? I guess I have just heard too little lately about sin. We can never forget just how powerful the forgiving power of God is in our lives. He didn't just cover our shame! He covered our sin—with the precious blood of His Son. Jesus died for us! Jesus even died for Barabbas, whether Barabbas ever acknowledged that or not.

Please don't water down the gospel to try to make it more palatable for your little ones. They need to know that without Jesus in their lives, they are no better than Barabbas. But through Jesus they are released and are free in Christ. Amen? Amen!!

Father, if it wasn't for Your grace, I would stand condemned for all eternity before You. You are my Redeemer. Praise You!

NOVEMBER 7

HALF TRUTHS

Genesis 20

BEST VERSE: 12

"Besides, she actually is my sister, the daughter of my father, but not the daughter of my mother, and she became my wife."

Isn't it amazing how we can justify our lies? We always think we have a very good reason to lie, don't we? We even see Abraham, whom God declared righteous just five chapters earlier, lie in a similar way about his wife, Sarah. He was afraid for his life. God had just told him in the previous chapters that He was going to give him a son and make him a great nation. Why couldn't he trust Him to protect him against a pagan king? So, he tells a lie to save his hide.

Before we jump to judgment, we are just as bad. We say we trust God to save us and take us to heaven, but we don't trust Him with our power bill. We believe He sent His son to die for us, but we don't believe He can rescue us from a pagan boss. Wow! We will justify our actions and even lie to protect ourselves.

TEACHING MOMENT

Children are prone to lie. It's just part of their sin nature. You don't have to teach them to lie. "Johnny, did you break that lamp?" "No mom.", as he hides a piece of it behind his back. "Susie, did you eat that cookie?" "No way!", as she wipes the crumbs from her mouth. But do you teach them to lie?

Have you ever told them when someone calls you don't want to speak to, "Tell them I just can't talk right now." Lie! Or they hear you tell the sales clerk that the item YOU broke came that way. Lie! Just know they are watching you. They are filing away those "lies" and will remember them when they need to justify their own lies.

Just tell the truth. Just show them and the Lord that truth is what you want guiding you. The Word is called truth.

God of Truth, remind me each time I am tempted to tell a little white lie that I am still lying. A half-truth is a whole lie. Let me be very aware of the lessons I am teaching my children.

NOVEMBER 8

BE CAREFUL THE NEWS YOU SHARE

2 Samuel 1

BEST VERSE: 16

David said to him, "Your blood is on your head, for your mouth has testified against you, saying, 'I have killed the Lord's anointed.'"

Oops! This Amalekite thought he was bringing David good news! Saul, David's persecutor for so many years, was dead. Now David could be king. This Amalekite even lied to make himself look better by saying he had killed Saul. Perhaps he was hoping for a reward. He obviously didn't know that David had spared Saul twice in the past when God had placed Saul in his hands.

Children love to tattle, don't they? They think they may gain some ground on brother or sister by informing you, Mom and Dad, when they have some "news" of their sibling's activities. Tattling will drive you crazy! It is hard to know what is true or untrue.

We adults tattle too, but we disguise the "news" as prayer requests. Have your children ever overheard you telling "news" about someone else that you were asked to keep to yourself? We just can't help ourselves, can we? Will you stop and think about the message you are showing your kids? If they hear you doing that, do you think they are ever going to share their deepest thoughts with you? Not hardly.

Your children will probably never come to you with a life-threatening decision, but their struggles at school or with friends sometimes seem life-threatening to them. And in this day and time, who is to say they are not? Your kids need your counsel and advice. Don't ruin that opportunity by being a tattle-tail yourself. To put it bluntly, keep your mouth shut. God knows your heart. Tell Him what you want to tell others. One thing's for sure—He can keep a secret!

Guard my lips, Lord, from spreading gossip. Keep me from spiritualizing my conversations. Help me, Lord, be truthful at all times.

NOVEMBER 9

SACRIFICE IS COSTLY

2 Samuel 24

BEST VERSE: 24A

However, the king said to Araunah, "No, but I will surely buy it from you for a price, for I will not offer burnt offerings to the LORD my God which cost me nothing."

David had gotten a little cocky. He decided to number the people, and upon realizing he had sinned he sought the Lord's forgiveness. So God sent Gad to give David His message. All this led to David needing a place to build an altar to offer sacrifices to God. He was offered the land and everything he needed to conduct the sacrifice for free from Araunah. Sounds like a deal to me! But not to David. He knew his sin demanded that he make this his sacrifice, not one provided by another.

TEACHING MOMENT

Teaching our kids about making sacrifices has a different meaning today. We don't take them out and kill a lamb and burn it on an altar. Of course, roasted lamb is pretty good. No, making sacrifices today means giving up something that may be okay but just not right at that particular time. It may mean letting someone else get the bigger piece of pie. It may mean offering all your allowance to help someone who has a greater need than you.

However, we teach them, sacrifice is a lesson that can only be learned by the individual doing the sacrificing. Your children can't learn sacrifice by watching someone else. Now they can appreciate their sacrifice, but they can't really understand the true nature of sacrifice until they willingly give something up.

Look for that "special" opportunity for your child to "sacrifice" something. God will show when it's time to teach this lesson. Your child has to be ready to make the sacrifice on their own. Forcing a sacrifice is just as bad as providing it for them. God will tell you. Just listen!

I lay myself upon the altar today, God. I present my life and my desires to You as a burnt sacrifice. I give it freely and willingly.

NOVEMBER 10

WORSHIP THROUGH GIVING

Exodus 25

BEST VERSES: 1–2

Then the LORD spoke to Moses, saying, "Tell the sons of Israel to raise a contribution for Me; from every man whose heart moves him you shall raise My contribution."

One of the hardest lessons we teach our children is the gift of giving. Most children (even most adults), had much rather receive than give. But teaching this gift is so important. When children learn at a young age that giving to the Lord is an act of worship, and when we model that for them, they are much more likely to give when they grow up.

In this passage the Lord instructs Moses to ask the people to give the articles needed to prepare the Tent of Meeting, commonly known as the Tabernacle. This would be the place of worship for many generations to come. It would be the place Moses would meet God and intercede for the people. It is here that Joshua would stand and wait on Moses to return from the Holy of Holies. It was their "church."

TEACHING MOMENT

Children need to learn that giving to the church is important because it allows the church to provide that place of worship for the body of Christ. Their giving provides for the Pastor(s) and staff who are serving the Lord. Their giving can literally change the world as the church sends part of their giving to other ministries and missionaries.

But their giving starts with you, Mom and Dad. They need to SEE you giving. They need to see you write that tithe check or give online. And when you give, do it joyfully so they can rejoice with you. Amen? Amen!

Lord, all things belong to You. I love to give back to You what You have given me. Help me to not only give, but to give sacrificially.

NOVEMBER 11

DID YOU HEAR THE ONE ABOUT...?

Genesis 18

BEST VERSE: 15

Sarah denied it however, saying, "I did not laugh"; for she was afraid. And He said, "No, but you did laugh."

We have all heard the saying "Laughter is the best medicine." Well, it appears from this verse that may not always be true. When Abraham and Sarah were told by the angel that they would have a son in their old age, they thought they were having their leg pulled. They laughed. "How could this be?" They doubted God.

Now we may be quick to judge them, but we do the same thing. We may not laugh out loud, but we doubt God's power and presence in our lives every day when we try to accomplish things on our own.

TEACHING MOMENT

Kids love to laugh, don't they? Probably in the past few days or so, you and your kids have had a good laugh about something (hopefully not at someone). What a perfect verse to pull out and teach about laughter. After you all get your breath back from laughing at whatever, say, "Hey, that reminds me of a verse about laughing in the Bible." Your kids will probably say, "What? Laughing in the Bible?" Then give them the lesson on this verse.

What are you "laughing" about today? What are you striving to do on your own? Why don't you just rest in the Almighty and let Him have His way in your life? Show your kids that laughing at the right thing is fun and can even be healthy. But laughing at God is not very smart. After all, He always knows the punch line.

God, You are the God of laughter. You gave us humor. Help me to enjoy it while pointing others to You. I really do laugh out loud when I think of the joy we have in You.

NOVEMBER 12

CONSEQUENCES

Deuteronomy 32

BEST VERSES: 48-52

The Lord spoke to Moses that very same day, saying, "Go up to this mountain of the Abarim, Mount Nebo, which is in the land of Moab opposite Jericho, and look at the land of Canaan, which I am giving to the sons of Israel for a possession. Then die on the mountain where you ascend, and be gathered to your people, as Aaron your brother died on Mount Hor and was gathered to his people, because you broke faith with Me in the midst of the sons of Israel at the waters of Meribah-kadesh, in the wilderness of Zin, because you did not treat Me as holy in the midst of the sons of Israel. For you shall see the land at a distance, but you shall not go there, into the land which I am giving the sons of Israel."

No one is exempt from the consequences of disobedience. I had to include all these verses today so you could be reminded of why Moses could not enter the Promised Land. Of all people, didn't he deserve to go? He was the one who led the people. He was the one who confronted Pharaoh. Why wouldn't the Lord allow Him to enter the land promised to His people?

Today we think we can "get by" with the things we do. We should be reminded that we all have consequences for actions that go against God's commands. And we, as leaders and parents, face even more strict consequences. We are leading others. We cannot be allowed to lead them to destruction.

TEACHING MOMENT

This teaching moment is much more directed at you, Mom and Dad. What are you doing, in word or deed, that could mislead your children? What are you showing them that is not pleasing to the Lord? Do you think the Lord would be happy with everything you model for your children?

I am NOT trying to be legalistic. I am far from that. But I do mean we need to be very careful how we lead. There are always little eyes watching us. We cannot afford to be lax for one second. One small act kept Moses from entering the Promised Land. Wow!

Lord, direct my every step. Show me where to place my feet along the path. It may not seem like the best route to me, but I trust You. You know the way much better than I do.

NOVEMBER 13

IDLE HANDS

2 Samuel 11

BEST VERSE:

Then it happened in the spring, at the time when kings go out to battle, that David sent Joab and his servants with him and all Israel, and they destroyed the sons of Ammon and besieged Rabbah. But David stayed at Jerusalem.

David should have been at war leading his men. But he stayed behind, thus began a nightmarish decision. You know the story, don't you? If you don't, read the rest of the chapter and even chapter 12. David turns one bad decision into a series of bad decisions (adultery, lying, murder to name a few).

Have you ever made one bad decision that led to a series of other bad decisions? Sometimes our failure to be where God intended can cost us. We choose to do something our way, rather than God's way, and it ends up bad. We are just as sinful and disobedient as David was here. So, don't act all high and mighty.

TEACHING MOMENT

Parents, keep your children focused. Keep them busy with God. I don't mean just busy stuff. I mean keep them looking at God. Keep them listening to God. When our children get "lazy" with their quiet times and prayer life, their minds can wander to areas that are not pleasing to the Lord.

As parents, we need to be checking with our kids daily about their walk with Christ. You don't have to have a Sunday School lesson every day with them, but you can definitely share what the Lord has taught you that day. Then ask them what the Lord spoke to them. Keep their eyes looking up.

Are you on the rooftop looking at things you shouldn't be looking at? Are you trying to find a way out of the mess you've gotten yourself into? Stop digging yourself into a deeper hole. Put the shovel down, and look up. Listen to the Lord, and do what He says. He always knows the way out.

Father, keep my eyes off things that don't bring honor to You. Keep me focused on serving You and doing Your business. I know I can't keep myself holy without Your indwelling Spirit.

NOVEMBER 14

PICK YOUR NEIGHBORHOOD CAREFULLY

Genesis 19

BEST VERSE: 16

But he hesitated. So, the men seized his hand and the hand of his wife and the hands of his two daughters, for the compassion of the LORD was upon him; and they brought him out, and put him outside the city.

Sometimes, even we put ourselves in harm's way, God rescues us from our stupidity. That may sound kind of harsh, but it's true. Look at this verse again.

Lot had intentionally chosen to live in a place that was ungodly, immoral, and dangerous. He should have had enough sense to leave this God-forsaken place a long time ago. But he had seen the green fields and wanted to be successful with his flocks and herds.

Have you ever wondered why, if Lot was a herdsman, he was living in town? I have. Why was he not living as Abraham, a nomadic life? Perhaps he was living "high on the hog," as my daddy use to say. Perhaps he was seen as wealthy and had some prestige in the town.

Be careful! The world can blind us to the dangers around us until it is too late. It took angels (and I believe the Lord Jesus Himself) to come and take them by the hands and lead them out before they would leave. Don't be that stubborn. Flee the evil around you and allow the Lord to protect you.

TEACHING MOMENT

How can you apply this verse to your children? They need to know that everything that glitters is not gold! What may look appealing at first could have hidden traps. Teach them to be careful in choosing their close friends without snubbing the lost. It's okay to have unbelieving friends as long as you don't take on their lifestyles and habits. Now that's a lesson worth learning.

Thank You, Father, for leading me to those You want me to live around. I trust Your judgment in choosing who is best for me. Help me recognize them when You point them out to me.

NOVEMBER 15

DON'T MISS THIS!

Joshua 3

BEST VERSE: 17

And the priests who carried the ark of the covenant of the Lord stood firm on dry ground in the middle of the Jordan while all Israel crossed on dry ground, until all the nation had finished crossing the Jordan.

God performed another miracle for the Hebrew children. This time He parted the waters of the Jordan. But instead of sending a strong wind to part the waters right in front of them, like He did at the Red Sea forty years earlier, He simply had the priests step into the flood level Jordan and the water stopped about 12 miles upstream and the rest flowed on down.

But God didn't stop there. He DRIED the ground. With all the women, children and livestock, walking across a recently emptied riverbed would have been messy and slow. So, what did God do? He dried the ground so they could cross without getting stuck. God is a God of details.

TEACHING MOMENT

One of the things I grab from this story is that God doesn't just haphazardly work in our lives. He is deliberate and thoughtful. He does things right. He wants everything to be perfect, as He is perfect. In fact, He demands that we be perfect, too. Now, He knows we can't be, but He still expects us to strive toward perfection by allowing the Holy Spirit to direct us.

Can you imagine what those little children thought when they saw the waters flowing on by and the riverbed dry up? Talk about that with your kids. They may have been looking for fish or frogs or other "critters" on the riverbed. Wouldn't your son have been doing that? I sure would have. Visualize this story with your children. Talk about the miracles God continues to do in our lives every day.

Do you believe God is still a God of miracles? I do. I have seen Him do miraculous things. I got to hold a newborn baby recently. That's a miracle. I had the privilege to lead three people to Christ. That's a miracle. I have seen Him heal people who should have died and have also seen Him heal others by allowing them to die. Those are both miracles. Don't ignore God's handiwork all around you.

Too many of us want to see a "Jordan" parted. We ask for those kinds of miracles or signs. But God is working all around us. He works in ways we cannot see. Open your eyes and ask Him to reveal Himself to you today. You might just be surprised at what He is doing in your presence.

God of miracles, open my eyes so I can see You work all around me. Let me recognize the everyday miracles You are performing in my life. I praise You for being a miracle working God.

REVENGE?

Genesis 34

BEST VERSE: 7

"Now the sons of Jacob came in from the field when they heard it; and the men were grieved, and they were very angry because he had done a disgraceful thing in Israel by lying with Jacob's daughter, for such a thing ought not to be done."

Now before you jump to conclusions (and that might be the only exercise you get today), I am not going to ask you to share this story in context with your children. This is one of those stories that is best explained in full when they are older. With that said, let's look at what really happened.

Jacob's daughter, Dinah, had been assaulted by a local man where they lived, and her big brothers were not happy. They decided to get revenge on this man and all who lived in the city. They took up the offense of their sister instead of letting the Lord deal with it. That's the lesson to be learned today.

TEACHING MOMENT

I guarantee you that your children will be faced with a difficult decision one day. They will have a friend who has been hurt by someone else. They will get pulled into a situation where they will be asked to "side" with their friend and "get back" at the other person. You've seen it happen so many times in school. Kids gang up on someone else to teach them a lesson. Wrong! God is not pleased with that.

Righteous anger is biblical, but revenge is best left to the Lord. There is nothing wrong with being upset over seeing someone mistreated. There is nothing wrong with coming to their defense. But plotting to get even with them is not the same.

If Jacob's sons had been there when Dinah was being assaulted and defended their sister, they would have acted correctly. But scheming to kill and destroy a whole city was not pleasing to their father or to God.

Teach your children to be courageous and bold in the face of injustice. But teach them also to let the Lord administer justice. He is the Judge after all.

Father, we are reminded that You are the only Judge and Lawgiver. Help me to give my vengeful heart to You and let You handle my hurts and avenge my enemies. You know best how to deliver justice.

NOT TEN SUGGESTIONS

Exodus 20

BEST VERSE: 1

Then God spoke all these words, saying,

Verses 1–17 of Exodus 20 are God speaking to the people and Moses on Mt. Sinai. He came down in a dark cloud with flashing light. They could hear Him but not see Him. And He gave them the Ten Commandments. The people heard God give Moses these ten laws for living long before they ever saw those stone tablets. And they were scared.

Now, I have to admit. If I was standing there near the mountain and witnessed this, I might be a little nervous too. We think we would have acted differently than the people did then. But would we have? I doubt it. Flesh is flesh, no matter what century it is.

TEACHING MOMENT

So, take a minute and read these ten commandments to your kids. Help them memorize them. There are several ways you can do that using your fingers to remember each one. Just google "memorizing the 10 commandments using your fingers." You will see tons of websites and YouTube videos.

However you learn them, make it fun for your little ones. But don't just stop there. Make sure they understand each commandment. Each one is as important today as it was then. Through Christ, we can follow them. Through Christ we have the Spirit to remind us daily of each of these.

If you are like me, you have failed one or more of these commandments. Praise be to God that my salvation does not rest in keeping a list of rules, no matter how important they are. Now hear me out. Christ has fulfilled them all perfectly. And because He has, I can rest in Him. Hallelujah.

Father, thank You for giving us these ten laws to follow. But thank You more for giving us the example to follow, Your Son Jesus. Help me be obedient to all your commands so that I can draw others to You.

GOD WORKS IN MYSTERIOUS WAYS

Judges 14

BEST VERSE: 4

However, his father and mother did not know that it was of the Lord, for He was seeking an occasion against the Philistines. Now at that time the Philistines were ruling over Israel.

The saying "God works in mysterious ways" does not appear anywhere in Scripture, but it does reflect the basic meaning behind several passages. What does the famous expression mean? It means God doesn't think like we think. He doesn't act like we act. His ways are way beyond our ways. Sometimes the way He works makes absolutely no sense to us.

Samson's parents were just like us in that they wanted their son to marry a good and godly young woman. But who does he pick out? A Philistine woman! The enemy of Israel! Why would God allow this? To prepare Samson to defeat the Philistines. Mom and Dad, God will use our children in ways we can't imagine.

TEACHING MOMENT

Our job, then, is to get our children ready for WHATEVER God chooses to do with them. We can't force our desires and wishes on our children, even if we think they are godly plans. We have to love them enough to let God have them. Wow! I know! That is hard, but it is the right thing to do.

God may ask your son to do something that makes no sense. He may struggle with it. Your task is to stand beside him as he follows the Lord. When others, even in your own family, mock him and you, stand firm. Trust God's wisdom and direction. Just look at how God used Samson to deliver Israel for twenty years.

Are you fighting against the Lord right now? You may not even see it as fighting, but if you are not yielding, you are fighting. We have only one right choice—to surrender daily. Anything else is just . . . well . . . disobedience. Do the mysterious thing with God.

God of mystery, surprise me today. Liven up my life in a way I can't even imagine. But Lord, when You do, let me point only to You.

NOVEMBER 19

GOLDEN WHAT?

1 Samuel 6

BEST VERSE: 4
Then they said, "What shall be the guilt offering which we shall return to Him?" And they said, "Five golden tumors and five golden mice according to the number of the lords of the Philistines, for one plague was on all of you and on your lords."

I have seen a lot of golden gifts, but I have never seen golden mice or tumors, especially tumors. Who in the world would think that would make a good gift? The Philistines, that's who. They had been plagued with mice and tumors since they had captured the Ark of the Covenant and brought it to their land. God was letting them know they had no business with His Ark.

Have you ever given God a gift that was less than desirable? Have you offered Him your leftovers or something you really didn't want anymore? I used to oversee four thrift shops at a ministry. I can't even begin to tell you the literal trash we received from people. And they wanted a tax receipt for it since they were giving to a ministry—in other words, to God.

TEACHING MOMENT
We have to teach our children to give God our best. The Lord deserves it. We don't give out of guilt, like the Philistines did. We don't have to "come up with" what we think is a good gift for God. The Word tells us how and what to give. We need to give Him our first fruits and our best. We need to give Him our ALL.

So, how do you teach your kids that? Help them decide how to invest their lives in service. The Ark represented the very presence and power of God. We already have that in us in the form of the Holy Spirit, if we are believers. Pray with your children every day to surrender their lives and will to Him. That's much better than golden mice or tumors.

How are you doing with that? Have you surrendered your ALL to Him today? Have you laid down your desires for His? Have you tried to "capture" the presence and power of God when you should have realized you already have it?

Powerful and ever present Father, envelope me today. Remind me I am Yours. Remind me I have to surrender to You today. I love You, Lord.

DREAMER

Genesis 37

BEST VERSES: 5, 9A
Then Joseph had a dream, and when he told it to his brothers, they hated him even more. . . . Now he had still another dream, and related it to his brothers.

Joseph was a dreamer. But where did those dreams come from? I believe God was preparing him for his future before he even knew it. We have the luxury of seeing the whole story in God's Word. Joseph, and his brothers, did not see the big picture. These dreams were irritating to his brothers and probably confusing to Joseph. But God spoke through them.

If Joseph and his family could have known what was ahead, they may have listened a little more closely to the dreams. Instead, they thought only of themselves and how they felt betrayed and belittled. Hmmm, sounds like us today. If it's not about us, we tend to shun it.

TEACHING MOMENT
Do your children ever share their dreams with you? I mean, literal dreams you have while asleep, not dreams for the future. I love hearing about kids' dreams. Some are funny, and others can be scary. Some kids don't remember

dreams at all. But the next time your child shares dreams with you, tell this story about Joseph. Explain how God can speak to us through our dreams.

But it is so important to make sure they understand that even our dreams must agree with Scripture. If God is speaking through a dream, He will not contradict a biblical truth. He will only reinforce it. If that is true, then watch and see how He reveals Himself. It can get very interesting sometimes.

Do you remember dreams where you knew God was speaking to you? He may just use His Holy Spirit to speak His message clearly and distinctly. But…you have to be listening. You have to be open to Him. Allow Him to speak.

Father, I know You can speak in whatever way you want. You can speak through my night dreams or my daydreams. Open my eyes and ears to see and hear Your message.

NOVEMBER 21

HOW DO YOU SPELL SUCCESS?

Joshua 1

BEST VERSE: 8
"This book of the law shall not depart from your mouth, but you shall meditate on it day and night, so that you may be careful to do according to all that is written in it; for then you will make your way prosperous, and then you will have success."

The world defines success differently than the Lord. Just look at this verse. The Lord is speaking to Joshua. Now, don't miss that point. Up until now He had only spoken to Moses, but now Moses is dead. He has been buried somewhere on the mountain, and Joshua is the new leader of Israel. Joshua was uniquely qualified because he had been Moses' right-hand man for forty years. He had heard the Lord speak to Moses, so he knew His voice. And now God tells Joshua to go into the Promised Land.

But God tells Joshua that the measure of his success won't be the amount of land he captures or the amount of gold, silver, and precious stones he collects as the booty of war. No, the measure of success that the Lord uses is how well one keeps God's Word. Do you understand what He is telling

Joshua? He is basically saying, "Joshua, the battles you will fight over there are the easy part. What is hard and will determine your success is how well you keep my Law."

TEACHING MOMENT

Your children are going to have wins and losses. They are going to fall flat on their faces at times. They are going to bring home the 1st place trophy. Both of those, the triumph and the defeat, are part of growing and learning. But the real victory they will have in their lives is knowing and living the Word of God. That is where you play a huge role, Mom and Dad. How well are you doing helping them learn the Word?

Helping your child memorize verses will be a gift of success that YOU can give them for the rest of their lives. And YOU get to watch them succeed in life each and every time a verse is recalled in a life experience and lived out. Don't measure your child's success by the grades they make or the jobs they obtain. Watch success follow them as they apply God's Word in their daily walk "'. . . for then you will make your way prosperous, and then you will have success.'" Amen?

I know I am successful, O God, each time I turn to You. I know You see my heart, and You measure my success according to Your measuring rod, not the world's.

NOVEMBER 22

REJECTED

Luke 10

BEST VERSE: 16

"The one who listens to you listens to Me, and the one who rejects you rejects Me; and he who rejects Me rejects the One who sent Me."

If there is one thing our children need to learn, it is how to handle rejection. No one likes being rejected. Our feelings get hurt. We wonder why that "someone" doesn't like us. Not only that, but sometimes that person rejecting us will get others to join with them to ostracize us. It just doesn't feel good.

So how can we help our children who experience this hurt? Look at the verse. If our children are truly trying to live like Jesus, they can expect rejection. But it's not so much them that are being rejected. It's the Lord Himself. The kind of rejection I am talking about here is rejection from people who do not want to do the right thing. Being around you or your children simply illuminates their wrong decisions or lifestyle. They don't want that because it makes them feel uncomfortable. We can expect nothing but rejection from them.

The lesson for this passage is simple. Just love them! Even when they turn their backs on you, love them. Even when they hurl insults, love them. You don't have to keep company with them, but you do have to love them. Why? Because God does.

Perhaps one simple forgiving act by you or your child will draw them back to the Light. Just keep being Jesus to them. He has the power and will work through you to love them.

Remind me, Lord, that the world's rejection of me is really aimed at You, if I am living for You. Give the toughness to continue to stand firm and represent You to others, no matter their response.

NOVEMBER 23

FRUITLESS

Mark 11

BEST VERSES: 13-14
Seeing at a distance a fig tree in leaf, He went to see if perhaps He would find anything on it; and when He came to it, He found nothing but leaves, for it was not the season for figs. He said to it, "May no one ever eat fruit from you again!' And His disciples were listening."

Many are puzzled about this act of Jesus. If you read on down to verse 20 of Mark 11, you will see the results of Jesus' words on the fig tree. Why would the Lord destroy an innocent fig tree? It wasn't about His hunger not being satisfied. It was about fruit production.

The Lord expects us, as believers in Christ and possessors of the greatest gift, to share that gift with others. Just as a fig tree exists to produce figs for food, we exist in Him to bear fruit for others. Jesus was sending a message to His disciples. Everything Jesus said or did was done on purpose. He did not just do things for no particular reason.

TEACHING MOMENT

We have the opportunity to teach our children how to use their God-given gifts for others. Once they come to Christ, they are given gifts in order to produce fruit for the body of Christ (the church). Discovering those gifts and using them is a blessing. So many believers never experience the joy of bearing fruit.

When our children experience this joy of fruit bearing, they get a glimpse of the body of Christ in a way that few experience. I have seen children as young as six and seven years old who are exercising their gifts for others. It is a truly beautiful thing.

But let me ask you, Mom and Dad. Do you know your gifts need to be shared too? Your children need to see you bearing fruit. They need to see you being a benefit for others. How can you bless another believer today? Ask the Lord. He will show you.

Lord, You are my gift giver. You give me exactly what I need to bless others. Give me the boldness and courage to use my gifts to be a blessing for someone else today.

NOVEMBER 24

WRONG CHOICE?

1 Samuel 15

BEST VERSE: 11

"I regret that I have made Saul king, for he has turned back from following Me and has not carried out My commands." And Samuel was distressed and cried out to the Lord all night.

This passage makes me wonder if God made a mistake in choosing Saul. I know the answer to that. No, He didn't. God is not capable of making mistakes. He is perfect. He is holy. He is just. So, how do you explain the verse? The Lord God tells Samuel that He regrets choosing Saul as king. The word "regret" is also translated as "repent." The Lord altered His method of dealing with Saul after Saul turned his back on Him.

God longs to bless us and see us fulfill His will for our lives. But if we choose to go our own way, He will let us. He will not force His will on us. God's will for Saul was for him to be a great king and leader. Saul's ego and self-will went against God and because of that, God changed how He dealt with Saul.

TEACHING MOMENT

This is an important lesson for our kids. We, as parents, may be forced to show some tough love to our kids because of their disobedience. We do not want to, but in order to shape and mold them we have to use some techniques that would not have been employed if our kids had followed our direction. Their disobedience does not change the fact they are our children, but it does change how we have deal with them at the time.

Have you ever known exactly what God wanted you to do, but you chose your own path? Have you ever felt the sting of His discipline in your life? He does not love you any less, but He will be just and loving during the whole time of His corrective action in your life.

As you parent your child, let them know exactly what your expectations are and that those expectations are a direct result of God's Word. They need to know that the guide you are using is God's guide. He is the one who directs you as well.

Lord, my desire is to always make choices that honor you. Use Your Spirit within me to stop me cold in my tracks if I start down the wrong path in a decision. Let all I do give praise to You.

NOVEMBER 25

HARDENED

Exodus 10

BEST VERSE: 1

Then the LORD said to Moses, "Go to Pharaoh, for I have hardened his heart and the heart of his servants, that I may perform these signs of Mine among them."

Probably one of the most difficult things in the Bible to understand is the statement that says God hardened Pharaoh's heart. What does that mean? Did God make Pharaoh refuse to let His people go so He could punish him? Did Pharaoh have a choice in the matter, or was it fully decided by God?

Actually, God just allowed Pharaoh's natural inclination to come out. He did NOT try to persuade Him by His Spirit. Pharaoh was a hard man and thought he was a god. His tendency was to be harsh and cruel. Why would he ever allow the slaves to leave Egypt?

TEACHING MOMENT

But before you are too harsh on Pharaoh, remember we are the same way. Our children are the same way. We are born sinners with hard hearts. Only through the softening of the Holy Spirit can we ever yield to a holy God. Only through His Spirit can we show anything other than hardness to those around us.

As parents, we introduce our children to grace and mercy through Christ. As they surrender to His will, they receive the ability to be tender and understanding to others. Nourish this. Model this. No one wants hard children who are rude and intolerant of others.

There's the rub! You have to show them this daily. As you soften your heart, they will learn. As you show that tender side, they will want to be like that. I promise it's true. But only through the power of Jesus in you can you do that. Don't even try to do this on your own.

Sweet Jesus, You are the perfect example of one who had ultimate power but showed mercy and grace. You, God's Son, the God-Man, can show us, the hard-hearted, how to be like You.

NOVEMBER 26

BUT I SWEAR

Deuteronomy 23

BEST VERSE: 23

"You shall be careful to perform what goes out from your lips, just as you have voluntarily vowed to the Lord your God, what you have promised."

I bet you've never done that, right? You have never said, "I swear . . ." We have all said that. But do we realize the gravity of that statement? The Lord warns us of making such vows. We have to be very careful of "swearing" to do something. It can really come back to bite us if we are not careful.

Now, not all vows are bad. Marriage vows are good. Vows to uphold an office you are elected to are good. The Pledge of Allegiance to our country is great. Just make sure that your vow to uphold these is real and that you are willing to be held accountable to the vow.

TEACHING MOMENT

The next time your son or daughter says, "But Dad/Mom, I swear I didn't break that . . ." take the time to explain what he just said. Pull out this verse. Talk about what that means. Make sure he understands that when we "swear" to something or make a vow, it means something.

One great way to do that is to model it for them. Make a vow to them that you plan to keep and then keep it. Show them by modeling good behavior. When we break our promises to our children, they learn that's okay. Promises always broken are promises that should have never been made.

Are you guilty of that? Are you guilty of broken promises? Who do you need to go to today and ask forgiveness for breaking a vow to them? Maybe it's your spouse. Maybe it's your child. Whoever it is, make it right. Your word matters.

Promise Keeper, remind me of the power of a vow. Help me keep my word to all I have sworn to. Help me be that person people know will keep his word.

NOVEMBER 27

FORGETFUL GAWKERS

John 12

BEST VERSE: 9
The large crowd of the Jews then learned that He was there; and they came, not for Jesus' sake only, but that they might also see Lazarus, whom He raised from the dead.

Don't you just love this verse? The crowd came not just to see Jesus but to look at Lazarus. I mean, after all, most of them had never seen a dead man living. Right? And Lazarus hadn't just died. In fact, he had been dead for four days. He was, according to his sister, already stinking! He was real dead. So, the crowd comes not so much to see Jesus but to see the miracle He had performed.

Aren't we just like that? We want to see a sign. We want to stare at something miraculous. Jesus is right there all the time, but we had rather look for the new amazing thing.

TEACHING MOMENT

It's a bit like when we buy our children that very special thing they have been asking for. We shop and shop. We look online. We finally track it down, wrap it special and give it to them. They are overjoyed—until the newness runs out. Then they are looking for the next best thing. They simply forgot all about the great gift you have given them. But not only that, they have totally forgotten about the motivation behind the gift.

We need to teach our children the importance of the Giver, not the gifts. We need to point them towards the reason behind the blessings He bestows on us. It is all about love. He loves us with a never-ending love. He loves us despite our short memories of His blessings. He loves us even though we look past Him to the thing given.

The next time you buy your child a gift (and there is nothing wrong with that) watch for that first sign of disinterest in the gift. Take that moment to teach this lesson. It is not about guilting your child to appreciate anything. It's about teaching them about recognizing the motivation behind the gift giving, whether that be from us or our Savior.

Don't let my eyes stray from watching You, O Lord. Don't let my eyes seek the miraculous. Remind me that the only miracle I need to see is You, my Savior and Lord.

NOVEMBER 28

TELL EVERYONE

Psalms 9–10

BEST VERSES: PSALM 9:1–2

I will give thanks to the LORD with all my heart; I will tell of all Your wonders. I will be glad and exult in You; I will sing praise to Your name, O Most High.

How can you read this psalm and not get excited about telling someone about Jesus? Look how it starts out. "I will give thanks to the Lord with all my heart." Do you do that? With all your heart? What else do you do with all your heart? Giving thanks to the Lord should be easy.

All these things the psalmist mentions here can be heard—give thanks, tell, be glad and exult, and sing praise. It's hard to stay quiet when your heart is full of praise. It's hard to keep your mouth shut when you are exalting the Lord. Let it out!

TEACHING MOMENT

Get your kids together and have a shout fest. That's right. Find a time and place when you can "let it all out." Make a list of things for which you are thankful as a family. Then make sure your family knows each one. One by one shout them out. Thank God out loud.

Then make a list of people you want to tell about Jesus. It can be friends, family, or someone you don't know that well. Then, with your kids, make a plan to tell each one. Put a date by each name and check with each other to see how the list is doing. Don't forget to pray for these people, too.

Are you thankful today? Are you rejoicing in what the Lord has done for you? Do that right now. Praise His name. Make His name known. Make sure everyone around you knows you are thrilled to be called His child.

Lord, I am guilty too often of not telling others about You. I get lazy. I get silent. Forgive me.

NOVEMBER 29

SEEING WITH THE HEART

John 9

BEST VERSE: 38

And he said, "Lord, I believe." And he worshipped Him.

Do you remember playing "Pin the Tail on the Donkey?" I loved that game. We almost always played this at childhood birthday parties. Mom or Dad would put the poster of the tailless donkey on the wall for us. Then we would blindfold someone, usually the birthday boy or girl, spin them around several times and point them in the direction of the donkey. They held the tail in their hands along with a pin or tac. Trying to find the poster was always a challenge, much less trying to find the right spot to pin that tail. Once they had pinned the tail on the poster "somewhere" they would yank off the blindfold to see how close they had come to the right spot.

As exciting (and frustrating) as it was to be blindfolded, we knew when we pulled off the blindfold, we would be able to see again. But to be born blind! Can you imagine? I can't. I take my sight for granted, I know. Now that I am getting older it is harder to read small print, but I still can see. But not being able to see from birth? That I cannot understand.

And then . . . this man meets Jesus. Can you imagine the excitement that must have been coursing through his veins as he went to the pool of water and washed the clay from his eyes? Do you think he was really expecting to see? He must have been. Why else would he have even asked for healing?

And then the doubters came. They didn't believe he was ever blind. They questioned the validity of the healer. They questioned the parents. Some people just can't believe.

But not this man. When he went back to Jesus and discovered exactly who He was, he simply says, "I believe." Blind eyes opening also opened his heart. So many walk around with sight but are still blind to the truth of the gospel.

TEACHING MOMENT

Show your children the importance of not only seeing physically but seeing spiritually. Show them the importance of helping others remove the blindfolds off their eyes so they too can see Jesus.

> I am so blind to so many things, Jesus. But I know You are still the one who gives sight to blind eyes. Open my eyes so I can see!

NOVEMBER 30

THE VOICE OF AN ANGEL

Genesis 16

BEST VERSE: 9

Then the angel of the LORD said to her, "Return to your mistress, and submit yourself to her authority."

I truly believe each and every time "the angel of the Lord" appears in the Old Testament it is our Lord Jesus. Why? Because after His incarnation (coming in the flesh to earth) there is never another mention of Him. I may be wrong, and there is no definitive way to prove it, but I believe it.

Just think, if I'm right! Jesus appeared to Hagar, the mother of Ishmael and the Arab world. Just think! If Hagar and Ishmael had remained with Abraham and Sarah, would their descendants have continued to follow Jehovah God and relied on the words of the Angel of the LORD when He appeared to her here, how the world might be different.

TEACHING MOMENT

Oh, but the same is true for us. If we will just stop and listen to the Lord, our world could be so much different. Our children have to be taught how to stop and listen. All those times you grab the chubby little cheeks of your little one and say, "Listen to what I am saying" are teaching moments. They need to learn to listen to those in authority.

If Hagar had been a submissive servant to Sarah (Sarai here), perhaps Ishmael would have been submissive also. If your children learn to be submissive to your leadership, they will be better employees. They will be better listeners. They will be better followers of Christ.

Are you listening to those in authority over you? Are you seeking to serve them? Are you allowing your fleshly desires to get the better of you? Your children are watching. Other believers are watching. We ALL need to be more submissive, especially me.

Lord, show me my faults of non-submission. Point out my arrogance and stubbornness. Let me lead my children to be submissive servants to whomever they have in authority over them.

PLEASED

Matthew 2

BEST VERSE: 17

... and behold, a voice out of the heavens said, "This is My beloved Son, in whom I am well-pleased."

Have you ever wondered why Jesus was baptized? He had no need to be. We get baptized to show everyone we have made a public profession of faith in Christ as our Savior. He certainly wasn't doing that. So why? Simple—He wanted to please His Father.

And what did God do? He spoke from heaven. God, the Father, said to God, the Son, that He was pleased. One part of God said to the other part of God, "That was good." I don't even begin to understand all the complexities of the Trinity. I just know Jesus was being obedient to His Father.

TEACHING MOMENT

I think this lesson could teach itself to our children. Obedience is the theme. Do your children need to learn obedience? Perhaps your children are getting into the tween or teen years. Obedience is certainly a major issue with most kids at that age. You should show them this passage. If they are believers, they need to see that even Jesus chose obedience.

Kids today are less and less obedient, it seems. But I don't blame the children. Children have always been children. We parents are the ones who have allowed our children to become disobedient, for the most part. I know there are exceptions, but we are the ones who have allowed the world to dictate to us how to raise our children. Stop it. Let the Word guide you.

But maybe the problem isn't the children. Are you being obedient? Are you allowing the Lord to guide you? Do you rebel at His commands? We must allow the Lord to speak to our hearts and direct our paths. After all, don't you want to hear, "This is My beloved child, in whom I am well-pleased"?

O Lord, I will obey You today. I want to be obedient in all things. When I begin to stray, bring me back.

WE NEVER FAIL GOD'S TESTS

Joshua 8

BEST VERSES: 1-2

Now the LORD said to Joshua, "Do not fear or be dismayed. Take all the people of war with you and arise, go up to Ai; see, I have given into your hand the king of Ai, his people, his city, and his land. You shall do to Ai and its king just as you did to Jericho and its king; you shall take only its spoil and its cattle as plunder for yourselves. Set an ambush for the city behind it."

What a setback! This bunch, under Joshua's leadership, come to the second city in Canaan and gets whooped! They get run off. Thirty-six men die as they turn their backs and run from the men of Ai. But what Joshua doesn't know is there is sin in the camp. Achan had taken forbidden spoil and the nation (yes, the entire nation) is now suffering.

So, here we are in chapter 8, and God sends them back to Ai but with a different battle plan. God is saying, "You aren't done, yet. You just have to obey me, and I will be with you." In the same way, God tells us today, "Get back up! Listen to me this time. I will give you instructions on how to be successful. But you have to obey me."

TEACHING MOMENT

If this isn't a perfect story to teach obedience to our kids, then I don't know of one. How much clearer could it be for our kids? Read them chapters 7 and 8, though. They need to see the whole story. They need to see that God gives specific instructions for us. We don't have to guess what He wants us to do. It is very clear.

When we obey the Father, He fights for us. When we disobey, we suffer the consequences and can even cause others to suffer. That is why we, as parents, must be clear with our discipline. We are teaching them spiritual truths through our parenting. Or at least we should be doing that.

Are you following the Lord's instructions? Are you being obedient to what He has called you to do? Or are you intent on doing things your own way. I truly believe that we don't fail God's tests. We just repeat them until we get them right. It is so much better to do it right the first time. Don't you agree?

Lord God, I am thankful that You are the One who lifts me up. Remind me today that I am dire need of a Savior, One who has the power to not only lift me, but to also sustain me. Hallelujah!

THE GLORY GLOW

Exodus 34

BEST VERSE: 29

It came about when Moses was coming down from Mount Sinai (and the two tablets of the testimony were in Moses' hand as he was coming down from the mountain), that Moses did not know that the skin of his face shone because of his speaking with Him.

Seriously? Really? He didn't know his face was shining? Well, for the past forty days and nights, Moses had been so focused on hearing from God that he had forgotten about himself. The glory of the Lord was so bright and glorious that his eyes had become accustomed to the glow. So, as the Lord released him to return to the people with the Second Edition of the Ten Commandments, the glow was normal for him.

Dads, is the glow of Christ on you? Moms, do your faces shine with the glory of God? Are your children seeing the "glory glow" on you? Do they shy away from approaching you because of the powerful presence of God that they see in you?

TEACHING MOMENT

If you are like me, that is probably NOT the case. There have been times when I've felt that glow. But those times seem too infrequent. You see, the problem is we aren't spending the time we need with God to absorb the glow. Moses had spent forty uninterrupted days with God. He had absorbed His radiance. Now, I know you can't spend forty days alone with God. But how about forty minutes? I bet if you did, you would absorb enough of His radiance from His Word that your kids could tell a difference. What do you think?

God of Glory, give me Your glow today. I want to shine so bright that others are shocked when they see me. I desire the shekinah glory all around. Flood me today with the glory of Jesus!

CHOSEN

Deuteronomy 7

BEST VERSE: 6

For you are a holy people to the LORD your God; the LORD your God has chosen you to be a people for His own possession out of all the peoples who are on the face of the earth.

Don't you remember choosing teams in grade school? At recess, everyone would gather, two captains were picked, and then they would take turns picking their team. I always felt sorry for the last one who was picked. You know how that was, right? Usually, it was the same kid every time.

Maybe you were that kid. Or maybe you were the one picking. It doesn't matter now, does it? But back then it was so important. Aren't you glad God doesn't do that? He chooses ALL OF US! He wants us ALL on His team. But we have to be willing to join it.

TEACHING MOMENT

I promise you there is going to come a time when your child is NOT picked for a team. It could happen early or when they are grown. But it will happen eventually. This is the verse to share at such a moment. They need to know that God will ALWAYS choose them. He is just waiting for them to say, "Yes Lord, I want to be on Your team."

Our job as parents is to get them ready to respond to that "choosing." We need to help them learn to recognize the voice of God, so when He does "call them" to Himself, they will know it is the Lord. That means they need to know as much about the Lord as we can tell them. If we do our part in sharing what the Lord has done in our lives and how He speaks to us, then they will know Him when He speaks.

Are you listening today? Are you attentive to the voice of the Master? He has chosen you, or have you forgotten? You are His special child whom He loves dearly. He wants to pull you close today and love on you.

Put me in, Lord! I am ready! But I know when You are ready You will use me. I am on Your team, which means I am ALWAYS a winner!

MY QUIET PLACE

Mark 1

BEST VERSE: 35

In the early morning, while it was still dark, Jesus got up, left the house, and went away to a secluded place, and was praying there.

Is there a better lesson we can teach our children than this? Even Jesus, the Son of God, part of the Godhead, found time to get away to pray. It says He found a "secluded place" so no one or nothing could bother Him. If He took the time to do this, how much more do we need to do it?

Years ago, I had an office which had been a dorm room at a children's home. It had two closets as you walked in the door, one on the right and one on the left. I turned one of those into a prayer closet where I could go each morning and pray. I loved that little closet. I could literally "hide" and pray for the staff and children.

TEACHING MOMENT

Moms and dads, why not help your children find a spot where they can pray? It could be the corner of their rooms or another place in the house where it is safe and quiet. Wouldn't you love to be like the disciples when they searched for Jesus and find your child praying in secret? That would bless my heart.

Teaching our kids to pray is so easy. We just have to model it for them. I love to hear children pray and I guarantee you God does too. Surely, He smiles when their prayers reach His ears.

Father, nothing is sweeter than time alone with You. Help me to crave more of it. Teach me to pray in a way that honors You and not me. Teach me to pray for others first.

READ THE INSTRUCTIONS

Deuteronomy 12

BEST VERSE: 32

"Whatever I command you, you shall be careful to do; you shall not add to nor take away from it."

Why do we men always think we can assemble any toy or contraption BEFORE we read the instructions? We have this macho, I-can-do-it mentality that makes us too proud to read the instructions.

I remember back in 1990 or '91 we bought our son, Christopher, one of those Powerwheels. It was a red jeep with a black top. It was cool. It had those big plastic tires. We just knew he was going to love it. The problem was it came in a box to be "assembled." I was up half the night on Christmas Eve putting that thing together. After wrestling with it for an hour or so, I finally pulled out the instructions. There actually was a method to the madness.

TEACHING MOMENT

Our children have to be taught to follow the instructions. It is still true that we need to be careful to do all the Lord commands. That's why we require them to follow our commands and instructions. We are modeling for them what the Lord requires of them. If we do not require them to follow our instructions why would we think they would follow God's?

Too many parents today are so "child-focused" that they do not require obedience. God still does! When we do not discipline our children and give clear guidelines, we are doing them a disservice. Of course, our guide for them is God's Word. And we must also be obedient to Him as a model for our children.

What are you disobeying today? What are you NOT doing that the Lord has asked you to do? Are you being careful to follow His commands? It's hard sometimes, I know. We all like to have our own way. But obedience precedes the joy.

I will be obedient today, Father. I will be careful to keep Your Word and, thereby, set an example for others. They are watching!

BFFs

1 Samuel 20

BEST VERSE: 42

Jonathan said to David, "Go in safety, inasmuch as we have sworn to each other in the name of the Lord, saying, 'The Lord will be between me and you, and between my descendants and your descendants forever.'" Then he rose and departed, while Jonathan went into the city.

How many of you have ever had a best friend? I mean one you could not see for years and then pick up right where you left off. I have one of those. We may go years without seeing each other due to the distance between us. But when we are together it is like no time has passed. Pretty cool.

Jonathan and David had a covenant-friendship. They loved each other. But it went beyond that. Their friendship extended beyond themselves to their descendants. They promised to love each other's families. That's true friendship. That's rare. But it is possible with God.

TEACHING MOMENT

Making these kinds of friends isn't easy. It requires us, as parents, to invest in our children's friends. My wife and I made a decision to allow our children to spend time with their friends, either at their house or ours, to develop deep relationships. Both of our children have childhood friends to this day. But they could not have done that without our help.

You may not can choose your children's friends, but you can sure guide them in their choosing. You surely can invest in their friends' lives. My wife and I are "Mom" and "Dad" to many of our children's childhood friends to this day. Why? Because we loved them. We showed them Jesus.

Are you loving your children's friends? Are you being a witness to them? Are you praying for them and with them? That's how you impact your children's choice of friends. Make them your friends too.

O God, thank You for allowing me to invest in the lives of others, especially my children's friends. Thank You for the joy of seeing them grow in Christ.

WILL THEY EVER LEARN?

Matthew 16

BEST VERSE: 7

They began to discuss this among themselves, saying, "He said that because we did not bring any bread."

How many times do your children have to be told and shown how to do something like cleaning their rooms? Every day you show them how to make that bed. Every day, or ten times a day, you tell them to pick up their toys. Will they ever get it? Will they ever learn?

Jesus probably felt the same way right here. The disciples had just seen Him feed over five thousand people and then over four thousand people, and they still were thinking He was worried about bread to eat. He probably was thinking, "Will they ever get it?"

Well, of course, the one advantage He had over you is He was (and still is) God. He knew what His disciples were thinking. He also knew that they would get it. Those eleven faithful disciples, in fact, would change the world.

TEACHING MOMENT

Your children can too. We can't see the future. But we know the one who can. He knows exactly what your children will become. Ask Him! Pray to the Father that He will guide you as you guide them. Let Him give you a glimpse into their future. They are in His hands.

Father, You are the one who teaches all things. Will You give me the ability to learn it from You the first time. Help me to teach my children as You teach me.

MIGHTY MOUSE

2 Samuel 23

BEST VERSE: 17D
These things the three mighty men did.

"Here I come to save the day! That means that Mighty Mouse is on the way! Yes sir, when there is a wrong to right, Mighty Mouse will join the fight!"

I am really dating myself. Those words above are part of the Mighty Mouse theme song, and Mighty Mouse was a popular cartoon figure in the 1950s and 60s. I loved Mighty Mouse. He would fly (yes, a flying mouse) and save the day. He never ran from a fight to uphold justice.

Don't ask me why, but I thought of Mighty Mouse when I read these verses today in 2 Samuel about the mighty men of David. Some of their exploits are recorded, but I bet they had many more stories. I can't wait to ask them about those one day. They will be remembered for their valor, courage, and loyalty to God and David.

TEACHING MOMENT

Kids love hero stories. Well the stories of the mighty men make good reading then. But it's not just about *what* they did. It's more about *why* they did it. They loved David, their king. They loved the Lord for whom they fought. They loved their nation and were willing to die for it. Aren't those character traits you want to see in your children?

And just like most traits they learn, they look for them in us. Are we sold out to Jesus to the point that we would die for Him? Are we loyal to our country where we live? Will we defend our families against, not only physical threats, but spiritual threats? I don't expect you to be "Rambos" and take on the world. But I do want you to have the courage to do whatever the Lord tells you.

Father, I can do nothing without You. But I am willing to fight the most dangerous foe for You. Give me the courage to stand and fight as a soldier in Your army.

NOT YOUR NORMAL PINKY SWEAR

Genesis 24

BEST VERSE: 9

So the servant placed his hand under the thigh of Abraham his master, and swore to him concerning this matter.

This passage has often puzzled me. Why did the servant put his hand under Abraham's thigh? Why didn't he just raise his hand or pinky swear? Why didn't he just say, "I promise"? Because this binding ritual had significant covenant meaning.

By putting his hand under his thigh, he was putting his hand near the location of circumcision, which is a sign of covenant between Abraham and man. Of course, Abraham was the first to be circumcised, so it had even greater meaning. This wasn't just a promise made by the servant. It was a binding vow which reminded the servant of the powerful Jehovah God who had literally "cut covenant" with Abraham.

TEACHING MOMENT

Now we don't expect our children to put their hand under their father's thigh in order to promise to do something. But we do expect them to take their promises seriously. Why? Because keeping their word is a characteristic of an honorable person. If people can't believe them when they say something, they will struggle all their lives in relationships.

Do your children make promises they don't keep? Do your children lie? Do they tell untruths to make themselves look better? Do they lie about their siblings to get them in trouble? You must deal with these habits now. You might want to use this story about keeping promises. (Just leave out the whole circumcision part until they are older.)

What "promise" do you need to keep today? What untruth are you tempted to tell? Whom have you hurt by saying things about them that you know are not true? Keep your vows. Keep your word. And most importantly, let the words from your mouth always speak truth.

Little ears are listening!

Father, help me to train my little ones to keep their word when they make promises. Most of all, teach me to be truthful to others so my children will learn from me.

WHAT IS IT?

Exodus 16

BEST VERSE: 15

"When the sons of Israel saw it, they said to one another, 'What is it?' For they did not know what it was. And Moses said to them, 'It is the bread which the Lord has given you to eat.'"

In my travels I have been offered some strange things to eat. I almost always partake of it, even if I don't really want it. I don't want to be rude to my host. But here are the Hebrew people in the wilderness faced with a new food source they had never seen. They had been grumbling and complaining since they left Egypt about not enough to eat or drink. So, God gives them "what is it," manna.

The word literally means "whatness" or "what is it?" We would call that mystery meat when I was in college going through the cafeteria line. Not only did God provide them their "daily bread," but He also told them when to gather it and how much. He told them how to prepare it and store it for the Sabbath. If that's not attention to detail, I don't know what it is.

TEACHING MOMENT

Are your children picky eaters? Many kids are. I truly believe too many parents give in to their child's desires rather than concentrating on providing for their needs. How many of your kids would have eaten manna that they had gathered off the ground each morning? How many of your children would have said, "Mom, I am tired of this manna stuff. That's all we ever have to eat."?

The next time your children complain about the food on the table, pull out this story. Remind them it is NOT about what's on the table. It's all about how the Lord provides for us daily. Turning up their noses to prepared food is thumbing that same nose at God. It's as if they are saying, "God, you don't know what I need."

But how about you, Mom and Dad? Are you doing the same? Do you question God's provision in your life? Are you grumbling about where He is leading you, as if you have a better plan?

Let Him lead. Let Him provide. He ALWAYS knows what we need when we need it.

Thank You, Lord, for the daily provisions in my life. You provide my daily needs despite my doubt at times. You are faithful to me.

DECEMBER 22

IF THEY HAD ONLY KNOWN

John 7

BEST VERSE: 42
"Has not the Scripture said that the Christ comes from the descendants of David, and from Bethlehem, the village where David was?"

I find it kind of funny that as the people were arguing about just who Jesus was, they actually remembered the prophecy about Bethlehem. They knew the prophecy but didn't know He had fulfilled it. They seemed to know Him, but they didn't.

Have you ever thought you knew someone, only to find out later you really didn't? If the people had really known Jesus, they would have been ecstatic. They would have been dancing in the street. They just *thought* they knew Him. But let me ask you a question. Do *you* really know Him?

TEACHING MOMENT
Our children begin asking questions about the Lord at an early age. They have inquisitive minds about spiritual things. It is important that we feed that curiosity with the truth. They need to know all we can give them. We need to inform them as they are able to digest the truth.

But in order to do that we must have the knowledge. You can't impart something you don't have. So, I'll ask you again. Just how well do you know your Savior? Do you really know Him? Do you want to know Him more? You can only know someone you spend time with. How much time are you spending with Him? Your children will see you doing that and want to know Him too.

I have some good friends whom I love to be with. I have other friends that I had rather not spend a lot of time with. But there is no one I had rather be with than my Savior. Why? Because He knows me like no one else and still loves me.

O God, I want to know You. I want to know You fully. I desire to know You as You know me.

DO NOT HINDER

Matthew 19

BEST VERSE: 14

But Jesus said, "Let the children alone, and do not hinder them from coming to Me; for the kingdom of heaven belongs to such as these."

I can't tell you how many times parents have come to me questioning whether their children are old enough to accept Christ as their Savior. I understand that they want to make sure they understand the importance of this decision. But, let me tell you, children get it. It's we adults who don't understand.

In today's verse Jesus tells the disciples to "not hinder" the little children from coming to Him. In other words, don't stop them. Jesus loves children. The passage goes on to say He laid His hands on them and blessed them. How much more do you need to read? When children come to Jesus, He touches and blesses them.

TEACHING MOMENT

Okay, Mom and Dad, hear me out. I am not going to try to convince you to allow your seven-year-old to get baptized. What I am saying is this. Believe your child! If they understand that Jesus was God's Son sent to die for them, if they see themselves as a sinner in need of salvation, if they believe He was buried, rose again the third day and ascended to heaven, and if they have confessed this with their mouth—guess what? The Bible says they are saved.

They may not understand all the deep theological truths of Scripture, but I bet you don't either. Don't be like the disciples. Don't hinder your children from coming to Christ. Let them come. Let Jesus lay His hands on them and bless them. There is no better feeling than knowing your child's eternity is sealed.

Have you been guilty of hindering anyone from coming to Christ? Have your actions or words persuaded someone to go in the opposite direction? Repent of that and do all you can to introduce others to Christ. Lead them to His feet for His blessing of salvation.

Thank You Father, for sending Your Son to bless my children. Let me get out of the way and allow them to go to Him. Help me teach and disciple them with Your Word.

DECEMBER 24

WORTH REPEATING

Deuteronomy 5

BEST VERSE: 1

Then Moses summoned all Israel and said to them: "Hear, O Israel, the statutes and the ordinances which I am speaking today in your hearing, that you may learn them and observe them carefully."

The Ten Commandments were repeated by Moses here before the people began to enter the Promised Land. Why? Didn't they know them? Didn't they understand them? I guess the Lord and Moses felt they needed to hear them again. Read them again in verses 7–21. Which one of those hits you the hardest?

How many times have you had to "relearn" something? Boy, it happens to me all the time! If I don't do something a lot, I have to get out the instructions again. It was the same with God's directions to the Israelites. They had to be reminded of His expectations over and over again.

TEACHING MOMENT

I bet you never have to repeat yourself with your kids, do you? I can hear you laughing now. Sure, you do. Our children may hear you the first time, but for some reason they don't understand it the next time. Repetition is needed for them to get it.

Aren't you glad we don't have to "repeat" salvation? Oh, our children need to understand this. "Once saved always saved" is true if you are truly saved. Repetition is NOT needed here. The repetition comes in our need to die daily to self. Every day we have to surrender to Christ and say no to our flesh. Now that's worth repeating.

I don't know about you, but I have to do that every second of every hour of every day. My flesh is wicked and strong and wants to rule my life. But when I say "no" to it and "yes" to Christ, life makes sense. Joy returns! Peace reigns. Repeat! Repeat!

Lord of all creation, You have made us flesh and blood. You knew we would have to choose to follow You. Help me today to choose You in all I do. Thank You for salvation that is sure!

DECEMBER 25

DO YOU SEE WHAT I SEE?

Daniel 10

BEST VERSES: 5–6

"I lifted my eyes and looked, and behold, there was a certain man dressed in linen, whose waist was girded with a belt of pure gold of Uphaz. His body also was like beryl, his face had the appearance of lightning, his eyes were like flaming torches, his arms and feet like the gleam of polished bronze, and the sound of his words like the sound of a tumult."

There are a few appearances of Jesus in the Old Testament, and this is one of them. The Lord Jesus Himself appears to Daniel on the bank of the Tigris River to encourage and strengthen him. But notice what Daniel had been doing? Go back and read verses 1–4.

He had been fasting and praying for his nation. He had prepared himself to hear from the Lord. He was ready. Those who were with him did NOT see Jesus. It doesn't say whether they had been fasting or not, but they obviously weren't ready to see Him. Are you?

TEACHING MOMENT

Our children must be prepared to see Jesus. Now I don't mean to say they will "see" Jesus with their own physical eyes. I don't want to put Jesus in a box and imply He can't appear to them, but I am saying they need to be able to see with their hearts our living Lord and Savior. It is up to us, their parents, to prepare their hearts.

Do we force them too fast to see Him? Do we force them to wear sackcloth and ashes? No! But we do lay before them an environment that invites them to pursue Him. We live a life that draws them to Him. We give them opportunities to experience what holy living is. By doing these things they will be sensitive to His call and will "see" Him when He "appears" to them.

Will you be that Jesus to someone else? Will you show them what Jesus looks like? Will you let your life be so surrendered to His will that all people see is Jesus? Then others will see what you see!

Dear Lord, when You show Yourself to me through others, or through a song or sermon, or even prayer, don't let me keep it to myself. Inspire me to tell those around me what You have revealed to my heart and not to hide Your light.

DECEMBER 26

SPECIAL RECIPE

Exodus 30

BEST VERSE: 34
Then the Lord said to Moses, "Take for yourself spices, stacte and onycha and galbanum, spices with pure frankincense; there shall be an equal part of each."

How many of you remember the TV show *The Waltons*? Do you remember the Baldwin sisters? They were two older unmarried sisters who had a "special recipe." It was their own special recipe from their father who was famous for his moonshine. They didn't make much, and they didn't sell it, but everyone knew about it. That recipe was a guarded secret.

God had his own "special recipe." The incense used by Aaron and the priests was not to be made for any other purpose. They were not to share the exact recipe with anyone. This was a holy recipe, unlike the Baldwin sisters' recipe. This recipe was to be used daily in the worship of a holy God. It had a specific purpose.

TEACHING MOMENT

Our children should be told often that they are a "special recipe" prepared by God. They have a specific purpose which can only be discovered as they surrender their hearts and life to Jesus. Your role as parent is to point them in His direction. You are to prepare their hearts to receive Him by praying with them, by reading them His Word and by listening when they ask questions about Him.

Some recipes take longer to prepare and cook. Your child may respond at an early age to God's calling. Others may come to Him later. Don't stop preparing them. Don't give up. Keep doing your part in God's plan for them.

Are you frustrated with your "recipe" right now? Maybe you need to let it simmer for a while. Let the Great Chef cook your life to perfection. He knows when it is "done." Trust Him.

Heavenly Father, I want to be the sweet incense in Your nostrils. I want my life to smell like You, not me. Help me spread Your fragrance all around, especially to my children and family.

DECEMBER 27

ARE YOU SAD?

Luke 20

BEST VERSE: 27

Now there came to Him some of the Sadducees (who say that there is no resurrection),

THERE'S NO REASON

You have probably heard why the Sadducees were called Sadducees. They were Sad, You See, because they didn't believe in the resurrection. Well, that could be a reason, couldn't it?

I would be sad if I didn't believe in the resurrection. But I do! I know one day I will either be resurrected from the grave or raptured alive. I know that!

Why? Because His Word tells me so. His promises are true. His promise to take us home is real. Do you believe?

TEACHING MOMENT

Tomorrow morning when your children wake up from their night's sleep, greet them like this, "Good resurrection day!" They will probably give you a strange look and will think you have lost it. But then explain what you mean. They have arisen from sleep to a new day.

In the same way, one day, we believers will awake to an eternal resurrection. We who have passed away before that time will see our bodies erupt from the grave and resurrect. If we are alive at the time, we will "resurrect" immediately to our eternal reward. That will be a happy, blessed day. It's no wonder the Sadducees were sad.

Are you ready to go? I pray you are. I pray you have made that decision to follow Christ, so that when He returns in the air to call His bride home, you will be one of those who goes. He will come. We will go. Will you?

Lord, thank You for the promise of resurrection. Praise You for the promise of an eternal home. Help me share the joy of this coming day before it comes and too many are left behind.

DECEMBER 28

THE LACK OF CORRECTION

Proverbs 9–10

BEST VERSE: 9:8

Do not reprove a scoffer, or he will hate you, reprove a wise man and he will love you.

As a children's pastor, I get to see firsthand how children respond to correction. Some accept it and change their behavior. Others simply ignore you, and finally some question your right to correct them. It is to this third one I want to focus today.

With today's verse in mind, as parents, we must reprove those we love, but we must do it in love. I am not saying that every child is a "scoffer." But direct disobedience is, in a sense, scoffing at authority. I have had children, when corrected, look at me and say, "You're not my parent!" My first thought (notice I say thought and not reply) is "And I am so glad."

Seriously though, we see way too much of this attitude today, even in our churches. There seems to be more and more direct disrespect for those in authority. Why are our children behaving this way? In many cases, they learn it from us. Ouch, that hurt.

TEACHING MOMENT

How do you teach your children to receive reproof? By being reprovable yourself. (Is "reprovable" a word? If not, I just made it up.) A scoffer (one who laughs or ignores truth) will not receive correction. They get mad if you even mention their sin. But a wise person accepts correction and makes the necessary confession to the Lord. Are you demonstrating that for your children? Are you teachable? Are you correctable?

My flesh hates correction. I want to do what I want, when I want. How dare you point out my waywardness. Who do you think you are? But the Spirit of the Lord in me convicts me and makes me absolutely miserable until I make things right with the Lord and others. Correction can be embarrassing, true. But not receiving correction is outright dangerous.

Will you be the one to bow before all the authorities that the Lord has placed over you? Little ones are watching to see how you respond. Be the example of obedience they need.

Thank You Lord for reproving me when I need it. I don't always appreciate it, but I know it is necessary. I accept it as one more way You are making me more like You.

DECEMBER 29

WORDS NOT HEEDED

Deuteronomy 17

BEST VERSE: 18

"Now it shall come about when he sits on the throne of his kingdom, he shall write for himself a copy of this law on a scroll in the presence of the Levitical priests."

If you read verses 14–17 of Deuteronomy 17, you will see that God knew the people would ask for a king one day. Later on, we see that happen when Saul is anointed king. And lo and behold, everything we just read in those verses in Deuteronomy came true. The kings imported horses galore, married multiple wives, and got rich. But if they had only done what He said to do in verse 18, they could have avoided all the heartache. Verses 19–20 continues,

"It shall be with him and he shall read it all the days of his life, that he may learn to fear the Lord his God, by carefully observing all the words of this law and these statutes, that his heart may not be lifted up above his countrymen and that he may not turn aside from the commandment, to the right or the left, so that he and his sons may continue long in his kingdom in the midst of Israel."

What a difference that would make?

TEACHING MOMENT

Children need to learn to keep God's Word close to their heart. They don't have to write a copy of it, but they should memorize and learn to meditate on it. Keeping God's Word close can prevent a whole world of hurt. It keeps us focused on pleasing Him and doing what He expects.

Ask your children what they think would happen in their country if the President or national leaders kept God's Word close to them. I bet they will have some great examples. Bottom line—God's Word is preventative medicine. God's Word directs our paths. God's Word gives us focus. Why wouldn't you want your children to keep it close.

Are you keeping it close? Do you start each day or end each day with a reading of the Word? Allow it today to point you in the direction God would have you go. Ask the Lord to use His Word to teach you to make those everyday decisions.

Lord, Your Word is full and rich. Help me to depend on it even further. Let it direct me this day.